Personal Development and Management Skills

Dr Chris Routledge is a Researcher and HR Consultant, specialising in Skill Development. He was formerly a
Principal Lecturer at Huddersfield University Business School.

Jan Carmichael is Head of Division of HRM within the Department of Management at Huddersfield University
Business School.

The CIPD would like to thank the following members of the CIPD Publishing editorial board for their help and advice:

- Pauline Dibben, Sheffield University
- Edwina Hollings, Staffordshire University Business School
- Caroline Hook, Huddersfield University Business School
- Vincenza Priola, Keele University
- John Sinclair, Napier University Business School

The Chartered Institute of Personnel and Development is the
leading publisher of books and reports for personnel and training
professionals, students, and all those concerned with the effective
management and development of people at work. For details of all
our titles, please contact the publishing department:
Tel: 020 8612 6200
Email: publish@cipd.co.uk
The catalogue of all CIPD titles can be viewed on the CIPD website:
www.cipd.co.uk/bookstore

Personal Development
and Management Skills

Chris Routledge and Jan Carmichael

Chartered Institute of Personnel and Development

Published by the Chartered Institute of Personnel and Development, CIPD House,
151, The Broadway, London, SW19 1JQ

First published 2007

Typeset by Kerrypress Ltd, Luton, Bedfordshire

Printed in Spain by Graphycems

British Library Cataloguing in Publication Data
A catalogue of this manual is available from the British Library

ISBN-13 978 1 84398 148 0

Chartered Institute of Personnel and Development, CIPD House, 151, The Broadway, London, SW19 1JQ
Tel: 020 8612 6200
Email: cipd@cipd.co.uk   Website: www.cipd.co.uk
Incorporated by Royal Charter.   Registered Charity No. 1079797

Contents

FIGURES AND TABLES

Acknowledgements

We wish to acknowledge all colleagues, students and managers that we have worked with over the years who have contributed to the development of our ideas on management skills and personal development.

In particular, we would like to recognise the contributions of our colleagues the late Don Abel, the late Richard Graham and Chris Mills.

We would like to thank Peter Richardson and Pam Dyson for their help with the diagrams and sketches.

Chris Routledge and Jan Carmichael

Introduction

THE BOILERMAKER

There is an old story of a boilermaker who was hired to fix a huge steamship boiler system that was not working well. After listening to the engineer's description of the problems and asking a few questions, he went to the boiler room. He looked at the maze of twisting pipes, listened to the thump of the boiler and the hiss of escaping steam for a few minutes, and felt some pipes with his hands. Then he hummed softly to himself, reached into his overalls and took out a small hammer, and tapped a bright red valve, once. Immediately, the whole system began working perfectly, and the boilermaker went home. When the steamship owner received a bill for $1,000 he complained that the boilermaker had only been in the engine room for 15 minutes, and requested an itemised bill. This is what the boilermaker sent him:

For tapping with hammer:	$ .50
For knowing where to tap:	$ 999.50
Total:	$1,000.00

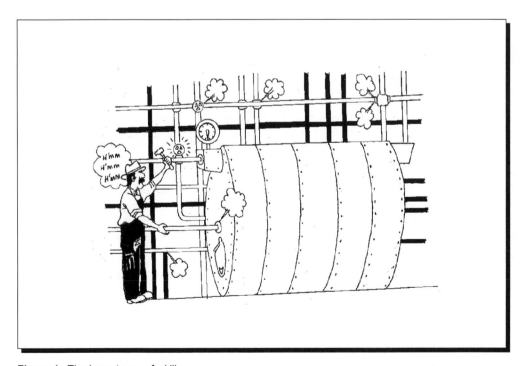

Figure 1: *The importance of skills*

This is an engaging story which demonstrates the premium our society places on skill. As our world grows more technologically complex, the demand and necessity for managerial skills is ever more apparent.

Astronomical sums of money are now invested in public and commercial enterprises. Millions of people are employed in these organisations and depend on them for their economic needs and the quality of their lives. Organisations have a profound effect on our environment and the way they are managed may even affect the survival of our planet. Never has it been more urgent to manage these enterprises effectively.

The growth in managerial jobs has been one of the phenomena of the late twentieth and early twenty-first centuries. Surely this growth can only be justified if, like the boilermaker, managers can be seen to make a difference. It is our contention that they can do this by the deployment of managerial skills. Managers are valued and rewarded in organisations because of what they do, not purely for what they know. Although knowledge and capability are linked, their development is usually through different means. It is this distinction that led to the writing of this book. There are many excellent books which emphasise knowledge, but this book is firmly in the territory of skill development. We describe a *process* and examine factors which enhance or inhibit this process. So it is essentially a practical book, but informed not only by professional practice but by research and academic work.

For a number of years the institutions which represent managers and most of the professional bodies have recognised the importance of demonstrating that their members are competent and up to date with current knowledge and skills. In some institutions these requirements are made transparent through the process of continuous professional development (CPD). Although the aims and intentions of the institutions are similar, there are wide variations in the methods used to achieve these aims.

This book has come about through our work with groups of professional students and managers mostly following the Professional Development Scheme of the Chartered Institute of Personnel and Development but also with students and managers studying for an MBA and a DMS qualification as well as corporate programmes.

In many ways it is the story of a journey of discovery of the skills, processes, benefits, issues, frustrations and problems involved in developing and honing a programme of continuous professional development. In doing this we have discovered a great deal about the processes of developing management skills.

Until recently the development of management skills was often regarded as the sole responsibility of the employer of managers. In many organisations the individual somehow 'picked up' the many skills needed to do the job and remain competent and up to date. In the larger organisations this was backed up with a number of courses to develop particular skills.

Lately there has been a trend to view the development of management skills as a lifelong exercise and as part of an ongoing programme of continuous professional development. Our view is that this trend is very timely and should be extended to all managerial employees in all organisations and underpinned by the idea that this responsibility belongs not only to the employer but also to the individual managers, and to their professional bodies and institutions such as business schools, colleges and universities.

The skill of the boilermaker is not exactly transparent or transferable in the above story, and there is a long tradition and belief that managers are born or forged on the experiences of life but certainly not trained or developed. We hope our work will help to redress that balance.

ISSUES IN DEVELOPING MANAGEMENT SKILLS

In our work with managers we are often asked crucial questions the answers to which may underpin any progress in personal and skill development. Indeed, until learners have satisfactory answers to such questions, or at least have been able to understand the debate that surrounds them, there may be a barrier to further development. We intend to present a selection of these key questions to help provide a foundation for the ideas presented and the issues that are addressed within the book.

Why is it important to continually develop skills?

Although the arguments for continually developing skills have been widely aired they are worthy of repetition. In our work with managers, in most organisations the one core feature of life common to all is change. Although there may have been a time when managers took a job, stayed in that job and experienced little change over a long time, the reality for most managers today is that the organisations in which they work change, and so do managers' roles within them. Often managers also have to manage the change process for other colleagues at the same time. There may, additionally, be personal change through a manager's choice to move into a new role in the same or a different organisation. The relative size and impact of these changes may vary but each one will require skills to be developed or updated. This requirement to change and develop skills affects not just managers but all professions and many employees.

The factors that precipitate change are also varied but can be grouped into:

- work role choices in the manager's control
- internal factors from the business that impact on the manager
- external environmental factors that impact on the organisation.

Whatever these reasons are, their outcome usually corresponds to changes for individuals.

This requirement to focus on change is not new. Writers such as Senge (1990) have discussed its influence, and both suggest that the need for change is likely to continue and grow. One major outcome of constant change is the focus on continual professional development for managers, seen as a requirement by all institutes and professional bodies and increasingly used in organisations. Growing interest in continuous professional development (CPD) has had an impact on approaches and methodologies in learning. In a fast-changing environment it is often not possible and certainly not cost-effective to take many months to undertake detailed training needs analyses and then to design and deliver expensive corporate training initiatives over long periods of time, even if resources are available to do it. If this approach is adopted, often the skills or behaviours that were the subject of the training have subtly transformed in the time taken to analyse and deliver them. There will always be the need for some large training initiatives – but what is increasingly required is a much quicker response which can be used individually or with small groups, preferably as part of CPD.

Is there a set of skills that is common to all managers?

If people are asked to list management skills, they are generally able to identify a wide range of relevant skills and leadership characteristics about which there is usually agreement. Each of us, therefore, has an implicit model of what we believe constitute management and leadership skills.

There is a long history of research into what managers do (Perren and Burgoyne, 2002; Boyatzis, 1982) and into connections between management and leadership style. So there would seem to be commonly agreed models, notably that of Mintzberg (1973) or the Chartered Management Institute framework for Chartered Managers, as well as those referenced above which are often used as a basis for training programmes for managers.

However, most of the models were developed at a specific time when organisations had certain expectations of managers which may not now always be appropriate, whether for strong task-focus or involving partnership approaches to leadership. Research over many years has indicated that lists of skills are inadequate to describe the reality of managerial work which is influenced by organisational context, culture, hierarchy, and pressures at work (Boyatzis, 1982; Quinn et al, 2003). Managerial work is also highly individualised due to differences relating to managers' individual styles that they bring to any role. Even if there was agreement about what knowledge, attitudes and behaviours constitute each skill, it is probable that individual managers would use these skills differently.

In today's organisations there are many competing priorities and complex changes for managers to have to contend with. Quinn *et al* (2003) suggest that managers must learn to cope with cognitive and behavioural complexity which requires them to use skills and leadership behaviours that previously would have been considered contradictory. For example, managers must be able to provide clear priorities, monitoring detail to achieve organisational outcomes while innovating for new business initiatives, and also coach employees as required.

To further their development, therefore, managers can only be provided with generalised models of skill and from them learn how to develop these skills to suit their own personal style and the situations in which they find themselves. Managers must learn to examine circumstances and decide on how to use appropriate skills to achieve an objective through other employees.

We believe that the focus in skill development is better directed to a process that has general applicability both to the generic skills and to the other skills and activities relevant and recognised in particular organisations.

Do we learn management skills in the same way as other things?

Bass and Vaughan (1966) defined learning as 'a relatively permanent change in behaviour that occurs as a result of practice or experience'. Learning, then, seems to involve a number of key characteristics related to action and understanding, as well as involving a learner's experience.

Reynolds, Caley and Mason (2002) have described four clusters of approaches to learning:

- learning as behaviour change or shaping, in which reward and punishment are used to modify behaviour (Skinner, 1974)

- learning as understanding (Festinger, 1957), which emphasises the importance of knowing facts and information and which forms the basis of much of modern education today

- learning as constructing knowledge, emphasising the importance of personal involvement and action in learning, so that people construct their own learning (Rogers, 1996; Senge, 1990)

- learning as social practice that emphasises the social aspect of learning (Vygotsky, 1978); organisational culture and 'communities of practice' (Wenger, 1998) influence learning at work.

One of the issues we have found key in facilitating the development of management skills is not whether individuals are familiar with these four approaches but in which contexts they believe the approaches are appropriate. Many managers and students believe that education in a business school or university is about knowledge and understanding. This leads them to believe that lectures and reading are the main methods for learning.

Some managers and students believe that skills are about learning from role models and 'communities of practice'. This can lead to the belief that skill cannot be learned in a setting outside their organisation.

Some managers and students believe that trial-and-error learning and the use of personal experience are appropriate for more mechanical operations such as using mobile phones and computers but not for soft skills. This can lead to students hearing about a soft skill associated with, for example, performance interviewing in a lecture – and subsequently in a workshop designed to develop this skill the initial comments are, 'We have done this before.' They do not always appreciate that experience in using these skills is necessary.

Often the main challenge facing a facilitator of skills is one of reframing beliefs about methodologies rather than familiarising the learner with a particular approach. A second and closely related challenge is to dispel the myth that every approach can work for everyone in every situation. It is just not possible to facilitate skills development using one approach delivered in the same way at the same time to everyone.

The clusters above summarise most learning theories which we use in all learning, and they all play a role in developing skills, although certain clusters may be emphasised in skills development and others be more pertinent in learning in different contexts. One thing our experience tells us is that people can become more effective learners by widening and deepening their learning styles and methodologies.

What is the role of education in developing management skills? In particular, can business schools offer the appropriate environment?

There are few organisations that provide a comprehensive training for those who wish to leave education after school. Even Government-led initiatives to help young employees or those who have been out of work for some time often rely on education and training to provide elements of development. Following reports of low levels of skill being detrimental to our national competitiveness (Handy, 1987; Constable and McCormick, 1987), national vocational frameworks were introduced to try to improve the qualification levels of employees and managers. Reviews of these systems have found only limited application in certain areas and suggested that higher-level vocational qualifications require more explicit knowledge to underpin workplace competence. This is, then, an important role for education. Education, in turn, has realised that it cannot remain separate from the needs of business and that higher education has an important role to play in preparing graduates for employment, so that personal development planning is part of most degrees and graduate employability an important measure in assessing institutions' performance.

Today, an increasing number of managers have experience of higher and further education, and for most managers and professionals continued education and development through a business school is an increasingly common occurrence. As a greater number of people have the opportunity to go through the higher education system it will become even more essential to get a higher level of qualification, or training, for those who wish to differentiate themselves in the labour market. Higher-level qualifications seem to continue to grow in number, and many of them include elements of CPD or 'work-related learning'.

Many people are therefore continuing their relationship with higher and further education and there is an acceptance that universities and colleges, often in combination with employers, are an appropriate place to continue work-related development, not just to acquire knowledge. Universities are also increasingly becoming involved in organisational training and development, and there is a greater acceptance of the reciprocal relationship between theory and practice (Burgoyne and Reynolds, 1997).

In light of the history of the relationship between education and work organisations it seems to us that higher and further education seems an ideal environment for students and managers to develop appropriate skills and attitudes for CPD.

What are the characteristics of our approach to skills development?

We use an experiential learning approach, developed and tested over a number of years and with many different groups of managers and students.

We use and recommend any facilitator to use a range of methods and approaches to facilitate effective development of skills and competence. We usually adopt one of a number of formats which include short inputs, demonstrations, stories, metaphor, discussions, role plays, group activities and observation of others. We try not to repeat similar formats too frequently, and each session is developed to focus on specific skills – for example, presentation skills – and to encourage the use of a range of skills, which may be different for individual learners.

Each learner is individual and has gathered a multitude of experiences through his or her life, developing attitudes and preferences for learning, understanding, and managing. It is not possible to control the learning of any individual, and managers often work in small groups so that it is not usually a neat orderly experience but relies on the active involvement of managers as learners. However, the benefits are large because it encourages managers to develop skills that are relevant to themselves, building on previous experience and learning from other managers. A learning community can be created and used in ways to benefit managers, organisations and tutors as part of CPD.

Our approach recognises that individuals do not all develop skills at the same pace and in the same way, and so allows an individualist approach.

It is flexible because it can be used both within the workplace and in an educational environment and provides a suitable vehicle for the integration of academic theory with organisational practice.

However, it can challenge some students' beliefs about learning and requires more commitment and motivation on the part of the manager and students than does a conventional series of lectures. It also requires flexibility on the part of the tutor or facilitator.

WHO SHOULD READ THE BOOK?

Anyone who wishes to develop new management skills or hone existing ones. Although it is suitable for the general reader there are a number of groups who might find it of particular value.

Students, studying on a university programme to gain a qualification for membership of a professional body – for example, the Chartered Institute of Personnel and Development or the Chartered Management Institute. On such programmes students learn about management, organisation theory and a range of related academic disciplines, and gain knowledge related to the standards of the professional institute. However, knowledge alone is insufficient in professions today and this book would accompany a skills or personal development module on these programmes or would provide a practical perspective alongside other more theoretical books. Students must be able to demonstrate related skills and be able to continually update knowledge and skills, once the qualification is completed, as part of continuous professional development (CPD). This is an ideal accompaniment for such a programme because it addresses both skill and knowledge elements.

Tutors of academic management and professional programmes such as Diploma in Management Studies or MBA could find this book useful in planning their schemes. Increasingly, there is a requirement for a more practical, professional development element in the programme. The book could equally lend itself to accompany a 12 x 3-hour workshop programme of personal and professional development or a residential programme. It is particularly useful in this context because it contains both the practical and the theory behind it.

Practising managers should also find the book useful. Any manager interested in developing his or her skills should find something of interest in the book – in particular, any manager starting a new job with new skill requirements, anyone promoted to a managerial position for the first time or a manager working within a competency framework or undertaking a development programme within work. All of these managers should find the book helpful and relevant because it provides a practical, flexible approach to help in making personal and work change.

Professional trainers could find this book useful. They are often called upon to design skills programmes for managers and employees. The ideas used in this book could well be incorporated into training programmes. The theory and research supporting the ideas would add credibility to the programmes.

THE STRUCTURE OF THE BOOK

The book is structured in two sections (parts), each presenting a different perspective on the development of management skills.

Part 1

In the first section of the book we describe our model and each element in the process, supported by theoretical and practical models. We also provide examples and activities to illustrate the process and encourage active participation.

The outline of the basic process includes four elements:

A Awareness

D Decision

A Action, and

X Excellence.

This illustrates how managers become *aware* of the need to develop a certain skill; how they *decide* whether or not to pursue the development of the skill; what *actions* they take to develop a methodology for the skill; and how they attain a certain level of competence or *excellence*.

Part 2

This section of the book examines some issues and themes which we believe are most pertinent to the above process and allow the reader to explore them and their effect on the process.

The first theme examined is *experiential learning*, how it differs from other approaches to learning, and its role in adult learning (Knowles *et al*, 1998). We review the role of different stages in the experiential model and its application to skill development (Kolb, 1984) and how some of the criticisms of experiential learning may be addressed. We consider issues surrounding reflection (McAlpine and Weston, 2002), reflective practice (Beard and Wilson, 2006) and learning from experience (Boud, Cohen and Walker, 1993), and identify a range of practical activities that draw on experiential learning.

The second of these themes explores the link between *how the brain functions* and the process of skill acquisition, and how neuroscience is beginning to suggest answers to why some approaches to learning are more successful than others. The work of Sylwester (1995), Ratey (2003), Smith (2004), Greenfield (2002) and Jensen (2005) informs this exploration.

A good deal of research and writing suggests that a person's physical and mental *state* has a significant effect on learning and skill development (O'Connor and Seymour, 2003; Kenyon, 1994; Jensen, 2005). Csikszentmihalyi (2002) suggests that there is a 'flow' state, an optimum state for skill acquisition. This is the third theme to be explored.

The next theme reinforces the role of *the senses* in how we develop and execute skills. It examines the power, capacity and flexibility of our senses (Hannaford, 2006; Sylwester, 1995). We also examine the highly refined distinctions that can be made in the various sensory systems which contribute to variability in skill performance (Woodsmall, 1999).

The final theme is concerned with how *personal styles, preferences and difference* inform skill development. In particular, we examine different preferences in learning and understanding (Lawrence, 1993), and how the Myers-Briggs model is used to assist the development of skills in managers (Bayne, 1995). We briefly explore the application of research into multiple intelligences, how learning and cognitive style impact on learning from experience, and how this work is being used to develop skills in the workplace.

Applications and examples are provided throughout the book, along with reviews of our personal experiences to 'ground' the book. Most of the activities can be done alone for those who are reading this book to aid personal development, and can also be integrated into a programme of personal and professional development. Most of the examples use common management skills to illustrate the process, which once learned, can be applied to any skill.

In the final conclusion we provide our views on the way forward on a personal development journey, and we also provide an outline of how our approach to professional development progresses over time on an educational programme.

THE ORGANISATION AND LAYOUT OF THE BOOK

Within each chapter there are a number of techniques and formats which help emphasise the main points and findings:

- *Key questions and objectives* – At the outset of each chapter there are a number of questions which anticipate the major issues associated with the topic as well as a brief structure of the chapter.

- *Examples, metaphors and illustrations* – Throughout each chapter there are a number of examples, stories, metaphors and illustrations that support understanding of the key points.

- *Summaries and ways forward* – These help to pull together the main ideas of each chapter and recommend how the material can be developed and taken forward.

- *Further reading and resources* – This resource section provides the reader with sources of the ideas in the book and further reading that may develop these ideas.

We have met many students and fellow professionals who approach the reading of a book differently and we do not want to prescribe a 'right' or 'wrong' way of using this book. We have tried to design the book so that it can be used in a number of ways. We suggest that the following methods might be useful to different people at different times:

- Start at the beginning and work through.

- If you want to start with a practical perspective, start with the applications, cases, examples.

- If you want to get a feel for the territory of the book, look at the key questions and structure at the beginning of each chapter.

- The summaries give a succinct potted version of the contents.

- The sketches give a lighthearted way of getting an overview of the learning from the book.

- Use the index and the references/bibliography as a resource for the topics.

■ Let it fill a space on a bookshelf and promise yourself you will read it one day.

Whatever way you use it we hope you will find it practical, useful and enjoyable.

REFERENCES

Bass, B. M. and Vaughan, J. A. (1966) *Training in Industry: The management of learning*. London: Tavistock Publications

Bayne, R. (1995) *The Myers-Briggs Type Indicator: A critical review and practical guide*. London: Chapman & Hall

Boud, D., Cohen, R. and Walker, D. (1993) *Using Experience for Learning*. Milton Keynes: SRHE/Open University Press.

Boud, D., Keogh, R. and Walker, D. (1985) *Reflection: Turning experience into learning*. London: Kogan Page

Boyatzis, R. (1982) *The Competent Manager. A model for effective performance*. Chichester: John Wiley & Sons

Burgoyne, J. and Reynolds, M. (eds) (1997) *Management Learning: Integrating perspectives in theory and practice*. London: Sage

Constable, J. and McCormick, R. (1987) *The Making of British Managers*. London: British Institute of Management/Confederation of British Industry

Csikszsentmihalyi, M. (2002) *Flow: The classic work on how to achieve happiness*. New York: Harper & Row

Festinger, L. (1957) *A Theory of Cognitive Dissonance*. Evanston, Ill.: Row, Peterson & Company

Gardner, H. (1999) *Intelligence Reframed*. New York: Basic Books

Greenfield, S. A. (2002) *The Private Life of the Brain*. Penguin Press Science

Handy, C. (1987) *The Making of Managers*. London: National Economic Development Office

Hannaford, C. (2006) *Smart Moves*. Arlington, Virginia: Great Ocean

Jensen, E. (2005) *Teaching with the Brain in Mind*. San Diego, CA: Brainstore

Kenyon, T. (1994) *Brain States*. Naples, FL: U.S. Publishing

Knowles, M., Holton, E. F. and Swanson, R. A. (1998) *The Adult Learner*, 5th edition. USA: Butterworth-Heinemann

Kolb, D. A. (1984) *Experiential Learning*. Englewood Cliffs, New Jersey: Prentice Hall

Lawrence, G. (1993) *People Types and Tiger Stripes*, 3rd edition. Gainesville, Florida: Centre for the Application of Psychological Type, Inc.

McAlpine, L. and Weston, C. (2002) 'Reflection: improving teaching and students learning', in N. Hativa and P. Goodyear (eds) *Teacher Thinking, Beliefs and Knowledge in Higher Education*. Dordrecht: Kluwer Academic

Mintzberg, H. (1973) *The Nature of Managerial Work*. New York: Harper & Row

O'Connor, J. and Seymour, J. (2003) *Introducing Neuro-Linguistic Programming*. London: HarperCollins

Perren, L. and Burgoyne, J. G. (2002) *Management and Leadership Abilities: An analysis of texts, testimony and practice.* London: Council for Excellence in Management and Leadership.

Quinn, R. E, Faerman, S. R., Thompson, M. P. and McGrath, M. R. (2003) *Becoming a Master Manager: A competency framework.* USA: John Wiley & Sons, Inc.

Ratey, J. J. (2003) *A User's Guide to the Brain.* New York: Random House

Revans, R. W. (1971) *Developing Effective Managers: A new approach to management education.* London: Longman

Reynolds, J., Caley, L. and Mason, R. (2002) *How do People Learn*? London: CIPD

Rogers, A. (1996) *Teaching Adults.* Buckingham: Open University Press

Senge, P. (1990) *The Fifth Discipline: The art and practice of the learning organization.* New York: Doubleday

Skinner, B. F. (1974) *About Behaviourism.* London: Jonathan Cape

Smith, A. (2004) *The Brain's Behind It.* Stafford: Network Educational Press Ltd

Sylwester, R. (1995) *A Celebration of Neurons.* USA: ASCD Publications

Tennant, M. (2006) *Psychology and Adult Learning.* London: Routledge

Vygotsky, L. S. (1978) *Mind in Society: The development of higher psychological processes.* Cambridge, Mass.: Harvard University Press

Wenger, E. (1998) *Communities of Practice: Learning, meaning and identity.* Cambridge: Cambridge University Press

Woodsmall, W. (1999) *Strategies.* Course notes accompanying a programme on Behaviour Modelling.

The Process

The background to ADAX

The development of the ADAX model was a 15-year journey. My colleague and I ran the Professional Development Scheme for the Chartered Institute of Personnel and Development. Our development of the ADAX process began as a consequence of the challenges we faced in dealing with the new requirements of continuous professional development and the format of the professional syllabus which separately identified knowledge and operational (skill) outcomes. We did not believe that a series of conventional lectures on their own could address knowledge outcomes, the development of management and HR skills and at the same time deal with professional development issues.

Initially, we made two decisions. The first was to introduce a series of three-hour workshops to mainly deal with professional development issues and the development of management and HR skills (Routledge and Carmichael, 1995). These workshops ran in tandem with our normal lecture programmes. The second decision was to use the Kolb/Honey and Mumford model to review and assess the activities of the workshops. Later, we extended this review process to a sample of the student's work experiences. We believed experiential learning was the most appropriate answer to the new challenges of developing management skills and exploring professional development issues. We also believed it was an appropriate methodology for linking academic work with a manager/student's organisational experiences.

Learners have different levels of experience and ability – from beginner to expert – so we attempted to provide an approach that allowed learners to develop skills, from whatever their starting point. We also identified a number of management and human resource skills that could be developed in the workshops and would be pertinent to their work environment and circumstances. We encouraged reviews of personal experience as part of this process to provide a rich repertoire of data that can be used in learning. Kolb observed (1984, p.38) that:

> **'Learning is the process whereby knowledge is created through the transformation of experience.'**

His model of learning attempted to explain how everyday experiences resulted in our learning from it, through developing understanding then planning to implement the learning in the future. Kolb (1984) provided one of the best-known models of experiential learning, which was thereafter developed and modified by Honey and Mumford (1992). They described a learning cycle, which examines what a learner might do – review experience, find personal meaning, and plan for future situations. Learners are perceived to go around the learning cycle, passing through each of the four stages for effective learning (see Figure 2).

The following is an account of how our own model was developed, as dictated by our experience. The order is not how we finally decided to present it, which is based on a more logical sequence.

The Kolb/Honey and Mumford models provided the first element of our evolving model: **action**. The main difference that we tried to emphasise was between *knowing* and *doing*, and how the learning experienced in doing differed from the learning experienced in knowing. To facilitate the application of the models we introduced a series of questions which enabled participants to work around the cycle. These are discussed in Chapter 5 later. As the participant's familiarity with the model increased, the idea of spiral learning was introduced. This emphasised the developmental nature of the reflection and understanding elements of the cycle and how this led to the second element of our model: **excellence**.

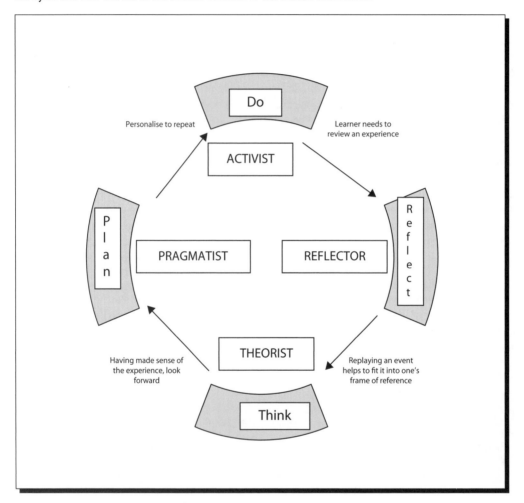

Figure 2: *Honey and Mumford's learning cycle, based on Kolb's experiential learning model*

As our experience of using the model increased, we realised that the generic nature of the review process meant that individuals could review any experience from a 5- to 10-minute interpersonal activity in the workplace to a three-year university business degree or five years' career development. Although this flexibility is a strength of the process, it is also a weakness for some people. We felt that other models or benchmarks would be useful for reviewing development and provide participants with different perspectives.

One of the most useful we have found in the context of learning is the competence model.

The model in Figure 3, which identifies the states that a learner seems to go through during learning, seems to us to be highly relevant to the development of management skills (May and Kruger,1988).

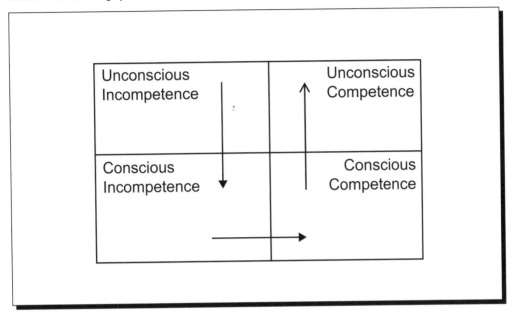

Figure 3: *A model of the stages in the learning process*

This model describes the learning process in terms of the unconscious/conscious mind and the states of competence and incompetence. The four elements correspond to key stages in the learning process. *Unconscious incompetence* is that state in which we are blissfully unaware of a particular skill – and we don't even know we are unaware of it. Before we begin driving, for example, we are often completely unaware of what skills are required to drive a car. Perhaps we have not thought about it much or have some ideally attractive idea of what it will be like.

The second phase of the model is *conscious incompetence*. At this phase an individual begins to realise what he or she lacks in terms of the skill – what he or she cannot do. The realisation of what it is like to steer, change gear, operate the indicator and brake all at the same time can come as quite a shock. This state can be very demoralising for some people and very motivating for others.

Most people who persevere through this state eventually arrive at the third state: that of *conscious competence*. Slowly but surely the individual begins to acquire the rudiments of the skill(s). There is a lot of conscious thought about the new movements, and these movements are probably not very smooth. Often you notice learner drivers talking to themselves, telling themselves when to brake, when to change gear, etc. There are still occasional faults when the driver 'crunches' the gears or oversteers into a corner, but competence is developing.

The final phase of the model is that of *unconscious competence*. In this state the skill actions are very much smoother and an individual is generally not even aware of deploying the skills. They have become automatic. The individual can carry out a conversation at the same time as he or she is driving. Sloboda (1991) describes skills in this phase as being fluent (the component parts run smoothly together), rapid (they can be executed almost immediately), automatic (they take little effort), simultaneous (they can be carried out at the same time as an unrelated activity) knowledge (because it is immediately available at the appropriate time).

This model seems to be useful in as much as it enables individuals developing skills to 'unpack' what is happening to them at significant and meaningful stages of the development process. Again, it very much enriches the 'reflection' and 'understanding' parts of the Kolb process.

The third element of our model came about by noticing that there appeared to be differences in the success individuals experienced in using the process. We report later in the book on observations we made with groups of students in using the process. Basically, we found differences in beliefs on how appropriate the workshops were for developing skills and professional development work generally. There appears to be a significant group of individuals who believe a university is for developing knowledge and being tested in examinations, and that skills are developed in the workplace. Also, some individuals demonstrate greater motivation than others. We ran those two findings together as our third element. **Decision-making** deals with whether individuals believe they can develop a particular skill and whether they can generate motivation in order to commit to developing it. A great deal of work remains to be done in this area.

The fourth element in our model is the most recent finding and one we are still developing: **awareness**. This is concerned with the individual's perceptual map. Initially we mistook this element for the third element, belief and motivation. For over 10 years now we have used the Myers-Briggs Inventory with students and have encouraged them to use the findings in their reviews. In the last five years we have also used Snyder's Self-Monitoring Inventory (1987) and Rotter's Locus of Control Inventory (1982) to give the individuals increased self-awareness of how they respond to the development process. The results of these inventories have convinced us of the importance of an individual's predispositions and perceptual map in determining how they experience the process. We now firmly believe that development is unique for each individual, and that everyone's individual map of the world will predispose each person to use the process in a different way. One of our current goals is to try to widen participants' perceptual maps to enable them to benefit from a greater variety of experiences.

We have reordered these four elements to give them an 'ideal' logic. However, we believe individuality rules and it will not be the same for everyone. Although the model appears to be a well-ordered neat garden, the reality may be nearer to a jungle.

SUMMARY

This section has described and explained how the ADAX process developed. This is our model for describing and understanding how people acquire skills. It is made up of four elements and we have identified and explained some of the key process skills which underpin the four elements. The reader should be able to acquire and practise these process skills as outlined within the appropriate section. The four elements are:

Awareness	(A)
Decision-making	(D)
Action	(A)
Excellence	(X)

This illustrates how managers become *aware* of the need to develop a certain skill; how they *decide* whether or not to pursue and commit to the development of the skill; what *actions* they take to develop a methodology for the skill; and how they attain a certain level of competence or *excellence*.

In Chapters 2 to 5 we examine how our thinking has been influenced by a number of writers and specialists around the issues of awareness, decision-making, action and excellence. We also describe techniques and approaches we have found useful in developing management skills.

In Chapter 2 we examine the role of awareness in the development of management skills, and the premise that if managers are to develop a skill, they must become aware that they do not possess the skill in the first place. There is so much information and stimulation out in the environment that individuals would be overwhelmed if they attended to all of it. We explore how individuals manage this situation by developing psychological processes that allow them to limit the amount of stimulation they attend to so that they can deal with it efficiently and effectively. We examine how differences in experience, beliefs, values and psychological predisposition lead to a wide variation in perceptual maps, and how this influences individuals' perspectives on management skills. We finally explore a variety of techniques and approaches, both individual and interpersonal, that can help managers extend and vary their perceptual maps to the benefit of their skill development.

For managers to decide and commit to developing skills they must want to develop them and believe they are able to do so. In Chapter 3 we examine the nature of beliefs and how they can exert such a powerful influence on our decision to pursue a skill and on the method we then choose to develop it. We also examine approaches to modifying and changing beliefs. We explore the nature of values and their influence on skill development, and how our beliefs determine how these values manifest themselves. We investigate techniques that enable us to experience what it feels like to work with and against our values. And we examine three motivational filters which predispose us to behave in certain ways.

In Chapter 4 we look at the 'action' part of skill development. First we explore the origins and nature of skill strategies – how organisational outcomes determine the content of management skills and how skill strategies are developed through our senses. We then examine three learning processes which shape action into skill outcomes: prior experience, trial-and-error and social learning. We investigate the nature of skill outcomes by looking into the relationship between simple and complex skills. We also see how skilled performance can be examined as a function of knowledge and action.

In Chapter 5 we examine a number of antecedents of excellence: business excellence, personal mastery, behaviour modelling, and high-performance teams. Each of these perspectives leads us to a fuller understanding of what excellence is. We also explore the idea that continuous skill development is a process to attain excellence and we examine practical ways of implementing this process. We further examine action learning as a methodology for excellence. Finally, we explore four issues we believe are fundamental characteristics of excellence in the process of developing management skills.

REFERENCES

Honey, P. and Mumford, A. (1992) *Manual of Learning Styles.* Maidenhead: Honey Publications

Kolb, D. A. (1984) *Experiential Learning.* Englewood Cliffs, New Jersey: Prentice Hall

May, G. D. and Kruger, M. J. (1988) 'The manager within', *Personnel Journal*, Vol. 67 (2)

Rotter, J. B. (1982) *The Development and Application of Social Learning Theory.* New York: Praeger

Routledge, C. W. and Carmichael, J. L. (1995) 'Managing the skills development process', *Journal of Industrial Training*, Vol. 25 (2)

Sloboda (1991) 'What is skill?', in A. Gellatley (ed.) *Skilled Mind.* Buckingham: Open University Press

Snyder, M. (1987) *Public Appearances, Private Realities.* New York: W. H. Freeman

Awareness

'As I wake from a deep sleep I slowly become aware of my situation and surroundings. I do not usually realise that this is happening, I do not need to do anything to make it happen, and I have little control over the process. While asleep I am not consciously aware of my surroundings, situation, or how my awareness levels change. However, as I wake I become aware of the birds and sounds outside my window; the warm and comfortable bed and coverings surrounding me; and of other people in the house and those going about their early morning business outside. I then begin to become aware of and focus on the day ahead of me.'

Something similar to this story probably occurs each day, for most people – I'm sure you can think of many occasions on which some event has drawn your attention to your surroundings, or some internal feeling, that you were not aware of previously. Yet you do not have to respond. If someone mentions my name across a noisy room, for example, I may immediately become aware of it – but if I am involved in another conversation, I may not overtly react although someone watching me closely might notice my temporary switch of attention. Our senses are constantly scanning our environment, internal and external, picking up cues, some of which we attend to, interpret and become aware of, whereas others remain unnoticed.

INTRODUCTION

Within the ADAX model, briefly described in the previous chapter, the initial stage of any development is for a learner to recognise that he or she needs to develop or improve a skill. This stage is important in specifying development needs and can help to provide motivation and to determine the direction that development might take. These factors are also part of the following stage of decision-making in our ADAX process. This chapter considers the process of becoming aware of a need to develop certain skills or to gain new insights about some aspect of work. Becoming aware of it may be unsettling for some people. However, others find this an exciting and interesting time, offering different challenges.

Within this chapter we introduce ideas about the importance of awareness and ask 'What is awareness?'

We reflect on the factors that influence our awareness to address questions to ourselves about ourselves, including 'Which characteristics most influence me, and where should I try to focus my awareness?' Throughout the chapter we provide activities to help readers to increase personal awareness to aid skills development.

WHAT IS AWARENESS?

We are concerned with how an individual becomes aware of potential opportunities for development. It involves a process of becoming conscious of internal or external cues in a situation. In every situation there is a great deal of information, and each potential stimulus can be selected by our senses to be processed, interpreted by our brain so that we become aware of it. Even when you are alone working intently on a task – for example, on an important report with your full attention focused on the keyboard and screen – your senses are still scanning your surroundings to pick up cues that might be important: the telephone, an email pop-up, a colleague outside your door, the surroundings outside. What is important is how any one of those cues captures your attention and diverts your focus from the task. There are, of course, stimuli that relate to our survival and that we share with other animals: a loud bang calls our immediate attention, or hunger pangs gnaw at us when we work too long and miss a meal. Unlike a wild animal that has to be constantly aware of potential predators, we have few life-threatening instances to react to but retain our ability to continually scan the environment and engage the same 'flight or fight' defence mechanisms. Certain stimuli have the ability to attract our attention and these are linked to our motivation, basic needs, past experience and interests. They may be internal or external cues. Internal cues include discomfort, as when first learning to trot on horseback, or embarrassment or pleasure, as when a new presentation goes particularly badly or well. External cues often come from direct feedback from colleagues or others involved in a situation and may be via comments or attitudes that you detect.

When we are working with others there is even more information that we may monitor – for example, speech directed at us, others talking away from us, body language, intonation, posture, and information that derives from the task in hand and the surrounding situation. This amount of information would be impossible to process all at once, and the cues from other people are therefore often perceived peripherally so that we are sufficiently aware of them without interpreting each piece of information individually.

Awareness may not always occur in the same way or in the same detail, but in learning it helps us in:

- recognising that we cannot do something as well as we would like to
- facilitating conscious remembering and learning of 'what works'
- continuing to motivate us to try harder
- reviewing the detail of what is required for ongoing improvement.

Awareness requires that we pay attention to and select appropriate cues around us. The process of attention requires a brief explanation.

Attention

When we see, hear or feel something, our attention is focused on that activity – but how *do* we focus attention? This is not a conscious activity for most of the time, and yet from all of the thousands of possible stimuli that are around us we make choices about what reaches our senses.

We have to select those that we process sufficiently to be interpreted and to which we direct our attention. Over years psychologists have worked to understand this process of stimulus selection and there have been different theories about how it occurs, from Broadbent's (1957) filter theory which suggested a bottleneck early in the perception process which resulted in information being filtered out and lost, to Norman (1968) who proposed a late-selection theory by which information was not filtered out but processed at an unconscious level and only certain features selected for conscious attention. Concern was raised about the possibility that unscrupulous individuals might find a way of planting stimuli in our unconscious minds to influence our behaviour without our realising it – for example, in advertising. But there is limited evidence that subliminal perception has any undue influence, so this idea is unlikely (Merikle, 1992). Some information is interpreted at this level of exposure, however, even if we are not aware of it. For example, we may be able to distinguish whether a photograph is of a male or a female after just a glimpse, even though we can describe little more about the person.

Treisman and Geffen (1967) suggested that there were two stages in the attention process – the first a 'preattentive' process, occurring prior to the conscious second stage and helping to direct attention toward specific stimuli. If people were asked to search for a target letter or shape, certain features of stimuli appeared to attract attention, including curvature, tilt, colour, contrast, brightness and movement. These features were suggested to be primitive features, each being perceived separately as part of the preattentive process (Treisman, 1989) and being brought together when the attention is focused on a particular item. Research found that people automatically process words for meaning, and that this can interfere in a visual perception task (described below) known as the Stroop colour-naming task, first conducted by Stroop in 1935.

EXERCISE

The Stroop colour-naming task

Write the words RED, BLUE, GREEN, BLACK, YELLOW and BROWN on two lists using pens with coloured inks – one list in which the coloured inks match the colours named, and the other list in which the colour of the ink never matches the colour named.

Ask a friend to read both lists aloud and observe time taken and any difficulties or incorrect colour names.

Most people find that the first list is easy to read because the cues of colour reinforce the names of the colours read out, whereas the second list suffers from interference caused by a mismatch between the colour of ink and the meaning of each colour name.

It has been found that emotions also influence which cues are attended to (Pert, 1997) and suggested that there is a high and low road to the processing of information. The high road is a logical, sequential activity over time during which decisions are made about required actions in relation to past experience. Yet the low road is a fast, instinctive and unconscious processing system that reacts when stimuli are perceived that might affect our survival (Smith, 2004). These two operate together and if we are overloaded or feel in another way threatened, the low road instinctive response takes over – and even when we do not run, our body reacts in ways to make it ready for either 'flight or fight'. Smith also explains how emotion is a key determinant in what we pay attention to, and that emotions are important in memory and learning through their influence on which cues are selected. For example, when hungry, we more quickly attend to the smell of food; or if we are interested in cars, we are more likely to recognise and remember details of a high-class sports car as it passes.

Attention is therefore a process that involves the filtering of information, either consciously or uncon-sciously depending on the circumstances, in order that cues that are important to an individual are perceived. It seems that emotion, certain visual characteristics, previous experience and motivation are important determinants in attracting our attention and becoming aware, and therefore in what we perceive, remember and learn.

THE ROLE OF AWARENESS IN LEARNING

Awareness plays an important role in learning. The following quote from Argyris (1985) emphasises its importance:

> **'The door to self-development is locked from inside. No one can develop anyone but themselves.'**

Argyris has written many books to aid our understanding of learning, both personal and organisational, particularly learning from everyday events in which learners have total responsibility for what they are aware of, what they learn, and how we facilitators of learning can help this process. The quote highlights the futility of attempting to train or educate people unless they are aware of a need to undertake development themselves, or at least unless they are open to new ideas and to trying out different ways of doing and seeing things. To extend the metaphor, the door must be at least ajar!

In ideal circumstances learners will be involved in identifying what they mean to learn, possibly how they mean to learn it, and what the intended outcome of that learning is. Or they may need help to become aware of each of these. As a learner progresses around the experiential learning cycle from doing to reviewing and then making sense of his or her actions or understanding, his or her awareness about actions, strengths and weaknesses grows. Learners may also become more aware of skills and behaviours of colleagues, customers or others who they deal with and of the situation that they are in, physically and politically. Being aware of relevant knowledge, of skills that we can use and of cues in a situation is important, although not sufficient for learning: we have to be able to interpret them all to form a whole picture and then learn how to react.

Some writers have criticised the experiential learning model because it does not provide a full picture of how someone learns (Tennent, 2006). It provides very limited consideration of which social and cultural knowledge and concepts influence learning and of how new ideas emerge (Beard and Wilson, 2006). We therefore believe that the awareness stage in our ADAX model adds an important element that is not sufficiently discussed in Kolb's model.

In order to examine the role of awareness in each of the models presented in the Introduction we will use an example of developing effective leadership in a poorly performing team. It is interesting to consider how awareness is essential in the learning process.

A leader may become aware that performance is below a required level through observation or through feedback from external measures of performance. However, the information may require more detailed analysis or more data before any action can be taken.

Through reflection on his or her own behaviour and that of the team, this leader will become aware of:

- any shortcomings in his or her personal style or attitude, or weaknesses in his or her team or ways of working
- skills lacking in himself or herself or other team members

- anxiety or animosity towards himself or herself (the leader) or other teams
- external factors that are affecting performance.

Reflection will help the leader to understand the problems and then to diagnose specific issues from among all of the possible factors contributing to the poor performance. This requires careful analysis and will be informed through reflection and understanding to become aware of skills that may require to be developed, behaviours or attitudes that do not match requirements, or impinging external issues. To take two possible scenarios:

- In scenario A, the leader – in this case let's call her a she – may reflect on the leadership style she has used with the team in different situations. Her natural style may be non-directive to allow team members to become involved and contribute in ways that they feel able, or want, to do. It may take some to reflect and come to this understanding; it may require the leader to read and gather information about different leadership models to identify her style; or she may be coached to this realisation – and there might be personal 'blind spots' or barriers to overcome along the way. However, having come to this insight about her personal style and considering whether in the particular situation, with this team, it is the most appropriate style to be using, the leader is now ready to plan how she might change in order to deal with the poor performance.
- In scenario B, the leader – and in this case let's call him a he – might reflect on the conversations and observations of the team and come to the understanding that the team is not functioning effectively. He could therefore gather information about teamworking and communication in order to diagnose the particular issues that require attention.

In both of these scenarios the team leader has become more aware of himself or herself – and of teamworking or other elements that may contribute to poor team functioning.

Greater awareness has provided a sound basis on which to make decisions and take action on the available options, so awareness is key in any learning situation. As we see later in the chapter, there are many different ways of working to raise awareness, whether working alone or with others.

Awareness and the competence model

Awareness is also important in the competence model and can provide the impetus for action in a situation. Taking the above example of a poorly performing team: if the team leader is at the stage of unconscious incompetence, he or she will not know how to improve the team's performance. Gaining greater awareness will therefore help in focusing on factors of the situation that may be a problem. This awareness may come from personal reflection and understanding or through external support from a coach or colleague, and can then be used to provide options and strategies to improve the situation.

Awareness is, then, a process that helps us to move from unconscious to conscious incompetence, and then is helpful as we move through decision-making and action onward to conscious competence. Throughout this process we are probably going around an experiential learning cycle numerous times becoming aware of more sophisticated cues and making incremental changes to what we do, until at unconscious competence we are not aware of the multitude of stimuli and skills we use to become excellent managers or leaders.

So awareness is important in the initial stages of development, and its importance continues throughout the process to help in redirecting learning. The following section considers a range of different techniques and activities that help to improve awareness of our skills and competence, ourselves and the environment in which we work.

GAINING AWARENESS

There are a variety of different practical ways in which our awareness of current competence can be increased. All rely on our wanting – or at least agreeing – to obtain this knowledge, and each is appropriate in different circumstances:

- either working alone
- or working with another, possibly a colleague or manager.

Working alone

Reflection

Everyone, at times, sits and 'replays' the events of a day, or a specific event – usually when it has gone particularly badly. For example:

Imagine you have just started working as a representative for an HR IT group and are asked to go out and demonstrate the system to a potential new client. You plan to start out early to reach the client for a 10:00am meeting. However, your car battery is flat so you have to ask a neighbour to help get the car started, and the motorway is busier than normal. Both are events beyond your control but put you behind schedule. You then experience great difficulty in locating the organisation, and the parking that has been arranged for you is a long distance from the building where you are to meet the client. So you arrive for the appointment about 30 minutes late. But the clients are still waiting for you, and allow you to catch your breath. You get into your discussions, which seem to start off quite well. When you are about 10 minutes into the presentation, however, your laptop shows 'low battery', so you have to ask to plug it into the client's electricity supply – only to experience problems linking to your network in order to continue the demonstration…

Most readers will be aware of the problems for the representative in this situation. Indeed, most people will be able to think of a similar example of when nothing seems to go right from beginning to end. We tend to reflect on these events to avoid such a situation happening again. There are some simple things that could have been avoided in the above example, and there were some events beyond 'your' control, but you might think, 'I'll be better prepared for them next time – leave earlier, check location and parking, and batteries.'

This is learning through reflecting on an event and may involve planning for a similar situation in future. Most of us seem to reflect on events that go badly, but do not always review good events, or even systematically review an event to tease out a balanced account of learning. Personal review questions can be used to reflect on what we do and how we achieve things throughout our day, and can be used at any time to ask:

- What am I doing now?
- Why am I doing this? What is it achieving?
- What is going well, and how do I feel about it?
- What is going less well?
- How are other people reacting to me?
- Are there things I would like to change in my behaviour?

This seemingly simple review of what we do is an effective approach to becoming aware of our development needs. Boydell (1985) recommends a 'backward review' to be used each day for reflection raising self-awareness to aid personal development. At the end of each day, reflect on the day, beginning with the most recent event and working backwards until you have thought back to the morning, using the questions above, or similar.

It is, however, somewhat more complex than the example suggests. Mumford and Gold (2004) make a distinction between retrospective learning – which takes place following an event, as in the above example – and prospective learning, where the actions, learning and review are pre-planned and systematic and so are thought to be more effective.

An example of planned action for prospective learning might run like this: 'I'll monitor what I do and how successful I am in persuading my colleague to do the presentation he doesn't want to do.'

Once you have completed the pre-planned activity it is helpful to use the review questions to raise your awareness of helping and hindering behaviours in achieving your objective. This is an effective way of gaining a better understanding of how you influence other people but relies on your self-awareness and can be used in any situation.

The CIPD's continuous professional development process uses the idea of self-review but usually covers a longer time-span. This process makes the reviewer aware of his/her actions, achievements and development needs, both personal and organisational.

ACTIVITY

With reference to the last 12 months, answer the following questions:

1   What have been your three main achievements at work?

2   In what ways have you added value to the business?

3   How can you ensure that you continue to add value – what specifically can you do?

4   What have been the three most significant learning events for you?

5   What have been the personal outcomes of this learning for you?

6   How can you continue your development in the coming 12 months?

Source: adapted from CIPD Membership Upgrade
form *Reflecting Back and Looking Forward*

Inventories

There are a range of inventories available to provide learners with information about their skills and competence and to raise self-awareness. An inventory is usually based on a model, research or opinion of what makes an 'ideal' manager so that each learner can self-assess himself or herself against the ideal to determine how he or she personally should develop. Examples of inventories to identify skills or competencies required by managers include CIPD Graduate Competencies, CMI Registered Manager, and MCI Vocational Qualifications in Management. These inventories are national frameworks against which anyone can assess himself or herself. For an inventory to aid awareness and personal development, however, it must be appropriate to the learner's personal circumstances, style and situation. (Examples of how the CIPD Graduate Competencies model may be used are included in the Appendix at the end of the book.)

It is also possible to use a framework of organisational skills or competencies to assess yourself against the most relevant skills for your current or future role in order to gain insight into areas for development.

This approach is likely to be useful if your organisation has more unusual – even unique – skills requirements which are clearly defined and related to success in the organisation.

An alternative approach is to develop a model of management, perhaps based on ideas about managers in your current organisation, that you can use to assess yourself against or to identify personal goals through a review of what you want to achieve. An exercise to provide such a model is presented below and can be completed either alone or with colleagues.

EXERCISE

The skills of an effective manager

Requirements for each group:

> 1 or 2 sheets of flipchart paper
>
> 'Post-It' notes in two colours
>
> Flipchart pens

Work in small groups of between four and six in number, although initially each group member should work independently.

Half of a group should think of one or more managers they have known who they believe is really effective as a manager. The other half of the group should think about managers they have known who they think are ineffective. Each half of the group must have Post-It notes of a different colour.

Each group member should spend approximately 10 minutes, working independently, identifying the key characteristics of the managers they are thinking about and to record one characteristic on each Post-It. During this time ideas should not be evaluated: the endeavour is to just record as many different characteristics as possible.

At the end of the 10 minutes the group should come back together and all identified characteristics should be listed on the flipchart. The group then works for approximately 15 minutes to discuss the characteristics identified and to group together the Post-It notes in order to develop and agree a model of effective and ineffective managers.

These models can then be used by each group member to assess himself or herself against the features identified.

Observation of others

An alternative way to begin to raise self-awareness of development needs is to observe other people and examine what they do, how they do it, and what they achieve. Using this approach it is possible to identify behaviour that we might want to learn or ensure we never use, so learning what to do and what not to do from others and widening our choice of available behaviours. Psychologists have studied social learning for many years and found it to be an effective route to development through cognitive processing of others' behaviour which may lead to imitation and adapting our own behaviour (Bandura, 2006). We watch, understand, and learn through watching.

A similar but more specific type of learning through observation is role modelling, in which a learner identifies a positive role model who they observe and attempt to imitate and learn from. The processes used in modelling are examined later in the book.

Working with other people

A learner is usually motivated to learn if he or she notices some shortcoming in himself or herself. Otherwise, a need may be identified by another person – for example, a manager – which may mean that someone has to try to persuade the learner to work to meet the need.

Feedback from others

Many people find it difficult to 'watch themselves' – that is, to be aware of their own behaviour, how and what they do, and its effect – so it can be useful to get feedback from other people. This can be in the form of spoken or written words, or via the completion of a questionnaire or skills analysis. The form of the feedback is less important than the willingness of the learner to understand and use the feedback and the skills of the person who provides the feedback.

The status of the person giving the feedback may be influential in how willing the learner may be to use the feedback. If the person giving the feedback is the learner's line manager or has high status in the learner's view, or control over the learner's destiny, or is trusted and recognised as effective in a relevant skill area, that person is likely to be regarded as important to the learner and so the feedback is more likely to be used. However, if the learner has no previous knowledge of the person who provides the feedback, or if previous knowledge suggests that this is someone not to trust or of little consequence, the feedback may be ignored or at best considered optional by the learner.

In addition, the personal characteristics of the receiver may influence whether the feedback is considered. There are therefore individual differences in openness to this type of information. Those who are more open to feedback tend to look for it from a wide range of people whatever their level of importance and connection to the learner. Such people may include:

- people unknown to the learner, who may provide informal feedback through their own behaviour towards the learner – eg pleasure or avoidance
- fellow students on a development programme
- colleagues at work who may behave as above, or from whom specific feedback can be requested
- managers as part of their role in developing the learner
- trainers whose primary role is to develop others.

We would probably assume that the detail and effectiveness of feedback would increase proportionately from top to bottom of this list, but as outlined earlier the learner's perception of whoever gives the feedback will determine its importance to the learner.

In our experience working with students, the more information learners are able to gather, from themselves and from others, and from different perspectives, the greater is their awareness of the effects of their behaviour, providing many options in developing skills. Feedback can, however, be very difficult to give and difficult to receive. Feedback is important in other parts of the ADAX process and is further discussed later.

Appraisal and personal development reviews (PDRs)

One occasion on which most employees are provided with formal feedback is a performance or personal development review. In most situations an appraiser has an organisational role to provide feedback as well as to make an assessment against organisational requirements. This may result in a 'pat on the back' or an objective action plan for improvement – and the employee is usually obliged to consider the feedback carefully. For most employees a PDR could be a way of finding out the organisation's view of them and their potential and, if effective, can help raising awareness about their own development needs and the time-scales for action on these immediately and in future.

Coaches and mentors

Coaching is an increasingly important role, often taken by a manager, and it is important in raising the awareness of an employee or colleague as well as helping the employee to address a learning need through coaching techniques. We use the GROW model of coaching (Brockbank and McGill, 2006) frequently found in books or on Internet sites. It is a useful model to fit any coaching situation and brings together many individual skills used in a manager's role. Using GROW provides a process and framework to help guide the coach through this process.

Mentoring is similar to coaching but usually much more wide-ranging and personal. It is a role most often taken on by a manager who is not the mentee's own manager. Raising the mentee's awareness of his or her needs is a key role for a mentor because mentoring is about long-term career intentions and how a mentor can steer and provide openings for the mentee. The exercise below is included as one approach to encouraging an individual or mentee to look forward and help to identify goals and how to achieve them. It is included with thanks to the local CIPD Branch CPD Adviser.

EXERCISE

What will my key achievements be?

This is an individual exercise although it can be done with a small group. The key intended output is a plan which identifies future goals or desires, and the skills and actions required to achieve those goals or desires.

1   Consider a day 12 months ahead of the current time. If you were looking back on your achievements from this time, what would be the most important things you have achieved during this period?

     These achievements can be personal or work-related – things that you want to have achieved when you look back.

2   Review the list and do a 'reality check' – of those things you have listed, which are really impossible, and what are the things that could realistically be achieved.

3   From the possible achievements select those that you think have the highest priority for you.

4   Take each of the goals in turn and make it into a SMART outcome. This means making the outcome:
     Specific – you must know precisely what you intend to achieve
     Measurable – so that you will know when it is achieved
     Achievable through being possible but stretching
     Realistic
     Time-bound – so you know by when it has to be achieved.

5   Think about what support you will need to achieve your goal, which people you will need to help, what resources or skills will be required.

6   Record your action plan carefully and keep it in a safe place to review in 12 months.

As can be seen from the above there are a range of different formal and informal situations for raising awareness about a learner's skills, knowledge and attitudes. The focus of attention raises awareness of different facets important in development.

AWARENESS IN PERSONAL DEVELOPMENT

Awareness is necessary in any planned sustained development and the above exercises are aimed at helping everyone become more aware. However, awareness can be focused on different aspects of a situation and thus provide different information for a learner. Such aspects, or areas of attention, are:

- WHAT: the skills that should be developed
- WHY: the relevance of those skills to the learner
- HOW: how the skills and competence should be developed
- CONTEXT: the context of the development – who else is involved, where and when
- SELF: self-awareness: becoming more aware of what we are or our preferences and our 'natural' ways of doing things and why we do them that way
- LEARNING: learning, linked to self but also learning about the process of learning that can be applied in helping others to learn.

Each of the different areas of attention above can be included in a review, and they are not mutually exclusive. However, each provides important information that ought to be useful in becoming excellent performers in whatever we do. We believe it is important to explore how each area adds to our awareness of a whole situation. In this chapter we now go on to examine the top four themes – the skills, their relevance and how they might be developed, and the context of that development. We briefly discuss the remaining two themes, although they are considered at length in chapters in the next section.

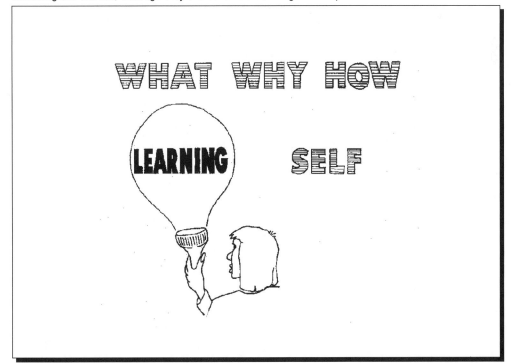

Figure 4: *Highlight different perspectives in review*

What skills should be developed?

Awareness of which skills have been used and how they might be developed is an important part of becoming aware of development needs and one that most people find easy to appreciate. However, when people talk about skills, although they may use the same general skill name, they may interpret what is meant by this skill name differently. Our work with students has taught us not to take for granted that when a group talks about a particular skill they all have a common understanding of this skill.

For example, interview skills are commonly used by all managers, and there are differences in the skills required depending on the type of interview involved – and there are also some underlying skills that can be employed in interviews, including questioning, summarising and developing rapport.

It is important that managers are aware of the skill 'building blocks' that are used in interviews and are as specific as possible about particular needs that they identify. It may be a very specific skill that is identified – for example: 'I don't know how to build rapport skills at the beginning of recruitment interviews.'

Knowing that a learner has identified a limited set of skills, it is possible in a specific situation to begin to work with the learner immediately on his or her development. But if a learner says, 'I don't feel confident that I get the best candidate in recruitment interviews', the learner is showing an awareness that a problem exists, but there are many possibilities to be investigated before any specific development can be recommended. Indeed, most advice on objective-setting suggests that it is important to be specific as well as realistic and measured when setting objectives for development.

Techniques to use

A number of techniques can be used to aid analysis, including observation of recruitment interviews by a colleague, specifically focusing on factors that influence 'how to get the best from a candidate'. These may include developing rapport, open questioning, probing, and maintaining rapport throughout the exchange. Alternatively, learners may choose to use role models that they can observe to aid analysis of their own style or may prefer to undertake a detailed review of their actions, feelings and attitudes in interview situations using review questions (as outlined later in the chapter) to identify what learning needs will improve their interviews.

Different learners use skills in different ways, so that although we may discuss how to undertake interviews and provide good practice guidelines, each learner is likely to use his or her skills uniquely and be aware of different cues in the situation. Guidelines are thus only a starting point from which each learner discovers his or her own personal approach.

Why these skills are relevant

Becoming aware of why he or she may have specific development needs helps to establish relevance for the learner, and this is important for each learner because he or she is unlikely to be motivated to develop skills that he or she believes are not personally relevant. If through future planning a learner is aware of longer-term development needs, those needs will be relevant to the learner but the learner may not have the opportunity to gain experience.

What can be more difficult is helping learners to become aware of the relevance of certain skills if they do not see that for themselves – for example, as part of a wider development programme, or having been sent on a training event without appropriate discussion beforehand. People do differ in their awareness of how and when particular learning may be important to them, and for some if the learning is not immediately relevant, motivation is compromised.

Techniques to use
PDRs and activities looking forward are useful in showing how important continual development and learning is.

The context: who should do what, where and when

Most situations are complex, involving a variety of people, conflicting processes and priorities so proving difficult to analyse, and it can take time to analyse events in detail as well as being difficult due to our personal involvement. There is a tremendous amount of information that our attention could be drawn to, in reviewing such a complex situation – for example, our own speech, behaviour and attitude in any encounter, as well as others' behaviour, speech and attitudes, which we interpret through their body language, intonation, expression and such factors, often unconsciously. There may also be group dynamics and our experience of others that also influence our understanding of the whole. It is useful to develop observation and listening skills to monitor full details of a situation so that these can be used later to aid reviewing. A review of each element in turn can be helpful, rather like turning a spotlight on each element of a situation one after another. Such a review helps to raise awareness not just about skills and development needs but about ourselves, other people and the mutual influence of these on behaviour. These factors are important in personal development and the review questions we use provide an opportunity to give attention to each factor in any situation.

We must be aware of the variability of complex situations because minor changes to the membership of a group in discussion, or different objectives or motivation, can change the whole dynamic of a meeting, may change our focus of attention, or result in other changes in the situation. In all of these situations it is essential to remain constantly aware of personal, contextual or skills requirement changes and of possibilities to adapt behaviour to the change.

Techniques to use
Techniques include the personal review questions and also using feedback from colleagues.

How the skills and competence should be developed

Awareness of how an individual develops skills and what approaches he or she learns most from is likely to be more consistent of each individual, although it also develops over time as their learning preferences change – for example, changes in learning styles (Honey and Mumford, 1982).

Learners will always, however, be encouraged to try out new approaches and to learn to develop skills of 'learning to learn' to further aid personal and skill development. It is also important in development to be aware of the processes used in understanding and developing skills: these are higher-order skills – eg 'learning to learn' *et al* – and provide important self-awareness of learning preferences and problem situations.

Techniques to use
Techniques include the final questions in the learning review as well as those from CIPD Continuous Professional Development.

Self and self-awareness

Our awareness of our own needs, preferences and motivations has been studied at length over many years and has generated many different models, some of which are discussed in relation to the whole of the ADAX model later in the book. However, one model that specifically includes awareness is that of emotional intelligence (Goleman, 1998). Within his model key competencies are identified that relate specifically to the awareness stage, taken from three competence areas:

- Self-awareness – knowing one's internal state, preferences, resources and intuitions:

  emotional awareness – recognising one's emotions and their effect

  accurate self-assessment – knowing one's strengths and limits

  self-confidence – having a strong sense of one's self-worth and capabilities

  self-control – keeping disruptive emotions and impulses in check

  conscientiousness – taking responsibility for personal performance

- Motivating oneself:

  using emotions for paying attention, for self-control and for creativity

- Empathy – awareness of others' feelings, needs and concerns:

  understanding others: sensing others' feelings and perspectives, and taking an interest in their concerns.

This model of awareness includes understanding and controlling ourselves and our own feelings, as well as understanding others' feelings. In organisations there is a growing body of research – particularly in relation to managers and executives – suggesting that EQ is essential to organisational success and in organisations for competitive advantage. Research into the skills and characteristics required by managers in organisations has found that technical skills are now less important to them than an ability to learn on the job and manage themselves and work with others effectively, as characterised by EQ. As Goleman *et al* suggest (2002; p.253):

> **'Leaders high in emotional self-awareness are attuned to their inner signals, recognising how their feelings affect them and their job performance... and can often see the big picture in a complex situation.'**

Awareness of our own and other people's personality preferences are important in learning and influence what we pay attention to. There is one dimension that seems to be particularly important in learning and that is whether we take and understand information from a holistic viewpoint or whether we prefer to break down information to consider detail. These and other stable, personal characteristics are discussed in detail in the second part of the book.

Techniques to use

Techniques are similar to those for how skills should be developed, and also include thinking about the Johari Window (see Figure 5).

The Johari Window is a helpful model to aid an understanding of the different views of a learner and how they contribute to development. It is a model representing a learner's personal characteristics and skills, based on:

- what the learner knows and doesn't know about himself or herself, and

- what other people know and don't know about the learner.

These two dimensions can be represented as the axes of a graph in quadrants, as shown in Figure 5.

For each one of us the Johari Window may be different, depending on our own self-knowledge and what information we have about others, through our experience. Of course, you have a slightly different set of panes for each important relationship you have. In any relationship we can use feedback from others to decrease the size of our blind pane, learning more about ourselves from other peoples' points of view. By disclosing information about ourselves to others we increase the size of our open pane (and decrease the size of our private pane). As we gather more information from other people and note their reactions to information we supply, we get the opportunity to become more aware of ourselves, our skills, attitudes and competence.

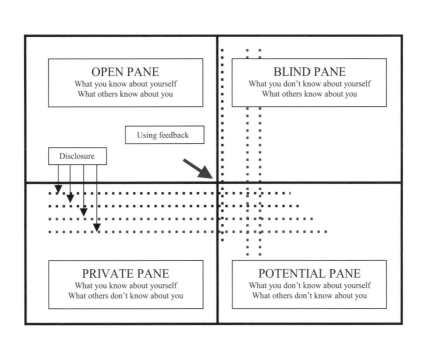

Open pane: what we know about ourselves and others know about us, so it includes physical characteristics, what we do and other visible features

Private pane: what we know about ourselves but what other people do not know. It includes how we feel, our feelings, values and beliefs but keep to ourselves

Blind pane: what others know about us but what we do not know – for example, what we look like from behind. It also includes others' interpretation of our behaviour, their views about us but may not articulate

Potential pane: what cannot yet be seen by anyone. This is what we might become, our future skills, development, and possibilities, as yet undiscovered.

Figure 5: *The Johari Window, showing how feedback and disclosure can improve relationships*

SUMMARY AND WAY FORWARD

This chapter has presented the first stage in the ADAX model, concerned with becoming aware of needs for development and discussing evidence related to how our attention in situations is focused, by providing an overview of known psychological principles of attention.

We have examined the major contribution of awareness to learning and the development of skills, and discussed factors that impact on individuals' awareness and ways to increase awareness.

Once a learner becomes aware of all the available information in a situation and chooses from amongst it what to focus on, he or she is effectively deciding to what extent greater awareness is welcomed and will be used in order to move a stage further in developing competence.

The activities included in the chapter are intended to promote greater awareness of skills that may require development and of the information that enables us to continually improve and develop skills and competence in our work. We recommend that you try as many of these exercises as possible because their outputs will help, whatever your current stage of development.

REFERENCES AND FURTHER READING

Argyris (1985) 'Human relations: a look into the future', *Management Record*, Vol. 2, No. 3

Bandura, A. (2006) 'Social cognitive theory', in J. Feist and G. J. Feist *Personality.* New York/London: McGraw Hill

Beard, C. and Wilson, J. P. (2006) *Experiential Learning: A best practice handbook for educators and trainers.* London: Kogan Page

Boydell, T. (1985) *Management Self-development: A guide for managers, organisations and institutions.* Switzerland: International Labour Organisation

Broadbent, D. E. (1957) 'A mechanical model for human attention and immediate memory', *Psychological Review*, Vol. 64: 205–15

Brockbank, A. and McGill, I. (2006) *Facilitating Reflective Learning Through Mentoring and Coaching.* London: Kogan Page

Goleman, D. (1998) *Working with Emotional Intelligence.* New York: Bantam

Goleman, D., Boyatzis, R. and McKee, A. (2002) *The New Leaders: Transforming the art of leadership into the science of results.* Great Britain: Little Brown

Honey, P. and Mumford, A. (1982) *Manual of Learning Styles.* London: P. Honey

King, K. (2005) *Bringing Transformative Learning to Life.* Florida: Krieger Publishing

Kolb, D. A. (1984). *Experiential Learning.* Englewood Cliffs, NJ.: Prentice Hall

Luft, H. (1984) *Group Processes: An introduction to group dynamics.* Mountain View, CA: Mayfield

Merikle, P. M. (1992) 'Perception without awareness', *American Psychologist*, Vol. 47: 792–5

Mumford, A. and Gold, J. (2004) *Management Development: Strategies for action.* London: CIPD

Norman, D. A. (1968) 'Toward a theory of memory and attention', *Psychological Review*, Vol. 75: 522–36

Pert, C. (1997) *The Molecules of Emotion*. New York: Touchstone

Riding, R. and Rayner, S. (1998) *Cognitive Styles and Learning Strategies: Understanding differences in learning and behaviour*. London: David Fulton

Smith, A. (2004) *The Brain's Behind It: New knowledge about the brain and learning*. Stafford: Network Educational Press

Stroop, J. R. (1935) 'Studies of interference in serial verbal reactions', *Experimental Psychology*, Vol. 18: 643–62

Tennant, M. (2006) *Psychology and Adult Learning*. London: Routledge

Treisman, A. (1989) 'Features and objects: the fourteenth Bartlett Memorial Lecture', *Quarterly Journal of Experimental Psychology*, 40A: 201–37

Treisman, A. and Geffen, G. (1967) 'Selective attention: perception or response?', *Quarterly Journal of Experimental Psychology*, 19: 1–17

Decision-making

Whenever I get the chance to listen to famous sportspeople who have achieved a significant goal, won a major event or broken a record, I always like to hear them talk about how they got to that position. What made them take up their sport? How did they maintain their motivation over their career? What drives them? It is not only famous people that prompt these questions. We all probably know a friend or relative who made a decision to take up some activity – whether in the social, sporting or work context – which required commitment, energy and the development of special skills and who has in his or her own terms made a significant achievement. It is the processes and the issues surrounding these events that we explore in this chapter.

In particular, we:

- develop the idea that deciding to pursue a skill and commit to it is a function of belief and motivation
- explore the function of beliefs in skill development, and in particular the role of self-efficacy, belief audits and approaches to managing and changing beliefs
- examine the role of motivation in skill development through the ideas of managing values and using motivational filters.

These are the elements which constitute *decision-making* in our ADAX model.

According to our ADAX model, once a person becomes aware of his or her potential or need to develop a skill (*awareness*), he or she is confronted by the decision whether to pursue it or not. The state associated with this decision can be very challenging. Some people have a strong emotional reaction to 'conscious incompetence'. There can be strong negative social judgements associated with not knowing something, which makes people feel afraid or embarrassed. Other people can find this state challenging and exciting. The outcome of 'conscious incompetence' is often connected to a person's self-perception, values and beliefs about himself or herself. Where people go to after the state of conscious incompetence is very dependent on their beliefs about the world and the values that motivate them.

My colleague and I run professional development workshops for students who are studying for a professional qualification. We noticed that some students seemed to derive far more benefit from the sessions than others. They would seem more motivated, have more energy, spend more time in review discussions and appeared to have more success in achieving the outcomes of the session. This made us wonder how they were different from other students who did not seem to perform as effectively.

Over several sessions we observed and interviewed a range of students who performed with differing degrees of success in the workshops. We attempted to pick out the students we considered to be effective learners. Routledge (1995) reports that the characteristics of effective learners are threefold. First, the learners find relevance and meaning in the training and can communicate this to others. Second, they can use their learning to set outcomes for events outside the training. Third, a considerable time after the training they can cite a number of examples of how they have incorporated their new learning into their repertoire of behaviours/capabilities/attitudes, etc, to their benefit.

One of the most striking differences that emerged was that the more effective learners expressed the following beliefs about the workshops and their learning:

- Learners operate the 'can't–want–will–can' chain. They start from the premise that they cannot do something at the present time, but they want to do it, and decide they will do it, and believe it will only be a matter of how and when. Although this does not guarantee success, it maximises the probability of success.

- Learners believe that success in anything needs a positive attitude – and this is very much the case with learning.

- Learners believe that a sense of fun and enjoyment is conducive to effective learning.

- Learners believe that it is necessary to receive feedback from a wide range of sources, not just the trainer.

- Learners believe that they can learn in a wide range of situations. They tend to be proactive and independent and do not always need an expert to learn from.

The story does not end there. Over the years my colleague and I have kept in touch with many of this group of students, both effective and less effective learners. One of the effective learners started his own training consultancy, and a second one went on to undertake a series of self-development workshops. Three other effective learners that we were able to track down had in some way pursued some kind of self-development for interest or career purposes. Something common to all members of this group is that in conversation with them they brought up the topic of skill/professional development without any prompting. All of them said how useful the skill workshops had been.

A small sample of the less effective learners did not mention the topic of skill/professional development without prompting. They did not link the workshops to any job changes or promotions they might have had. None of them mentioned how useful the skill development workshops had been. One individual did report a change of heart and said that although she had not realised the value of the skill development sessions at the time, she could now look back and see how they had helped her in her career.

The key finding in terms of our model was that all the effective learners stated that they had found the workshops useful in terms of achieving some personal or career development goal.

For our learners to make a decision to acquire a particular skill, they must believe that the process is possible. They must believe that they have the necessary attitudes and behaviours to acquire this skill. They must also believe that the workshop is an appropriate place to progress towards this outcome and that they will have the opportunity to practise the skill back in the workplace.

However, to believe skill acquisition is possible and that one has the means and capacity to achieve the end result is not sufficient. These beliefs must be energised through the process of motivation before full commitment can be made to the decision.

It is a two-dimensional process – one of belief and one of motivation. If you have to be at a certain place at a certain time, it is not enough to believe you have a reliable car and a tank full of petrol and you are an experienced enough driver to avoid an accident and negotiate the traffic. You must also have a compelling reason to reach that destination, such as picking up your children from school or meeting your new boss or organising a future holiday. These are the things that energise the process and enable you to fully commit to the outcome.

We feel that the two-factor theory proposed by Vroom (1964) may give some insights into the processes surrounding the decision-making. Vroom postulated that individuals make calculations on whether to pursue outcomes (decision-making and commitment) based on the subjective belief of the likelihood of the outcome and the value the individual places on the outcome.

Commitment = Subjective probability of outcome (belief) x Value placed on the outcome (motivation)

For example: if an insurance salesperson believes that the more clients she calls, the more sales she will make, and the more sales she makes, the more money she will earn – and she values money highly – then her behaviour will be to call as many clients as possible. She will be strongly committed to engage in this behaviour. Theoretically, we could put a score of 0 (impossible) to 1 (certainty) on the belief and a score of −1 (strongly negative value) to +1 (strongly positive value). Vroom was not implying that individuals actually do such precise calculations but that they do go through this process subconsciously, comparing outcomes and weighing their significance.

As in Vroom's expectancy model, the commitment and action to pursue the development of a skill is a function of the belief in the likelihood of developing the skill and the value placed on the possession of the skill. If a person believes he or she can acquire a skill and he or she values that skill, he or she will be more likely to take the decision to acquire it, be committed to it and remained committed to it until he or she has reached a significant goal.

In the rest of this chapter we examine some of the characteristics of these two components.

We explore some of the general characteristics of beliefs and how they impact on skills. From a practical perspective we look at some skills of managing, modifying and changing beliefs including self-efficacy, belief audits and approaches to changing beliefs.

In the final part of the chapter we explore two practical ways of operationalising the concept of motivation: managing our values and using motivational filters.

BELIEFS

A belief is defined in the dictionary as:

1   The mental action, condition or habit of trusting in a person or thing; trust, dependence, reliance, confidence, faith.

2   Mental acceptance of a proposition, statement or fact as true, on the ground of authority or evidence; assent of the mind to a statement or to the truth of a fact beyond observation, on the testimony of another, or to the fact or truth on the evidence of consciousness; the mental condition involved in this assent.

3   The thing believed; the proposition or set of propositions held true; opinion, persuasion.

4   A formal statement of doctrines believed, a creed.

5   Confident anticipation, expectation.

Dilts *et al* (1990) suggest that a belief is a generalisation about a relationship between experiences. O'Connor and Seymour (2003) describe beliefs as our guiding principles, the inner maps we use to make sense of the world. Hall (2005) makes a useful distinction between thoughts and beliefs. We can have the thought '$a = b$', but to turn this into a belief we have to confirm it, say 'Yes' to it. A belief is a thought we frame as 'valid, true and real'. Beliefs exist on a level different from thoughts.

In my work as a trainer and lecturer I have encountered students and delegates who believe they lack numeracy skills. Many cannot remember the first time this thought impinged on their conscious mind. If they could, they would probably remember times when they had 'difficulties' with numbers, such as negative comments made by maths teachers, failing numeracy tests or exams, and comparing themselves with individuals who excelled in quantitative subjects. Perhaps they had inherited their attitudes to numbers from their parents who also believed they did not possess numeracy skills. Each of these thoughts must have occurred at certain times in their lives. All of these thoughts come together to form beliefs about their competence at maths and numbers. Once an individual gives an interpretation to these thoughts, it does not matter whether the thoughts are real or imagined or the interpretation is realistic or not – at those particular times beliefs are created about what those thoughts mean to the individual.

Once an interpretation (belief) has been given to a thought, it then becomes a guiding principle to enable a person to understand his or her world. It also becomes part of the unconscious mind and organises and influences all future thoughts (Phillips and Buncher, 1999).

We can begin to develop beliefs before we can speak or interpret. Phillips and Buncher (1999) describe the process by which beliefs can be learned and expressed as one of SEE–DO.

'As children, before we can speak or interpret, we can watch and copy. We learn to grow up by watching and copying what others do. As children we cannot rationalise or justify, we just experience without interpretation everything that goes on around us. It is in noticing the subtle changes and variations in voice expression and closeness shown by our parents that the first beliefs in our childhood years are formed. These learnings are then integrated by our unconscious mind with other thoughts and are used as building-blocks with which to construct further beliefs. Our beliefs, including those which are not our own to start with, control who we are now and for evermore.'

Beliefs are not facts. Some beliefs are based on facts. We share many of these beliefs with other people. We do not try to overturn the laws of gravity by walking off high buildings or put our fingers in a fire to see whether it burns. Others – particularly those about the way people behave and our own capabilities – are unresponsive to logic. There is a wide variation between people when we consider these types of belief. This makes beliefs difficult to deal with. People act as if their beliefs are true. That is why it is often very difficult to change someone's mind. The fact that beliefs reside in the unconscious mind is an even greater barrier to modifying or changing them because we are often unaware of their effect.

Our parents are a major source of our beliefs, but there are many more. Some of the more significant ones are:

- siblings and their comments

- friends and their comments
- other people's beliefs
- our interpretation of other people's behaviour
- peer groups
- television, radio and films
- imagination
- stories
- incidents at work and work colleagues
- music
- celebrities
- politicians
- feelings.

Dilts *et al* (1990) tell a story attributed to Abraham Maslow.

> **'A psychiatrist was treating a man who thought he was a corpse. Despite all the psychiatrist's logical arguments, the man persisted in his belief. In a moment of inspiration, the psychiatrist asked the man, "Do corpses bleed?" The patient replied, "That's ridiculous! Of course corpses don't bleed." After first asking his permission, the psychiatrist pricked the man's finger and produced a drop of bright red blood. The patient looked at his finger with abject astonishment and exclaimed: "I'll be damned! Corpses do bleed!"'**

This amusing story demonstrates how powerful beliefs can be. One of the reasons beliefs are so powerful is that they are so pervasive in our make-up. They make sense of the world. They enable life to be simple because they are automatic and unconscious. Every time we have to make a decision or take some action, we do not have to work things out from first principles: there are our beliefs guiding our actions.

Tytherleigh (1997) suggests that beliefs are powerful because they directly influence our experiences. If we believe we are competent, we search for opportunities to demonstrate that competence. Our beliefs create our experience. Our experience of competence reinforces our beliefs. Beliefs become self-fulfilling prophecies. They are stored in our unconscious mind, and generalise across our behaviour without our even being aware of them. They also exclude and filter out experiences not consistent with themselves. Tytherleigh also lists three factors which determine the strength and influence of a belief:

- The longer the period of time a belief is held, the stronger the belief becomes.
- The amount to which a belief affects reality is determined by the measure of certainty and conviction with which it is held.
- The amount of agreement and collusion between people about a belief also affect the strength and influence of the belief.

Everyone has hundreds, possibly thousands, of beliefs, each one generated from individual thoughts. These beliefs reside in our unconscious mind. Phillips and Buncher (1999) describe the mechanism that holds these beliefs together as our ego. It is this mechanism that automatically chooses for us how to think, act and behave in any situation. It is our 'world map'. According to the beliefs stored, the ego allows us to experience the world in a particular way. Our emotions during this experience are often unrelated to the event that is occurring but are related to the emotions which surrounded the original thought which gave rise to the formation of the belief(s). We only notice life's experiences after they have been filtered through our belief system. Your ego will not let you see what does not fit with what you already believe to be true.

Figure 6: *The power of beliefs*

My experience in running skill development workshops convinces me that beliefs are the factors that most empower or limit learning. (I cannot prove it: it is just one of my beliefs.) They strongly influence what capabilities we develop, what behaviours we demonstrate, and where and when we develop them. O'Connor and Seymour (1994) suggest that empowering beliefs give learners permission to try out new things, to develop new skills. Limiting beliefs act as barriers to learning. They usually operate around expressions like 'I can't' or 'I must' or 'I should'. They take permission away, reduce options, limit outcomes. O'Connor and Seymour advocate that cleaning up personal belief systems is a central part of any personal development programme. The test of empowering beliefs is whether they are useful for learning. Do they produce the outcomes you want?

Beliefs about personal competence and potential capabilities are often installed when we are quite young and by the time we reach adulthood can be very resistant to change. It would be unrealistic and misleading to say that managing, modifying and changing these beliefs would be easy. However, many of us fervently believed in Father Christmas and the Tooth Fairy, and now do not. There are obviously natural mechanisms which work to install more appropriate beliefs, and the techniques we are about to examine build on these mechanisms.

Approaches to managing, modifying and changing beliefs

Some years ago, I attended a conference where the delegates where given a chance to learn to juggle during one of the sessions. They were given minimal instructions and a few demonstrations by the tutor before being allowed to practise for about 40 minutes. After about five minutes several of the delegates had sat down and were chatting or engaging in some other type of activity. Over the 40 minutes they were joined by about half of the delegates. Of the rest a few were relieved when the tutor called time. Some were disappointed they were not allowed more time, and some were downright indignant that they were not allowed to complete the task – and some were giving a very good demonstration of conscious competence in the skill of juggling. Talking to many of the delegates during the evening I now believe I was watching a manifestation of self-efficacy. The group expressed a wide spectrum of beliefs about their chances of being able to juggle by the end of the session. Some expressed the view that they had never been good at that sort of thing and knew they would never be competent, whereas others really looked forward to the session and were extremely competitive and promised themselves they would buy juggling balls and become proficient. There was also a range of views expressed between these. I remember thinking at the time what a great variety of beliefs were brought to bear on what seemed a fairly innocuous activity.

The concept of self-efficacy addresses the relationship between belief, skill and behaviour. Bandura (1977) suggests that self-efficacy relates to 'beliefs in one's capabilities to mobilise the motivation, cognitive resources and courses of action needed to meet given situational demands'. Bandura's theory of self-efficacy (1977) proposes that self-efficacy is fundamental to competent performance. Like many psychological traits self-efficacy is a function of genetic disposition and life's experiences. So we are born with some degree of self-efficacy and through our approach to certain tasks such as skill development we grow in the trait or we diminish it. Self-efficacy allows managers to increase their competence in skills and in turn increase their self-efficacy. It acts as a virtuous circle.

If we have a high expectation of success in achieving a skill (high self-efficacy), then performance seems to follow (see Figure 7).

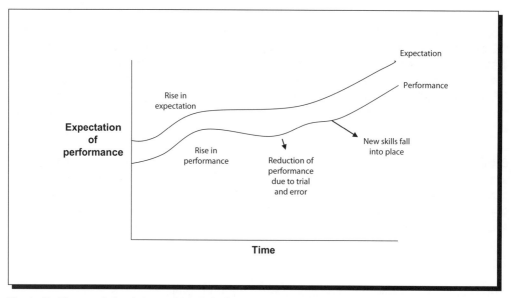

Figure 7: *The correlation between high self-efficacy (expectation) and performance*

However a decrease in performance can occur if the mismatch between expectation and performance becomes too great (see Figure 8).

The continued increase in performance depends on developing new skills and this is most likely where self-efficacy is high. Bandura states that self-efficacy is enhanced by successful performance, vicarious experience, verbal persuasion and emotional arousal. The most important and relevant to the development of management skills is successful performance. According to Bandura, successful performance raises expectations for future success; failure lowers these expectations. Cox (1995) states that repeated success through participatory modelling is the most critical aspect of Bandura's work when applied to performance. The subject first observes a model perform the task. Then the model assists the subject in successfully performing the task. The subject is not allowed to fail. As a result of the repeated success, strong feelings of self-efficacy develop.

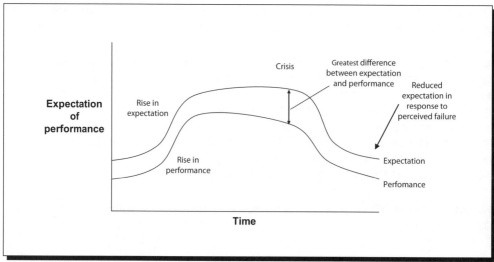

Figure 8: *The correlation between low self-efficacy and poor performance*

Below is an account of a management workshop to develop problem-solving interviewing skills for HR specialists.

Self-efficacy in action

After an initial introduction and overview of interviewing, the delegates were shown a video of a competent problem-solving interview. They were then asked to identify all the skills used by the interviewer. They were asked not to give any negative comments about the interviewer but stick purely to positive ones. The tutor then collected, verbally, all the feedback from the delegates and wrote them up on a flipchart. This was then displayed in a prominent place in the training room. The tutor then described verbally the processes involved in the problem-solving exercise they had just watched.

The delegates were then introduced to a practical exercise to carry out a problem-solving interview. This involved the delegates working in threes. One was to be the interviewer, one the interviewee and one an observer. They would then carry out the interview based on what they had seen and heard about the interview. At the end of the interview each person would give feedback on the interviewer's performance starting with the interviewer himself followed by the interviewee and finally the observer. Again the delegates were asked only to give positive comments.

At the end of this round all the people who had performed a particular role gathered in groups – so there was a group of interviewers, a group of interviewees and a group of observers. The three groups produced a list of 'top tips' for being the role they had just performed. Again only positive comments were used. These were flipcharted and displayed in a prominent place. The delegates studied the flipcharts for a while, and then two more rounds of interviews were carried out so that at the end every delegate had carried out every role. Each delegate took away three sets of feedback from his or her group.

The participants had used a competent model and skills from their fellow delegates which had worked for them. Because the emphasis was always on the positive, the delegates could become immersed in a success-based climate. We have found this approach to be effective both in developing skills and in raising the delegate's self-efficacy.

Self-efficacy and management skills

When you are next faced with the challenge of developing a management skill, you might consider your own self-efficacy in relation to the skill. Ask yourself the following questions and rate yourself on a one (low) to 10 (high) scale.

1   Do you feel very enthusiastic at the outset (high) or lukewarm about the idea (low)? ☐

2   Are you able to stay focused on the task (high) or do you lose interest quickly (low)? ☐

3   Do you rise to the challenge when faced with an unforeseen problem (high) or do you feel overwhelmed (low)? ☐

4	Do you feel you have plenty of energy for the task (high) or a lack of energy (low)?	☐
5	Do you feel you have plenty of personal resources to complete the task (high) or do you feel you lack personal resource (low)?	☐
6	Do you feel the task is important to you personally (high) or that it does not really matter (low)?	☐
7	Do you know how to deal with negative feelings about the task (high) or do you give up in the face of negative feelings (low)?	☐
8	Do you enjoy the task (high) or do you take no enjoyment in it at all (low)?	☐

If your total score is high, then you probably possess high self-efficacy about the task. If you score low, you might move on to the belief audit and examine your beliefs and expectations about skill development.

Belief audits

Because beliefs are so influential and pervasive in our lives, O'Connor and Seymour (2003) recommend that a belief audit would enhance any personal development programme. In my experience and the experience of other colleagues it is easier to work with beliefs when you have a particular goal in mind than to conduct a general/life belief audit. I find I am more motivated to deal with what can be a tricky issue when I perceive a future benefit. I also find if you are going to try changing your beliefs, it is a good idea to rank them in some sort of order of strength. If you are about to start a programme of personal change or skill development, you may find the following process helpful:

1   Identify the issue you want to deal with (this may be a change in your behaviour or the development of a new skill).

2   List as many beliefs as you can about this issue. Don't censor yourself at this stage; just let your imagination have free rein. When the ideas begin to dry up, you are probably ready to move on to the next stage.

3   Go through the list eliminating redundant items (repeats) and any beliefs that seem to have no significant impact on your goal.

4   Split your final list into what you consider helpful beliefs and limiting or unhelpful beliefs.

5   Check the validity of these two lists by visualising what it would be like living with these beliefs while trying to achieve your goal (skill acquisition or personal change).

6   Rank the items in each list in terms of its strength.

7   Think or discuss with a friend/colleague which of these beliefs you may want to change or modify.

The two lists in Table 1 below are the outcome of a belief audit carried out by a colleague of mine before she went on a presentation skills workshop. They are listed in order of strength.

Positive		Negative
This will prove to be a useful skill		I will panic and show myself up
I have already acquired some of the skills of presenting		I will get a poor rating which will be fed back to my boss
I have been successful on other workshops		Other delegates will be much better than me
I will come to enjoy presenting		I will be nervous when I have to present

Table 1: *Example of a belief audit before a presentation skills workshop*

Prior to embarking on a skill workshop or some personal change it may be that you want to reinforce some of your positive beliefs or change/modify some of your negative beliefs. Before we try to change a belief it is important to realise that all beliefs whether positive or negative have a positive intention behind them, and we want to change the belief, not the positive intention behind it. Consider the belief that most of us had as a child – that there is a fat, jolly man who dresses in a red cape and who drives a sleigh pulled by reindeer that can fly, and he delivers presents to us at Christmas. Most adults come to modify or completely change this belief. However, the intention behind this belief does not change. What this story of Father Christmas is really about is giving. We introduce our children to this idea of giving through this attractive and endearing fairy story. The story changes but we leave our children with one of the most wonderful of human traits: the idea of giving and receiving.

Even phobias, intensely negative beliefs, have positive intentions. A fear of heights may have lots of disadvantages to someone – but the positive intention behind this belief is to protect the individual. It is that positive intention that must be preserved when we change our belief.

It would be disingenuous of me to pretend that changing beliefs is easy. Some beliefs are easier to change than others. Some that have been with us for many years are central to the way we see the world (our core beliefs). These beliefs can be very difficult to change. However, even if we cannot completely erase a belief we can perhaps modify or reduce its intensity to our advantage.

There are a number of ways in which to deal with inappropriate beliefs.

The first approach you might try is to reduce the strength of a belief or begin to create doubt about its validity. Apply logic to the belief. Ask yourself questions that can create doubt about its validity. Look for counter-examples. Is it always true? So, for instance, my colleague who thought that she might get a poor rating that would be fed back to her boss, she might talk to other past participants and elicit their views, talk to the trainers of the workshops. If she is poor at presenting now, that is why she is going on the workshop – to improve. There are numerous ways to begin to undermine the limiting belief.

Another simple approach is to choose a limiting belief and think of a more empowering belief that would be more useful to have. I often meet delegates on training programmes who have difficulty with role plays.

One of the reasons they give for this difficulty is that they cannot get any value from the role play because it is not real. I ask them to 'as if' it were real. What behaviours would they use if it was real? Get the reality to start in their imagination and then bring it to life. Many trainees believe they have to play a role (ie someone else) – once they get the idea they can be themselves, the situation becomes less daunting.

One method of testing out the consequences of a new belief is to 'live with it'. Firstly, try it out in your head. Simulate what it would be like to live with this new belief for a day/week/month. What would be different about you and your behaviour? In what ways would people respond differently to you? Then try it for real. You can always tweak the belief if things do not work as you expected.

I have tried to bring some of these ideas together as a process that you might try out when you wish to change or modify a belief.

Changing or modifying a belief

Write down the belief. This will make it explicit. Beliefs are often quite vague entities and writing it down will bring it firmly into your conscious mind. You may want to tweak it before you are finally happy with it.

What was the positive intention behind this belief when it was formed? Where, when and from whom did this belief come? If you know these aspects of the belief, it becomes easier to understand and to deal with.

You then need to ask yourself if you are ready to change or modify this belief. Most people recognise the internal signals that tell you you are ready to change, when every part of you is saying 'Yes' and you have no reservations whatsoever. This is a really useful signal to recognise. If you are not aware of it, try to experience it by thinking of things you know you are one hundred per cent committed to. Note the feeling. It is a true friend. If you do not get this feeling, you must identify any objections that parts of you have to changing the belief. I find it helps to write them down. Do not proceed until you have dealt with these objections.

Then think about a more useful belief than the one you have. Write it down and play with the form of words until you are happy with it.

Note any objections that occur in connection with this new belief. Write them down and continue until there are no more. This process of writing them down helps to let go of the objections and in some cases they disappear like smoke.

Think about living with this belief for a period of time – for the next couple of hours, a whole day or a full week. Think of any problems or issues this would cause. If there are any problems, modify the belief until you are happy with it.

Finally, ask yourself if you could have this belief, would you take it? Listen for that hundred per cent signal. If you do not get it, try working through the three previous stages until you do.

There is a saying concerning beliefs that I think is appropriate for ending a discussion on the role of beliefs in the development of management skills:

'If you believe you can or believe you can't, you're right.'

MOTIVATION

As mentioned earlier, it is not enough just to believe that an outcome is possible. In order to commit to the outcome it is necessary to be motivated to achieve it. Deciding to go for an outcome is a function of belief in its attainability and motivation to achieve it.

In my work as a facilitator on skill development workshops the word 'motivation' crops up many times. It is what has been called a 'fat' word. It can mean many things to many people. I listen to participants on the workshops discussing motivation and it transpires that they often are referring to different aspects of motivation without being aware of it. In order to make the concept of motivation more accessible and meaningful it would seem more useful to examine some of the dimensions of the concept. I will explore two such dimensions: values and characteristic ways of behaving. The first explores the origins of motivation, and the second how individual differences can affect it.

VALUES

Values describe an individual's fundamental standards about what is worthwhile and worthless, desirable and undesirable, moral and immoral. They are the basic principles which guide our lives and greatly influence our personal preferences and attitudes, as well as our outcomes and the means by which we achieve them. We develop our values in the same way we develop our beliefs through life's experiences and by modelling significant people in our lives.

Smith (2004) suggests that values are very powerful and through the brain's emotional systems provide the energy and direction which enable us to reach our outcomes. Motivation is emotion in motion. When we become motivated, we feel different: physiological changes take place because different circuitry in the brain is activated. When people's values are met or matched, they feel a sense of satisfaction, harmony and rapport. When their values are not matched, they often feel dissatisfied, incongruent or frustrated. In this way values are keys to internal motivation.

The identification of values

Rokeach (1973) suggests that values can be classified as goals that we seek, 'ends', or the ways of achieving these goals, 'means'. There are times in people's lives when the goals are of primary importance (the end justifies the means) and times when the means are more important (taking part is more important than winning). Rokeach describes these two sets of values as *terminal* and *instrumental*. A selection of the Rokeach value system is shown in Table 2 below.

Terminal values		Instrumental values
Enjoying		*Being*
A comfortable life		Ambitious
An exciting life		Capable

Terminal values		Instrumental values
A world at peace		Courageous
Equality		Forgiving
Happiness		Independent
Inner harmony		Logical
Pleasure		Loving
Social recognition		Polite
Wisdom		Self-controlled

Table 2: *The Rokeach system of terminal and instrumental values*

Values can be identified by asking questions such as 'What is important to me?' For example, I asked a friend what was important to him about driving. After considerable thought – and a number of revisions – he came up with the following list.

> Test of competence
> Status (type of car driven)
> Excitement
> Sense of freedom
> Independence.

People may readily agree with most of these and hence consider they have similar values to my friend's. However, it is not quite as straightforward as it may seem. These values are what we call nominalisations. To extract a more specific meaning to the words we must supply more information.

Dilts (2003) suggests that the meaning of values are mediated by the beliefs underpinning them. He uses the model in Figure 9 below to describe such beliefs.

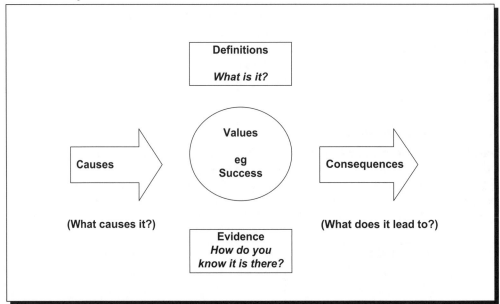

Figure 9: *Dilts' model of values mediated by underpinning beliefs*

Values are characterised by what is important to us. Beliefs are cognitive structures which connect values to life's experiences and give meaning to them. Values manifest themselves as behaviour and skills through the beliefs associated with them. Beliefs answer the questions, 'Exactly how do you define the particular value?' 'What creates it?' 'What are the consequences of this value?' 'How do you know if a particular experience is associated with a particular value?'

To give *meaning* to a value such as 'test of competence', for example, one must build beliefs about what competence is (definition); how you know if it is present (evidence of its existence); what causes it; and what it leads to (consequences). These beliefs add as much to the meaning as the value itself.

Two people can share the same value of 'test of competence' for the skill of driving, for example. One person may believe that competence is about how fast you can drive, how good you are at overtaking and whether you can take corners at speed without losing control of the car. On the other hand, the other person may believe that competence is about obeying the highway code, driving 'defensively' and being thoughtful of other road users. These two people will achieve competence at driving in different ways. Clearly, an individual's beliefs relating to his or her core values will determine how these values are put into effect.

So our motivation will be fuelled not only by our values but by how we interpret these values through our beliefs, and we must ask very specific questions about our values before we can understand them in the process of motivation.

Recognising and clarifying our values

In order to recognise and clarify our values it is probably better to start with the values associated with a particular activity – eg driving, participating in a sport, learning, working, etc.

Choose a particular activity (it is best to start with one that means a lot to you). Ask yourself what is important to you about this activity and list your answers. Do not censor yourself at this stage: just let the ideas flow. Then revisit the list making sure there are no repetitions or anomalies. You can then order the values in importance to you by selecting two of the values and asking yourself which you would most easily give up when taking part in the activity. Repeat this with each and every pair of values and produce a final ranking.

My friend's list with his values associated with driving turned out to be:

> Independence
>
> Status
>
> Test of competence
>
> Excitement
>
> Sense of freedom.

It may be that you want to work with a limited number (the first two). You now want to give specific meaning to these values so that you know how they affect your behaviours and experiences. Apply each of the following questions to your chosen values.

- 'Exactly how do you define the particular value?'
- 'What creates it?'

- 'What are the consequences of this value?'
- 'How do you know if a particular experience is associated with the particular value?'

This will lead you to identify the beliefs associated with these two values and make them easier to work with because you can now understand how they impact on your behaviour and experience.

Working with values

When we work with our values we tend to feel positive, in harmony with ourselves, with access to all the resources we need. We get a sense of personal power. This is obviously a useful state to be in when we are trying to achieve an outcome. However, when we work against our values we feel uncomfortable, we know intuitively something is wrong. We feel pulled in different directions. This is not a useful state when we have to make a decision or achieve an outcome.

Life throws up mixed situations, allowing us to work congruently with our values in some situations, but having to work with conflicting values in others. Sometimes we have to work in situations where our own personal values are compromised by the company values. In some situations our own values work in conflict with one another and we have to make difficult choices such as taking on distasteful work in order to earn more money. Most people are aware of differences in the way they feel when they are congruent as opposed to incongruent about an outcome or decision. However, most people could hone their awareness of these differences. Below is a technique outlined by O'Connor and Seymour (2003).

Recognising your congruence and incongruence signals

Think back to a time when you were about to undertake a project you were absolutely one hundred per cent committed to. Remember what it was like at that time. How did you feel? What thoughts and sounds were in your head? Think back and pretend you are actually there, having that experience. You can now recognise what it is like to be congruent. This is a really useful resource.

Now think back to a time when you had reservations about some plan or decision you had to make. You maybe thought the plan had some merits and other people had extolled its virtue. However, there was something that was not quite right and left you with an uncertain feeling. Try to imagine you are back there in that situation experiencing those thoughts and feelings again. What was it that gave you that sensation? A feeling somewhere in your body? Images or sounds in your head? This is your incongruence signal and it lets you know that you are not fully committed. It can be a very valuable resource and save you money and heartache.

Check these two signals across a number of situations and commit them to your memory.

MOTIVATIONAL FILTERS

Just stop reading for a moment and look around you. There are so many things that you can pay attention to and so many ways of perceiving those things. For instance, I have just looked out into my garden and noticed how windy it is. Also, the washing line is broken and the geraniums are beginning to flower. There are literally thousands of other things I might have noticed. Our environment provides us with so many stimuli that if we paid attention to everything we would be totally overwhelmed with information and unable to take any effective action. Knight (1999) has suggested that this is the reason human beings have developed perceptual filters. These filters cut down the amount of information we pay attention to and enable us to use it to behave effectively and efficiently. These filters begin to develop as soon as we are born and it may be that we inherit some of these predispositions from our parents. The filters act below conscious level and determine *how* we do things, not *what* we do. They lead us to act in habitual ways and give consistency to our behaviours although they may differ across different contexts. What we pay attention to at work may be different from what we pay attention to in a social setting. These filters manifest themselves in many aspects of our lives – the way we behave, the language we use, the beliefs we hold and the ways we perceive the world. Charvet (1996) describes three filters, outlined below, which give rise to characteristic ways of behaving in relation to motivation.

- Proactive/reactive: motivation level

  This motivational filter describes the level of activity and initiative a person displays in his or her behaviour. A proactive person is quick to initiate. Such people tend to act without much consideration. They do not think or analyse much before jumping into situations. They are good at going out and getting things done. They do not wait for other people to initiate. Reactive people tend to hang back and let other people initiate, or they wait until they have carefully considered or analysed the situation. They spend a lot of time waiting and procrastinating. They prefer to respond to other people's initiatives. They can make good analysts.

- Toward/away from: motivation direction

  This motivational filter describes what motivates people into action. What direction do they move in? Do they move toward an object or away from a problem? 'Toward' people think in terms of goals to be achieved. They are energised by goals. They can be seen as naïve because they do not take potential obstacles into account. 'Away from' people focus on what is to be avoided. Their motivation is determined by moving away from something. They are energised by threats. 'Away from' people may have trouble focusing on priorities because whatever is wrong attracts their attention.

- Internal/external: motivation source

  This filter deals with the source of motivation. Are the judgements a person makes sourced from within the person or outside the person? Internal people provide their own motivation from within themselves. They have difficulty accepting other people's opinions. Because they take orders as information, they can be hard to supervise. They do not need external praise, and tend not to give much feedback as managers. Internal people have standards within themselves. Their motivation is triggered by gathering information from outside and processing it against these standards and making judgements about it. External people need other people's opinions and feedback from external sources to stay motivated. Without feedback they do not know how well they are doing. They do not hold standards within themselves. They rely on external standards.

Each category represents behaviour on a continuum between the two pure forms. There are no rights and wrongs. Each type can have advantages and disadvantages in different contexts. Each type can be recognised by characteristic language and gestures, and it is a useful skill to be able to detect the various types and hence to know the motivational filters a person possesses. Table 3 below describes the language and gestures of the three types. You can use this to practise recognising and predicting how colleagues and friends might be motivated and to become more self-aware about which filters you use and in which contexts.

Motivational filter	Sentence structure	Language	Body language
Proactive	Speaks in short sentences Uses active verbs Tangible object Clear sentence structure Direct	Just do it. Take the initiative. Right now. What are you waiting for? Go for it.	Signs of impatience Speaking quickly Finger-tapping Lots of movement Inability to sit still
Reactive	Incomplete sentences Passive verbs Verbs transposed into nouns Long and convoluted sentences Conditionals: would, could, might, may	Let's think about it. Consider this. Now that you have analysed it… This will clarify it for you.	Lack of movement Willingness to sit for long periods
Toward	Talks about achievement Inclusive Goals	Attain Obtain Have Get Achieve	Pointing Head nodding Inclusive gestures
Away from	Exclusion Problems Things to be avoided	Won't have to Prevent Avoid Get rid of Fix	Shaking head Arms indicating avoidance Gestures of exclusion
Internal	Decides, or knows himself/herself Resists when someone tells what to do Outside instructions taken as information	Only you can decide. You know it's up to you. What do you think?	Sitting upright Pointing to self Pause before answering a judgement while evaluating it Minimal gestures
External	Other people decide Needs to compare to external source Outside information taken as an order	So-and-so thinks… The feedback you will get… The approval you will get… Give references.	Leaning forward Watching for response Facial expression looking for clues and/or approval

Source: based on Charvet (1996)

Table 3: *Recognition of motivational filters*

SUMMARY

In this chapter we have examined the second stage of the ADAX model: decision-making. Individuals who are successful at developing skills become aware of either their potential to develop a skill or their lack of a skill (*awareness*).They then seem able not only to decide to develop the skill but also to devote sufficient commitment and energy to sustain their effort throughout the process. We contend that this decision-making process is a product of the individuals' belief in their ability to develop the skill and the motivation with which they pursue this goal.

We have explored some of the characteristics of and issues associated with these two attributes and attempted to explain how they impact on the successful development of skills.

We have examined the role of beliefs generally in shaping how individuals view the world and how this can impact on skill development. We have used a skills perspective in demonstrating how we can manage, modify and change our beliefs.

We have explored two aspects of motivation. These relate to more precise characteristics of the concept which allow the description of more practical applications. Because values are fundamental to the motivation process we have focused on their identification and management. We have also explored motivational filters and how they explain some individual differences in motivation.

REFERENCES

Bandura, A. (1977) 'Self-efficacy: toward a unifying theory of behavioural change', *Psychological Review*, 84: 191–215

Charvet, S. (1996) *Words that Change Minds*. Iowa: Kendall/Hunt Publishing

Cox, R. H. (1995) *Sports Psychology: Concepts and applications*. Madison, WI: Brown & Benchmark

Dilts, R. (2003) *From Coach to Awakener*. California: Meta Publications

Dilts, R., Hallbom, T. and Smith, S. (1990) *Beliefs: Pathways to health and well-being*. Portland, OR: Metamorphous Press

Hall, L. M. (2005) *The Spirit of NLP: The process, meaning and criteria for mastering NLP.* Carmarthen: Anglo-American Books

Knight, S.(1999) *NLP Solutions*. London: Nicholas Brealey

O'Connor, J. and Seymour, J. (2003) *Introducing Neuro-Linguistic Programming*. London: HarperCollins

O'Connor, J. and Seymour, J. (1994) *Training with NLP*. London: HarperCollins

Phillips, P. and Buncher, L. (1999) *Gold Counselling*. Carmarthen: Crown House Publishing

Rokeach, M. (1973) *The Nature of Human Values*. New York: Free Press

Routledge, C. W. (1995) 'Strategies of effective learners on interpersonal skills courses', *Training and Management Development Methods*, Vol. 9, No. 2: 4.07–18

Smith, A. (2004) *The Brain's Behind It*. Bodmin: MPG Books

Tytherleigh, J. (1997) *Creating Your Experiences*. Plymouth: Seven Stars Publishing

Vroom, V. H. (1964) *Work and Motivation*. New York: John Wiley & Sons

Action

'The Management Guru'

'In the days when terms like "change management" and "process consultancy" were relatively new, a small British firm realised it had a need for some Organisational Development. Its senior managers decided to spend a significant part of its training budget to buy one whole day of a famous management guru's time. The entire board assembled to hear him speak.

'The great man took his seat and was silent. After a while one of the board members stood up and began describing their problems. The guru remained silent.

'Another board member then began to speak. And then another and another, but still nothing from the visitor. Soon the flip chart had been covered with words and diagrams and everyone except the guru was engaged in debate.

'His silence continued over lunch. At 3 o'clock the managing director had finished an elaborate diagram of a current problem and the famous man stood up, went to the flip chart, and repositioned a flip chart which was hanging loose from the wall. A hushed silence fell on the group.

' This man turned to the group and said, "I often find 'white tac' has better sticking power than 'blu tack'."

'He then sat down that was his last contribution.'

This may seem a strange story to illustrate 'action'. However, this guru realised that there comes a time when managers have to stop planning and discussing and actually *do* something. *Action* is usually the first observable outcome of the ADAX process – it is the manifestation of the *awareness* and *decision-making* stages of the process. Without the action all the learning and potential skills remain theoretical. You can read about how to delegate or negotiate, but this will not enable you to become competent in these two skills. There must always be an action component to skill development. Some of the questions to be addressed in this chapter are:

- How do managers know what to do when they are developing skills?
- What part do the senses play in developing skill strategies?
- How does prior learning and experience influence skill development?
- What roles do trial and error and social learning have?
- In what way can skill outcomes be described as simple or complex, and how are they related?
- Do all skills eventually become automatic?
- How do knowledge and competence interact in describing skilled outcomes?
- How do goal-setting and visualisation help promote *action*?

SKILL DEVELOPMENT AND ORGANISATIONAL OUTCOMES

The nature of the manager's job is largely determined by organisational outcomes. So the context in which a manager operates is a major factor in determining what constitutes a manager's skills.

Case study

Developing planning skills

A newly promoted manager wants to develop his planning skills. The content of these skills will be determined by the context in which he has to use these skills. Planning his own personal time and planning work to ensure that his team works effectively will require some common skills as well as a range of different ones.

Planning personal time will involve prioritising his work, using appropriate techniques – eg urgent versus important, delegating appropriate work and agreeing completion, and developing methods of personal time management.

Similar planning skills are relevant in planning the work of a team. However, also involved are skills of communication, target-setting, and monitoring and motivating colleagues, as well as dealing with changes and contingencies within the team.

In this case study the learner has to deal with a wider range of skills when planning and co-ordinating work of other employees than when planning for himself alone. .

Over time the skills and activities that managers use have been observed, chronicled and analysed by a number of researchers and authors (Mintzberg, 1973; Stewart, R., 1967, 1976, 1991; Boyatzis, 1982; CIPD, 2002; Quinn *et al*, 2003). These and similar studies underpin our knowledge of the content of management skills. It is not surprising that the results of these studies are none of them identical. Each study is only a single perspective of the enormous territory of management skills, and each one reflects the approach, experience and idiosyncrasies of the researchers. In many ways this is an advantage, for the studies as a whole help to widen and deepen people's understanding of management skills. However, no one single study can give us a complete understanding of the territory of management skills.

SKILL DEVELOPMENT STRATEGIES AND THE SENSES

The skills that we use in the practice of management involve the processes of thinking, of speaking and listening, and of doing (physical behaviours). In fact, any skills that we can think of are made up of some combination of these processes. Human beings enact these processes through their senses. This makes a study of the senses a very useful lens through which to examine skill development.

Most people are familiar with the idea of five senses:

- visual (our sense of sight)
- auditory (our sense of hearing)
- kinaesthetic (our sense of touch, movement and feeling)
- olfactory (our sense of smell)
- gustatory (our sense of taste).

We use our senses in a number of different ways to actuate the processes that allow us to develop skills. We can use our senses externally or directly, as when we see or hear or touch something. This is the most direct way of using our senses. When we think, we create these same sensory processes internally. The neuronal activity is just the same for thinking as it is for operating with our senses directly. When we speak, we are communicating our thoughts to someone else.

Crossing a busy road requires us to look for oncoming traffic, listen to the sounds around us, and vary our speed of movement. All these activities require us to keep our senses out towards the environment. Conversely, when we are thinking about booking a holiday, we tend to daydream – we form pictures in our mind of previous holidays, hear the sounds of the beach and recreate the feel of the sun on our backs. Our senses are directed inwards. When we want to tell someone about our holidays, we turn our thoughts into words.

Our daily lives involve a constant movement between the outward and the inward focus of our senses and our use of language. We pay attention to our environment; we think and reflect on our experiences; we communicate these experiences to other people.

To summarise, we can use our senses in the following ways:

- visual: internally (Vi) and externally (Ve)
- auditory tonal (how something sounds): internally (Ai) and externally (Ae)
- auditory digital (use of words): internally (Adi) and externally (Ade)
- kinaesthetic: internally (Ki) and externally (Ke).

For simplicity's sake I am including the gustatory and olfactory senses in with the kinaesthetic sense. Emotions and feelings are also considered within the internal kinaesthetic sense.

The strategies through which we achieve our skill outcomes are the ways in which we organise our thoughts, feelings, language and behaviours. So skill strategies can be represented as a sequence of sensory accesses. These accesses constitute the building blocks of skills. They enable us to describe skill in a common format irrespective of the outcome the skill achieves.

A couple of evenings ago I was watching a TV programme in which Rick Stein, the famous seafood chef, was preparing a meal for the Japanese ambassador. His approach reminded me of how we construct skill strategies from sensory accesses. First, he chose all the ingredients for the various courses. Second, he had to determine the quality of ingredients and the amounts to be used. Third, he determined the steps and sequences to optimise the preparation:

- The ingredients are akin to our sense modalities.
- The amounts and qualities of the ingredients are likened to the characteristics of our modalities or what we can do with them.
- The order of preparation is how we sequence our sensory accesses.

Sometimes we may use more than one strategy to achieve a particular outcome. Probably one of the most frequently used skill strategies that managers develop is a motivation strategy. Most managers are completely unaware of their strategies or the fact that they use different strategies in different circumstances.

O'Connor and Seymour (2003) describe two versions of a motivation strategy. The first one starts with a person looking at the work to be done (visual external, Ve). He or she then constructs an internal picture of the work finished (visual internal, Vi), gets a good feeling (kinaesthetic internal, Ki) and tells himself or herself to get started (auditory internal, Adi).

The whole strategy may thus be represented as: Ve, Vi, Ki, Adi.

In the second strategy, a person looks at the work to be done (visual external, Ve) and asks himself or herself 'What would happen if I did not complete this?' (auditory internal, Adi). He or she then constructs the possible consequences (visual internal, Vi) and feels bad (kinaesthetic internal, Ki). He or she does not want this feeling and those consequences, and so starts the work.

The whole strategy in this case may be represented as: Ve, Adi, Vi, Ki.

People have habits and patterns of doing, feeling and thinking, and they tend to follow these patterns regularly. They do this because in the past they have found these patterns useful, and they have been reinforced by repeated use. The patterns may not always be efficient or effective. Sometimes they are used in contexts other than the ones in which they were developed and they may work less well or not at all. Strategies are not good or bad *per se*: they are useful or not useful in achieving certain outcomes.

An effective strategy starts with choosing an appropriate set of sensory accesses and carrying them out in a particular sequence. If we can identify a particularly effective strategy, it can be taught to other people by having them access these appropriate modalities in the right order. However, although the building blocks of the strategy and their sequence are important, it is equally important to be able to make effective use of each of the senses when they are accessed. High levels of competence are often the result of a person's ability to make highly refined distinctions in the various sensory systems.

We develop this idea in Chapter 9, in Part 2 of the book.

TURNING ACTION INTO SKILL

Having examined the way organisational outcomes determine the content of the *action* and how individuals' sensory mechanisms enable this action, we now turn to the question of how this action is turned into skilled performance.

To do this we examine three processes from learning theory: the use of prior experience, trial and error, and social learning.

Prior experience

Bransford *et al* (2001) have reviewed a number of learning theories which emphasise understanding as a primary characteristic, their focus being on *knowing*. Individuals are seen as goal-directed and actively seeking information. They approach skill development with a range of prior knowledge, skills, beliefs and concepts which significantly influence what they notice about the environment and how they interpret it. This in turn affects their abilities to develop new skills. In general, the contemporary view of this approach to learning is that people construct new skills, knowledge and understanding based on what they already know.

One of the key issues regarding prior learning is whether the learning transfers to new learning/skills in a positive or negative way. For example, there are many advantages in having experience on the road with a bicycle before learning to drive a car, such as developing a knowledge of the highway code and being 'aware' in traffic. However, there are many manoeuvres that are applicable to cycles which are certainly not applicable to cars.

In our professional development workshops we aim to develop and build upon the delegates' prior experience. In some workshops with some delegates this works very well, but in other workshops the prior learning of some delegates seems to work against the honing and development of new skills.

We run a series of workshops on interviewing skills. Some of our delegates are experienced interviewers and when they work on role plays they interview with competence and elegance. This enables them to practise more advanced skills and routines and take their skills to an even higher level. These delegates appear to us to be using their prior experience in a positive and useful manner.

However, there are some delegates who attend our workshops who have previously developed in a dependency culture. They seem basically interested in any handouts we distribute and not in the practice and honing of skills. A typical comment from these delegates is 'I have done this before,' as if skill development is a one-off activity and not an ongoing, iterative process. It usually transpires that someone has given them information about the topic in the form of a lecture or handout. We find this attitude a great block in our workshops and we tend to spend a significant amount of our time challenging this unhelpful approach.

Trial and error

Most managers would understand the idea of trial and error as a basis for learning and could probably point out examples of their own learning where this principle applied. The school of learning which represents this approach is known as behaviourism, and was the first learning theory to be systematically studied. The behaviourists represented learning as a process of forming connections between stimuli and responses. The driving force for such learning was assumed to be the availability of external forces such as rewards or punishments. Bransford *et al* (2001) have reviewed the work of the main contributors to this theory.

A significant limitation of this approach stemmed from its focus on observable stimulus conditions and the behaviours associated with those conditions. It made it difficult to include such factors as understanding, reasoning and thinking, which are of particular importance in modern learning theory. This limitation led to much more research effort being directed to the 'cognitive' approach.

Modern approaches to management learning and skill development combine both the behaviourist and cognitive approaches. The combination reinforces the utility of trial and error in skill development within a framework of reflection and understanding.

The trial and error approach to learning is probably noticed most readily in young children. Much of what very young children learn is through trial and error. Walking is a typical activity developed by this process. However, young children are very vulnerable and their development and progress has to be carefully supervised. As adults we have usually learned enough about ourselves and our environment to keep us safe. However, there are occasions when in new circumstances we probably return to learning with an element of trial and error based on what has worked for us in the past when faced with similar circumstances.

For example: when visiting a foreign country for the first time, conventions from the UK culture are often inappropriate so we have to rely on tentatively testing out others' reactions to our behaviour. I recall the first occasion, many years ago, that I visited Greece and quickly discovered the locals' view of a woman's place in the world. If I wanted to buy an item in a shop, or a snack at a bar, it would be the man I was with who was expected to know or say what I wanted or to complete any financial transaction. I found this disconcerting at first, but after numerous transactions in bars and shops I came to accept that this was how women were seen and expected to behave. It was very different from the UK culture at the time. Foreign languages are an obvious skill that can be learned through trial and error, based on previous experience and through listening to other people.

Social learning

In the 1960s Bandura carried out what are now considered to be classic experiments observing children at play to assess the extent to which they imitated an adult model. The adult model had behaved aggressively towards a doll, and children who had observed this model were found to be more likely to behave in a similar way than children who had not seen this model (Bandura and Walters, 1963). Since the 1960s there has been a good deal of work confirming that individuals are influenced and learn by observing other people.

Along with several colleagues I have regularly run a negotiating skills workshop. We begin the workshop by explaining the three main parts of the negotiating process (the model we use is divided into three parts). After each part we encourage the trainees to practise the various elements and the associated skills through a series of exercises. The students are then given a case study to provide the basis for a run through the whole process. In the early days of the programme the tutors would lead feedback sessions on the case, which would enable the tutors and the trainees to evaluate their learning. We would then move on to another case, allow them to practise, and again use feedback sessions to evaluate their skill development. In effect we were using an iterative process of practice and feedback to develop and evaluate their skill development.

We were always a little disappointed with the results.

Some years ago a colleague and I decided to produce a video of the case we used for the first complete run of the negotiation process. We decided to show this video to the trainees immediately after they had negotiated the case. The extra element allowed the trainees to actually watch experienced negotiators demonstrating the process and the skills. The results during the rest of the programme improved dramatically. This was the only change we made to the programme. Incorporating a negotiating model into the training methodology brought about a step-change in the level of skill development by the end of the programme.

Since that time we have used this modelling opportunity with many other skill development workshops, and with similar success.

Training methodologies based on social learning can be used on both formal skill development workshops and with on-the-job learning where the model can be another manager or the learner's boss. There seems to be certain factors that influence the efficacy of the social learning process:

- The status of the model influences learning.
- Models are more effective if similar to the learner.
- Learning is more effective if learners can already perform sub-skills that make up the model's behaviour.
- Models are more likely to be copied if they are in similar surroundings to learners (Dworetsky, 1994).

Latent learning has also been found to occur in that a model's behaviour may be learned, not necessarily immediately repeated, but stored for a later time when it can be appropriately rewarded.

It is also important to be aware of the potential for employees to learn undesirable behaviours. For example, an employee may develop an overly aggressive management style if he or she sees this being used by senior managers to achieve their objectives.

CHARACTERISTICS OF SKILL OUTCOMES

The output of the *action* process is the skill outcome. Two characteristics of these skill outcomes help us to understand their nature and how they develop. The first is complexity, and the second is the interplay between knowledge and doing.

Simple and complex skills – the process of 'chunking'

It soon becomes obvious that many complex skills are made up of sets of simpler skills – eg the skill of leadership (a complex skill) is made up of many sub-skills such as those relating to effective communication, establishing rapport, problem-solving, motivating, and so on. Similarly, the skill of interviewing is composed of a number of smaller skills such as planning, rapport-building, questioning, probing, presenting information, evaluating, and decision-making. In this way we can recognise 'small chunk' and 'large chunk' skills. The small chunk skills can be viewed as building blocks to make up larger-chunk skills. This makes the development of complex skills less arduous because some of the components have already been learned. Dilts (1998) has described a generic model of skills which reflects this chunking phenomenon.

Simple behavioural skills involve specific, concrete, easily observable actions that take place within short periods of time (seconds to minutes). Examples of simple behavioural skills include: relaxing through breathing, arranging chairs for a meeting, demonstrating a physical routine during a training session, etc.

Simple cognitive skills are specific, easily identifiable and testable mental processes that occur within a short period of time (seconds to minutes). Examples of simple cognitive skills include: remembering names, spelling, acquiring simple vocabulary, creating a mental image, etc. This type of thinking skill produces easily observable behavioural results that can be measured and provide immediate feedback.

Simple linguistic skills involve the recognition and use of specific key words, phrases and questions, such as asking particular questions, recognising and responding to key words, reviewing or summarising key phrases, etc. Again, the performance of these skills is easily observable and measurable.

Complex behavioural skills involve the construction and co-ordination of sequences or combinations of simple behavioural actions. Abilities such as juggling, making a presentation, carrying out a role-play, demonstrating a multi-task training routine, etc, are examples of complex behavioural skills.

Complex cognitive skills are those which require a synthesis or sequence of other simple thinking skills. Creating a story, diagnosing a problem, solving a problem, planning a project, creating a budget, etc, are examples of complex cognitive skills.

Complex linguistic skills involve the interactive use of language in highly dynamic (and often spontaneous) situations. Abilities such as persuasion, negotiation, use of humour, storytelling, composing a complex memo, etc, are examples of skills involving complex linguistic skills.

Typically, it is more challenging and involved to learn complex skills than simple ones. Often, however, complex skills can be chunked down into a group or sequence of simpler ones. One of the key issues in learning new skills is to determine which level or 'chunk size' of skill one will be dealing with. The methods that are successful for learning one level of skill may not be effective in learning another level. For example, simple imitation or mirroring may be effective for learning a routine of rapport-building by matching someone's body language, but it may be inadequate and inappropriate for learning a complex linguistic skill such as negotiating.

The relationship between simple and complex skills

Anderson (1988) describes the process of chunking simple skills together to form complex skills in terms of declarative and procedural knowledge and how they interrelate in the skill development process. Neuroscience is now providing us with explanations of how this might work.

When a new task is being learned in the frontal cortex of the brain, many neighbouring neurons are recruited to assist in the process. A large amount of input is used from different regions of the brain. Once the task has been mastered and repeated a number of times, the firing patterns become established and the behaviour/skill becomes automatic. It no longer requires conscious attention. The programme is stored in the subcortical structures of the brain. The recruited neurons are free to return to previous duties or become available for new learning.

If an individual can push more and more automatic skills into the subcortical region, the higher brain is not so busy and is available to observe, monitor and make adjustments (Ratey, 2003).

Acquiring numerous repertoires of automatic skills is essential for coping with the complex activities of everyday life and gives us the capacity to develop a range of skills from the very simple to the very complex. Just the actions of getting out of bed, having breakfast, cleaning one's teeth and driving to work involves hundreds of such automatic skills and routines, and without them these activities would be impossible.

The same process holds true both for motor functions and cognitive functions. Just think how many of these automatic cognitive functions it takes to read your emails in the morning. The frontal cortex of the brain learns, routinises and processes motor and mental functions in parallel, which is why movement and thinking often seem so closely linked.

Processes and skills that are fundamental and learned automatically are stored in the lower part of the brain. Skills that are increasingly complex, or very new, are managed further up the brain, increasingly towards the frontal cortex, so that more brain regions along the way can have an input. This allows more neurons to be involved in producing a more precise final output. The most complex of skills may well use many levels of the brain co-ordinated by the actions of the motor function.

The motor function allows us to shift back and forth between deliberate and automatic movements. It enables us to perform many different tasks at the same time, as well as moving between skills as simple as signing our name and as complex as leading negotiations to determine pay increases for a multinational company.

Imagine an operations manager interviewing a prospective supervisor. The manager may well have many automatic skills that he has developed over the years, such as rapport skills, questioning skills, active listening skills, a capacity for evaluating the relevance of answers, and making notes. During the course of the interview he will call upon these automatic skills and routines and be able to use them without undue overload on his prefrontal cortex. This he can use to plan the shape of the interview depending on the evidence collected and gaps in the evidence. He can also be using this capacity to evaluate how this potential supervisor would relate to the other people in his department. So the planning capacity of his brain would be utilised by non-routine management and co-ordination activities while his automatic skills kick in as and when required.

Knowing and doing

Dilts (1998) suggests that skilled performance can be examined as a function of two fundamental dimensions: *consciousness* (knowing) and *competence* (doing). It is possible to know or understand some activity or skill, but be unable to do it (conscious incompetence). It is also possible to be able to carry out a particular activity well or perform a skill with a high degree of competence, but not know how one does it (unconscious competence). Mastery of a skill involves both the ability to 'do what you know' and to 'know what you are doing'.

One of the biggest challenges in learning from experts comes from the fact that many of the critical behaviours and psychological attributes which allow them to excel are largely unconscious and intuitive to them, and as a result they are unable to provide a direct description of the processes responsible for their own exceptional capabilities. In fact, many experts *avoid* thinking about what they are doing and how they are doing it because it actually interferes with their capability.

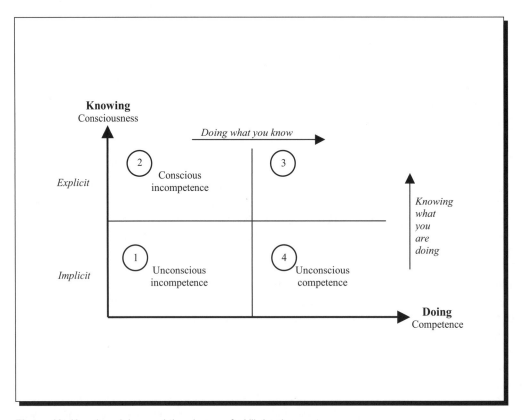

Figure 10: *Knowing, doing, and the phases of skill development*

Figure 10 shows the relationship between 'knowing' and 'doing', and how they can be superimposed onto the competence model. From this diagram we can explore four learning strategies – two concerned with knowing or awareness, and two associated with doing or competence.

Knowing

■ When we move from quadrant 1 to quadrant 2 we become aware of the skill we do not have and what the skill might look/sound/feel like. On a formal training course this might be brought about through a demonstration by a competent model and the learner 'having a go' at reproducing the skill. In the workplace it compares with seeing a competent model and trying out the skill in an informal setting. As we have mentioned before, the state of *conscious incompetence* may not be a very comfortable place to be, and it would be a good idea to begin to move the learner from quadrant 2 to 3 rather than just leave the learner in this uncomfortable state.

■ When we move from quadrant 4 to quadrant 3 (an apparently retrograde move that can only be undertaken once the whole skill development process has been accomplished, and even then only reflectively for analytical purposes), we become aware of how we do things – eg what our unconscious strategy is for 'knowing what questions to ask', 'coming up with creative sugges-tions', or 'adapting the non-verbal aspects of one's leadership style'. When these strategies are identified and described they can be enhanced, modified or improved. This may be done by demonstrating the strategies and having a modeller analyse the critical behaviours and psychological attributes. This type of analysis is probably the source of 'best practice'. If we analyse the processes and techniques used by someone who produces excellent results, we can train other people to use these processes and techniques. They might not be able to produce exactly the same excellent results but it might give them a more effective skill strategy and enable them to improve the results they do achieve.

Doing

- When we move from quadrant 2 to quadrant 3 we learn to do what we know. This is the basis for most skill development workshops, where we learn about the 'best practice' for a particular skill and then try it out, practise and hone it until we reach a certain level of competence.

- Most of our skill development in life is what we might call 'implicit' learning. This happens when we move from quadrant 1 to quadrant 4. We develop skills without being aware of going through the stages of *conscious incompetence* or *conscious competence*. We often copy the skills of other people and hone and personalise them through trial and error. This is all done unconsciously. Most of our skill base probably starts in this way. This is a critical factor for both learners and trainers in the process of skill development because it is very rare for this development to take place 'on a clean slate'.

Formal and informal skill development consists of some or all of these strategies. Different mixes are successful depending on the individuals concerned and their own personal history of learning and the context of the development.

TWO TECHNIQUES TO AID ACTION

Goal-setting

Stephen Covey (1999) eloquently describes the process of experience as 'twice-created'. He argues that all that happens to us in life is created twice – first in the imagination, and then in physical reality. Before you decorate your room you visualise it in your mind's eye. Before you plant a garden you plan it out in your mind. Before you give a speech you create it first in your head or as a mind map. This first creation can originate in our own minds or in the minds of others. In the first case we are in control of shaping our destinies whereas in the second case we are at the mercy of other people's agendas. What we are now is the second creation of our own proactive design or the result of other people's plans and goals, of circumstances or habits. Covey goes on to argue that we can become responsible for our own first creation by acquiring the skills of effective goal-setting and creative visualisation.

Many writers have described and evaluated the use of goal-setting across a variety of contexts. Locke and Latham (1990) have identified over 350 organisational and academically based research findings which support their view that specific and challenging goals lead to a higher level of performance. Whetton, Cameron and Woods (2000) identify goal-setting as a key element in an integrated motivation policy and in their model for short-term planning. Parker and Stone (2003) suggest that managers who know how to create meaning in the goals they set themselves and their subordinates are creating the conditions which encourage empowerment.

Locke *et al* (1981) argue that goal characteristics significantly affect the likelihood that the goal will be accomplished. Woods and Whitehead (1993) use the acronym FRAME to characterise effective objectives. They advocate Few key objectives in number; that they be Realistic and hence achievable; that if a third party is involved, the objectives be Agreed; that they are capable of being Measured; and finally that they are Explicit.

This is similar to the widely used SMART objectives list (Specific, Measurable, Agreed, Realistic and Time-bound). Both these acronyms are best used in a business context.

In the context of sports goals Cox (1994) has summarised the work of a number of writers describing the motivational characteristics of goals:

- Specific goals are better than general goals.

- Goals should be written or described in behavioural terms so that they are measurable.

- Difficult goals are better than easy goals.

- Use short-term goals to achieve long-term goals.

- Set performance goals instead of outcome goals.

- Outline a specific strategy or plan for meeting each goal.

Dilts (2003) has described a set of 'well-formedness' conditions that a goal should satisfy so that it is more likely to be achieved. This is described in the context of coaching, but it would seem to be the most useful and universally applicable of the different sets of goal characteristics.

A goal is considered 'well formed' if it meets the following conditions:

- It is stated in positive terms.

- It is practically and logically impossible to give someone the negation of an experience. Our brains can only respond to positives. So any outcome we wish our brains to focus on should be stated in the positive. I was given a vivid illustration of this at an NLP workshop when the trainer exhorted us not to think of a blue elephant and guess what happened! So if you don't want to feel anxious when you are giving a presentation, set yourself an objective to feel energised or relaxed when giving a presentation.

- It is described and evidenced in sensory-based terms.

   The only way you will know how the objective is of use is if you can understand explicitly what it means and how you will know when you have achieved it. The best way of doing this is to state the objective in sensory-based terms. What will you see? What will you hear? What will you feel? It is not much help to have an objective to find a nice beach. More specifically you want to find a sandy beach where you can sunbathe and hear the seagulls and feel a cooling breeze blowing off the sea.

- It is under the control of the person/group who has to achieve the goal.

   If you set yourself an objective, you must play an active role in its achievement. Goals that rely on other people taking action are not well formed because if people do not respond to what you want, you have nowhere to go. If you want people to be friendly with you, do not wait for them to make friends with you but decide what you can do to become friendly with them.

- It preserves the positive intention of the present state.

   If we wish to set a goal to stop smoking (for example), we should first identify what positive advantages there are associated with smoking – eg to calm yourself when you feel nervous or to help you in social situations. If you are to stop smoking, you must decide how you will substitute for these advantages when you adopt your new goal. If you don't, you may well adopt equally harmful habits such as overeating or drinking. Many people put off new goals because of the potentially uncomfortable consequences of taking action. Well-formed outcomes must account for these consequences.

- It fits the ecology of the surrounding context.

People all too frequently set objectives which are absolutes, implying that the goal is desirable in all cases or in all contexts. This is not always the case. For example, if you set yourself a goal to be more assertive with your subordinates when they are not meeting their targets, you may want to ask yourself if there are occasions when your subordinates are not meeting their targets and you do not want to be more assertive with them. With each objective you must specify the appropriate boundaries and limits for desired and undesired outcomes.

Below is a checklist of the above criteria for producing effective or 'well-formed' goals. Try them out now with some of your current goals/outcomes. Use them in the future whenever you need to set new goals or revise current ones. It is not meant to be a mechanical routine but it will help you explore the issues surrounding your goals and will help create goals that are achievable and sustainable.

Checklist of criteria for producing effective goals

- State the goal in positive terms.

  Say what you want, not what you don't want.

- Use sensory-based terms in your description.

  Describe the goal in terms of what it will look like, sound like and/or feel like.

  Describe how you will know when you have achieved the goal – what the evidence will be.

- Ensure that the person or group who seek the goal has control of doing so.

  Ensure that achieving the goal does not depend on others.

- Ensure that the goal retains all positive aspects of the present situation.

  List the positive aspects of the current way of doing things, and determine how the new goal when achieved will continue them and even improve on them.

- Think about the ecology of the surrounding context.

  List the contexts in which you would and would not want this outcome.

Visualisation

Anyone who is interested in and watches sport cannot have failed to notice top sportsmen and women using visualisation as an aid to performance. Most of us will have seen sprinters standing in their lanes before the race begins looking straight ahead or sometimes with their eyes closed in an almost trance-like state. What the sprinters are doing is probably running the race in their heads and visualising all the things they have planned and trained to do, and in particular visualising success. Visualisation – or imagery, as it is also known – is something all of us do. Daydreaming is one of the most familiar forms. We can use our senses both internally and externally, and it is the use of our senses internally that is the basis of visualisation. When imagery is used to help individuals to improve skills it is commonly referred to as 'mental practice' or 'mental rehearsal'. Although the terms used to describe the phenomenon are more associated with the visual sense, visualisation is not restricted to what we can see. It can also involve the auditory and kinaesthetic senses.

Figure 11: *The use of visualisation*

It is not only in the sporting world that visualisation has been used. O'Connor and Seymour (2003) describe a technique known in neurolinguistic programming as 'future pacing'. This has a number of applications in business and management as well as in sport. One such application allows people to mentally practise what it will be like to deal with a future situation with a new resource (such as a new skill or training routine). It is also a way of rehearsing what it will be like to achieve your goals and outcomes. By giving the brain very strong positive images of success we can make success more likely. Expectations can become strong self-fulfilling prophecies. You may also want to generate some new behaviours which may be helpful in difficult situations (conflict, giving a presentation). Future pacing is a way of testing some of these behaviours before you have to use them for real.

Future pacing is a way of coming as close as possible to a situation without being in it. However, there are no guarantees. The test of any change is when we encounter the real situation.

Block (1981) in his review of human imagery has identified two main theories: the pictorialist and the descriptionist. The pictorialist position is that when we imagine a scene in our mind we are scanning an actual image. The image is as real as the one that forms on the retina when we view a real object using our senses externally. The other main theory is the descriptionist. This argues that there is no such thing as a mental image when we see something in our mind. It is the detailed and graphic nature of language that makes it seem so. It is our thoughts that manufacture the image, and it is so clear that we believe we are actually seeing one.

Fisher (1986) suggests that imagery is the language of the brain and that the brain cannot tell the difference between a real image and one conjured up through visualisation.

I have used visualisation techniques in a number of training contexts and found that individuals vary enormously in their reported ability to form images. They seem to vary in two dimensions: clarity and stability. Some people report very clear images and sounds when they visualise – almost as clear as if they are seeing a real object or scene. Others report very vague, unclear images. Personally, I fall into the first category and find it difficult to imagine why everyone does not see things as I do. Some people report that they see very stable images and can keep them in their mind's eye just as long as they wish. Others see fleeting images lasting only a few tenths of a second. I fall somewhere in between these two extremes. My attention span for images is quite short. Some people report that they cannot visualise at all. I suspect this might be because they have images of a subliminal type and are not consciously aware of them, but this is only a surmise. One thing that seems to work for these people is to ask them what they think they should see – to 'as if' they can visualise. This has helped a number of people I have worked with to receive some benefit from techniques involving visualisation.

Mahoney and Avener (1977) have examined and described internal and external imagery. Internal is mainly kinaesthetic in nature, where people feel themselves in their own bodies when they are visualising. They see out of their own eyes and hear out of their own ears, but the experience is mainly 'feeling'. External imagery is mainly visual. People see themselves from outside their own bodies. In the sporting context internal imagery is reported as giving superior results. However, this is somewhat activity-dependent. For people to get the most from visualisation it seems better to have a facility for both.

Cox (1994) has summarised some characteristics of the successful use of imagery skills:

- Imagery skills can be developed.
- The subject must have a positive attitude towards imagery.
- Relaxation is a necessary prerequisite to effective use of imagery.
- Two kinds of imagery – internal and external – are used.
- Subjects who use imagery improve their skills to a greater degree than those who do not.
- Subjects who can form clear stable images usually get the best results.
- The more competent a subject is in mastering imagery skills, the more effective is its application.

As with most skills, imagery can be improved with practice. Below is a routine for using imagery/visualisation for goal-setting. The general routine may also help you develop visualisation skills.

Routine for using visualisation for goal-setting

Find a private, quiet and comfortable place.

Try some 'belly breaths' in order to help you relax. Breathe in slowly to the count of four. Allow your tummy to expand as you breathe in. Then breathe out to the count of eight. Repeat this four times.

Practise visualising by imagining a circle filling your visual field. Colour it blue, then change it to red, then green, and back to blue. Allow the images to disappear and any spontaneous images to appear. (If you find it helpful, close your eyes while you are visualising.)

Create an image of a glass tank. Fill it with a colourful liquid from a hosepipe. Listen to the sound of the water splashing into the tank. Add a bucketful of ice cubes into the tank. Hear the sound they make falling into the water. Put a large purple umbrella into the tank. Finally, put your hand into the tank and feel how cold the water is.

Imagine your work environment and visualise a number of scenes in this environment. Pick a work scene connected to one of your work objectives. Make this a significant objective. Picture the scene, the furniture, the people and you working on your objective. Try to make the scene as real as possible, with colour, sound and as much detail as possible. Run the scene forward to a time when you have just achieved your goal. How does it look?

Slowly walk over to the person who looks like you and step into his or her body and feel the success. What are you seeing out of your own eyes? What are you hearing in your own ears? What are people saying to you? Most of all, how do you feel?

Live with these scenes and these sounds and feelings for a couple of minutes, and notice how good they are.

End the session with four more 'belly breaths'. Open your eyes and adjust back into the environment.

SUMMARY

In this third part of our skill development model we have examined the *action* component – those processes which bring the skills to life.

Firstly, two inputs to this action were examined. The content of the management skills is determined by what the manager is required to do: the organisational outcomes. This requires a manager to lead, delegate, negotiate and manage his or her own time and countless other activities. These activities become the 'what' of the skills. The second input to the action is the manager's sensory mechanism which gives substance to these activities. A manager uses his or her senses to see, hear, feel, behave, think and speak. These processes give life to the skills. A manager chains together sensory accesses to form skill strategies which enable him or her to carry out the leading, delegating, negotiating, etc.

Secondly, three processes from learning theory: the use of prior learning, trial and error and social learning were examined to suggest how management skills can be developed to the necessary level of competence and how they become habitual.

Thirdly, two characteristics of skills outcome were examined to further understand the nature of managerial skilled performance. The process of 'chunking' was described as the mechanism for demonstrating the relationship between simple and complex skills. The mechanisms in the brain which deal with these processes were also described. The relationship and interplay between 'knowing' and 'doing' were also explored within the framework of the competence model. This suggested that there are skill development strategies associated with 'doing what you know' and 'knowing what you do'.

Finally, goal-setting and visualisation were examined as techniques which help initiate the *action* part of skill development.

REFERENCES

Anderson, J. A. (1988) 'Cognitive styles and multi-cultural populations', *Journal of Teacher Education*, Vol. 39 (1): 2–9

Bandura, A. (1986) *Social Foundations of Thought and Action*. Englewood Cliffs, NJ: Prentice Hall

Bandura, A. and Walters, R. (1963) *Social Learning and Personality Development*. New York: Holt, Rinehart & Winston

Block, N. (ed.) (1981) *Imagery*. Cambridge, MA: MIT Press

Boyatzis, R. (1982) *The Competent Manager. A model for effective performance*. Chichester: John Wiley & Sons

Bransford, J. D., Brown, A. L. and Cocking, R. R. (2001) *How People Learn: Brain, mind, experience and school*. Washington, DC: National Academy Press

CIPD. (2002) *Developing Managers for Business Performance*. London: Chartered Institute of Personnel and Development

Covey, S. (1999) *Seven Habits of Highly Effective People*. Hoboken, NJ: John Wiley & Sons

Cox, R. H. (1994) *Sports Psychology: Concepts and applications*. Madison, WI: Brown & Benchmark

Dilts, R. H. (2003) *From Coach to Awakener*. Capitola, CA: Meta Publications

Dilts, R. (1998) *Modelling with NLP*. Capitola, CA: Meta Publications

Dworetsky, J. P. (1994) *Psychology*. Minneapolis: West Publishing

Fisher, A. C. (1986) 'Imagery from a sports psychology perspective'. Paper presented at the American Alliance for Health, Physical Education, Recreation and Dance, Cincinnati, Ohio

Locke, E. A. and Latham, G. P. (1990) *A Theory of Goal Setting and Task Performance*. Englewood Cliffs, NJ: Prentice Hall

Locke, E. A., Shaw, K. M., Saari, L. M. and Latham, G. P. (1981) 'Goal-setting and task performance, 1969–1980', *Psychological Bulletin*, 90, 125–52

Mahoney, M. J. and Avener, M. (1977) 'Psychology of the elite athlete: an exploratory study', *Cognitive Therapy and Research*, 1, 135–41

Mintzberg, H. (1973) *The Nature of Managerial Work*. New York: Harper & Row

O' Connor, J. and Seymour, J. (2003) *Introducing Neuro-Linguistic Programming*. London: HarperCollins

Parker, C. and Stone, B. (2003) *Developing Management Skills for Leadership*. Harlow: Prentice Hall

Quinn, R. E., Faerman, S. R., Thompson, M. P. and McGrath, M. P. (2003) *Becoming a Master Manager: A competency framework*. Hoboken, NJ: John Wiley & Sons Inc.

Ratey, J. J. (2003) *A User's Guide to the Brain*. Toronto: Pantheon Books

Stewart, R. (1991) *Managing Today and Tommorrow*. London: Macmillan

Stewart, R. (1976) *Contrasts in Management.* London/Maidenhead: McGraw-Hill

Stewart, R. (1967) *Managers and Their Jobs.* London: Macmillan

Stewart, V. (1990) *The David Solution. How to reclaim power and to liberate your organisation.* Aldershot: Gower

Whetton, D., Cameron, K. and Woods, M. (2000) *Developing Management Skills for Europe.* Harlow: Prentice Hall

Woods, M. and Whitehead, J. (1993) *Working Alone.* London: Pitman

Excellence

> '**Complacency can come about because of our own expertise. We can become so comfortable with it that we assume we know all there is to know and stop growing. We come up with no new ideas and we are reluctant to consider new ideas from others. Meanwhile, the world has passed us by.**'
>
> *R. J. Sternberg, Yale University*

Excellence would appear to be a much sought-after commodity in almost every field of human endeavour, and management skills are no exception. The idea that managers can achieve excellent performance has a number of antecedents – business excellence, the field of personal mastery, behaviour modelling, high-performance teamworking and other miscellaneous examples of excellence from fields as diverse as sport, the arts and professional working. We review these three fields to explore the ideas associated with excellence.

Questions addressed in this chapter include:

- What is excellence?
- How do we know when we have achieved excellence?
- Is there a process which leads to excellence?
- Are there characteristics of excellence in skills?
- What is the role of learning in the achievement of excellence?

BUSINESS EXCELLENCE

One of the most influential models of business excellence was developed by Peters and Waterman (1982). This model suggests that the importance of people and an ability to continually learn through changing are key factors alongside economic performance. Hermel and Ramis-Pujol (2003) explore the difference between 'defining excellence' and 'guiding excellence' in organisations. The former they suggest to be the purpose and/or possible ways of achieving excellence. The latter is seen as related to choices about implementing excellence. Although identifying excellence usually relies on hard measures, the ways of achieving excellence usually involve 'soft data' particularly relating to individuals' style, learning and values.

The business excellence model commonly employed in organisations uses measures of leadership, HR issues, design and innovation, quality and customer satisfaction to assess excellent organisations.

Through research with organisations, Robson and Prabhu (2001) point to the main differentiators between 'leaders and laggers' in excellence as being in strategy and leadership, in which the leaders develop strong quality values, teamwork and customer orientation. Many models of business excellence focus on benchmarking and measurement of tangible assets. However, Marr and Adams (2004) have pointed out that Kaplan and Norton's most recent writings have a much greater focus on the intangibles. These are identified as human capital (employees' skills, talent and knowledge), information capital (systems) and organisational capital (leadership, culture, teamwork). Such intangible assets are considered by Kaplan and Norton (2004) to be of primary importance and assessed in more qualitative ways, and are much more reliant on the people employed than on measurable organisational processes and procedures. Research is emphasising the importance of the human and cultural elements of excellence on organisations. 'Excellent companies present strengths of innovation, ability to change and a leadership that excel through both their values and their action' (Hermel and Ramis-Pujol, 2003).

Although this definition relates to organisations, the characteristics identified belong to the employees who work in the organisation, and so the definition can be used equally to describe excellent people.

PERSONAL MASTERY

Senge (2000) identified five disciplines required for organisational excellence, relating his ideas closely to the concept of the 'learning organisation'. The disciplines are purpose, communications, flexibility, effective learning from experience and transfer of this learning, and personal mastery. This last requirement of personal mastery was described by Senge:

> **'People with a high level of personal mastery are acutely aware of their ignorance, their incompetence, their growth areas. They are deeply self-confident.'**

Although there may seem to be some inconsistency in the above ideas, they indicate that for someone to have personal mastery he or she must possess skills and competence compatible with self-confidence, yet at the same time be realistic, honest and always looking for ways to improve his or her performance, demonstrating appropriate personal values of constant improvement. Personal mastery is not about achieving a specified goal but about defining what the goals are, taking into account many personal and stakeholder views, and constantly working to achieve the best that the learner is capable of with self-awareness and motivation to continually develop.

Excellence, then, is not just about having skills and knowledge to achieve a goal that has been determined and provided by an outsider: it is about refining one's personal vision of where one wants to go and what one wants to become given the constraints of one's current reality.

Excellence is an ongoing process rather than something one achieves.

Covey (1999), in his highly rated book *The Seven Habits of Highly Effective People*, suggests that excellence is based on the following seven habits:

- being proactive
- beginning with the end in mind

- putting first things first

- thinking win/win

- seeking first to understand then to be understood

- synergising

- sharpening the saw.

In common with other advocates of personal excellence Covey focuses on the physical, mental, social/emotional and spiritual aspects of human nature although they are expressed in different ways. However, it is the final one, which addresses continual renewal and development, which seems to us to express the key element in excellence.

Gardner (1993) has studied the life and work of four of the most outstanding people of their generation: Mozart, who created many masterpieces in virtually every existing musical genre; Freud, who created the new and influential domain of psychoanalysis; Virginia Woolf, one of the greatest women writers of any generation; and Ghandi, who devised and practised a form of civil disobedience that continues to inspire millions around the world.

Through his analysis Gardner suggests there are three features that are regularly associated with extraordinary accomplishment:

- *Reflecting* – the regular, conscious consideration of the events of daily life in the light of longer-term aspirations

- *Leveraging* – the capacity of certain individuals to ignore areas of weakness and in effect ask: 'In which ways can I use my own strengths in order to gain a competitive advantage in the field in which I work?'

- *Framing* – the capacity to construe experiences in a way that is positive, in a way that allows one to draw apt lessons and, thus freshly energised, to proceed with one's life.

Gardner concludes by arguing that it is not only extraordinary individuals who can demonstrate these characteristics. Ordinary people can also produce improvements in their field of endeavour by applying the principles of reflection, leveraging and framing.

Behaviour modelling

Behaviour modelling and its use in the field of neurolinguistic programming (NLP) give a useful and practical insight into the concept of excellence. Behaviour modelling involves observing and identifying successful processes which underlie excellent performance. It is the process of taking a complex piece of behaviour or series of behaviours and breaking it down into small enough 'chunks' so that it can be reproduced. The purpose of behaviour modelling is to create a pragmatic map or model of that behaviour, which can then be used to reproduce or simulate some aspect of that performance by anyone who wishes to do so. The goal of the process is not only to identify the essential elements of thought and action required to produce the desired response or outcome but to tease out the more invisible elements which underpin those behaviours, such as beliefs and attitudes.

The field of NLP has developed out of the modelling of human behaviours and thinking processes. The NLP modelling procedures involve determining how the brain is operating (*neuro-*) by analysing language patterns (*-linguistic*). The results are then put into strategies or programmes (*programming*) so that they may be used to transfer skill to other people.

NLP began when Richard Bandler and John Grinder modelled patterns of language and behaviour of three outstanding therapists (models of excellence). The first techniques of NLP were derived from key verbal and non-verbal patterns Grinder and Bandler observed in the behaviour of these exceptional therapists.

Since that time NLP has been used extensively to study the mental strategies, language patterns and beliefs that influence a variety of educational and management-related activities including communication skills (Dilts *et al*, 1980; Laborde, 1998; Smith and Hallbaum, 1998), sales skills (Dilts, 1983; Bagley and Reese, 1987), negotiation (Dilts, 1980; Early, 1986), OD and training (Dilts, 1979; Maron, 1979), creativity and innovation (Dilts, Epstein and Dilts, 1991), recruitment and selection and leadership (Pile, 1998; Gaster, 1988).

NLP has identified an array of techniques and behavioural patterns that have produced excellent results and can be taught to other people to similarly produce excellent results.

High-performance teamworking

'High-performance teamworking' has become a common phrase in organisations and is another perspective through which excellence can be studied. There are examples of high-performing teams quoted in literature – for example, the Red Arrows whose guiding motto is *Eclat* ('brilliance'). They state (**www.raf.mod.uk**) that they represent:

> **'total teamwork based on mutual trust, incredible skill put to the test, a dedication to training for excellence.'**

These are members of the RAF selected for their skill and specific personal attributes and then in a small specialised team trained to the highest levels of personal mastery to work together. Within business high-performing teams also require similar skills, teamwork and focus. Reseach by the CIPD with the DTI (Sung and Ashton, 2005) evaluating case studies of the *Sunday Times* 100 Best Companies to Work For 2004 defined three 'bundles' of practices related to:

- high employee involvement practices (self-directed teams, quality improvement)
- human resource practices (recruitment, appraisal and mentoring), and
- reward and commitment practice (financial rewards, flexible working, etc).

The key findings suggest that continuous learning and focused development are essential elements, with people learning through their work and with an emphasis on tacit skills. Leadership is also crucial in developing high-performing organisations. Recent ideas have centred on a requirement for 'connected leadership' (Gobillot, 2007) in today's fast-changing environment which relies on personal impact and influence. Connected leaders are perceived to value being approachable and flexible, to enjoy good communication and to take risks, whereas less high-performing leaders are efficient, knowledgeable and tactful. In all of the above examples of excellence and high performance, personal attributes and determination are evident, whether individually or in teams.

EXCELLENT PERFORMERS

There are excellent performers in many different arenas, including sport, music and professional work, and research in each of these areas provides similar findings in relation to excellence.

Excellence in sport was initially defined by outcomes and achievement. Research was mainly focused on the identification of personal characteristics – eg the 'iceberg' personal profiles were deemed to lead to more successful outcomes. This is someone who scores low on intensity, fatigue, anger and confusion. The search for excellence then moved to psychological interventions and a range of techniques to training – eg cognitive interventions, motivational techniques and social psychological aspects of sport. Orlick (1998) and Danish and Nellen (1997) summarised these two components and suggested there should be a greater balance between the two:

- performance excellence, which relates to observable outcomes – winning major races or reducing a handicap in major sporting feats

- personal excellence, which refers to 'achievement in developmentally appropriate tasks across the length of one's life and the acquisition of personal qualities that contribute to optimal health and well-being' (Miller and Kerr, 2002).

To encourage excellence, therefore, it is important that individuals are involved not only in performance outcomes but in their own psychological, emotional, intellectual and social development. Coaches are for these reasons expected to encourage athletes to be concerned with and see the relevance of personal development as well as providing increasingly challenging environments.

Research undertaken with gifted musicians (Oerter, 2003) attempted to evaluate the contribution of biology and experience. It was suggested that musicians' higher performance was due to greater practice. However, there seems also to be an inherited component, possibly also linked to persistence and endeavour, which may contribute to greater practice. The research identified a process through which these high-performing musicians progressed (Oerter, 2003):

1   Play and have fun with music.
2   Practice with tutor assistance.
3   Make music a core value in life, leading to more intense practice.

Practice was found to be important, and resulted in the increasing complexity of related skills, including auditory and motor skills related to playing the instrument (so that long compositions were saved in the memory as one cluster), with many skill components.

In comparison, excellent professionals were defined by colleagues to have exceeded the usual benchmark standards of competence through determination and wanting to be the best (Courtney, 2005). This research (with occupational therapists) attempted to define excellence within a profession and found that it included personal characteristics or an attitudinal component – for example, consistency of standards, timeliness and responsiveness to clients – along with the idea of a role model to others and a public recognition of internal standards required for personal mastery. An important additional element was continual self-critique through reflection on experience, linked to current knowledge and skill and knowing one's limitations.

Circumstances or environment may also impact on our ability to reach personal excellence in anything. If we work in a very unsupportive or 'blame culture' environment, it may not provide the opportunity to reach standards and critique actions. Although the situation cannot be used as a reason not to try, it must be accepted that in an encouraging environment all of the required attitudes and actions are more likely to occur.

There are a variety of views expressed in the literature on the meaning of excellence. However, whether excellence is related to sport, business, managerial performance or performance in any field of endeavour, there are certain characteristics that seem to be constant:

- motivation to innovate or change
- continual learning
- questioning ways of doing things
- an ability to change with circumstances
- an understanding of the process of learning and determination to use it.

It is our contention that the practical application of these concepts leads to improved performance in any field of endeavour, and particularly in management skills, and will eventually lead to excellence. The rest of this chapter is devoted to our experience of the practical applications of these characteristics and how they may be further developed.

CONTINUING SKILLS DEVELOPMENT: THE QUEST FOR EXCELLENCE

In our professional development workshops we work with managers, professional employees and students to review, develop and improve their skills and work practices. This often calls for shifts and modifications in beliefs and attitudes to support the skill and work practice changes. We sometimes use simulations, games and role-plays to facilitate these changes. At other times we use a participant's past or future work experience to promote change. We always begin with an activity that the participants have been involved in, whether simulated or real. In order to review and learn from the experience, we give the participants a number of questions to work with (see box below).

Questions to aid reflection, learning and application

- What happened? (Give a full description.)
- Who else was involved?
- What did you do? (Your part in the activity.)
- How did you feel about what happened?
- What were you trying to achieve? (Your intention.)
- To what extent was it successful?
- What went well?
- What went less well?

If participants can answer these questions in detail, they have useful information about a situation they have experienced which helps them to gain an understanding about what occurred, why they behaved in the way they did and what influence they had on what took place.

We then encourage participants to plan for situations in the future by answering the following questions.

- What could you have done differently/better?
- What is your plan for the future in similar circumstances?
- How will you know when you have achieved it? (What evidence will you have?)

To facilitate understanding about learning we ask the following questions:

- What did you learn from the experience?
- What did you learn about yourself and the way you learn?
- What did you learn about learning?

These final three questions are much more challenging than the others and are testing the participants' knowledge of themselves (self-awareness) and their ability to use models of learning applied to themselves and other people.

The questions are initially recommended to all participants and some individuals find them challenging. Most people find them easier to complete when they have had some practice and they can see how monitoring their own and other people's behaviour can influence the outcomes of a situation.

Once learners become familiar with this review process, we encourage them to change, reduce and reformat the questions to cut down a prolonged review, and personalise it. If a reviewer is comfortable with the format of the review, he or she is more likely to use it. However, initially we do encourage detailed reviews to make sure that relevant information is not neglected. Later on in the process we encourage reviewers to use behavioural models and to benchmark themselves against these models. The case study below examines the information that can be obtained through the reviews of two different individuals.

Case study

Leading teams through change

Jen and Fran are two managers working in the retail section of a large financial institution and have to implement a new IT system. Each manager leads a team of call centre operatives who will be expected to operate the new IT system, once implemented. The teams have undergone change previously in their work with the bank and are somewhat concerned about the possible loss of work due to the new system.

Both managers are familiar with the new system and very competent with the old one, having worked with it for eight years and trained most of their teams in its operation.

Jen is competent with IT, outgoing, confident with employees, and as a team leader she is popular, easygoing, and encourages her team to work hard and look for ways of improving what they do and to take responsibility for making changes within the team.

Fran is also competent with the old IT and encourages her team to work hard but prefers everything to be done in the same way and likes to check all the work output. She, personally, found change situations previously stressful, so is worried and would rather not move to the new system. She has difficulty hiding this from the team so they are now anxious about the implementation.

There are minor problems as the new system is implemented, and while Jen's confidence and 'can do' attitude get her through, Fran becomes even more worried about the real and potential problems. She requires her team to note every issue they find with the new system, and so it takes longer for her team to gain confidence with the system's operation. There is some difficulty in transferring learning from the old to the new system, which is magnified by Fran's lack of confidence in her team.

EXERCISE

Questions on the case study

Imagine that you have a set of completed review questions for Jen and Fran (if you feel you must, you can cheat by looking at the box below):

- What main differences would you expect to see?
- What are likely to be the helping and hindering actions of the two managers?
- What might they learn from each other?
- Outline how Fran might reflect and then how and what she could plan to help in a similar situation in future.

Suggested responses of Jen and Fran, based on the list of questions to aid reflection above

What happened?

The IT change.

Who else was involved?

The team.

What did you do?

Both Jen and Fran are likely to describe the change situation, the issues and fears of their teams and the problems of implementation. Here the stories will probably diverge. Jen will tell how her team worked together, made any amendments and got through the situation, whereas Fran is likely to explain her reaction as wanting to ensure that the work was accurate and so 'helping' the team by checking all work.

How did you feel about what happened?

Both managers may have felt concerned in the situation, but Fran is more likely to include reference to her feelings of stress, not liking the change, the lack of confidence in her team, and her anxiety about the problems that occurred.

What were you trying to achieve?

Again, both managers are likely to mention wanting to make the changes effectively. However, differences are likely to centre on Jen's intention to keep her team working hard and looking for ways to improve and make changes. Fran's intention would probably be said to include wanting to ensure quality of output and to note difficulties to report.

To what extent was this successful? What went well?

The change was a success for both managers, eventually, and Jen may also evaluate her team's attitude to work and making changes as a success. Fran may mention the standard nature of the work completed.

What went less well?

Although both managers are likely to mention the problems that occurred and difficulty in transferring learning to the new system, it is likely that Fran will have the longer list, including needing to check work, the team's lack of confidence, and taking longer to reach the required output.

Answers to the later questions are dependent on each manager's being aware of her reasons for decisions, being aware of her impact on others, and being open to different ideas and learning.

What to do differently for Fran may come from seeing Jen in action (social learning) or from thinking about how to reduce work for herself and the team (cognitive problem-solving) or through review discussions with Jen (action learning). It all requires her to be motivated to do differently, to be willing to try something new. Hopefully, full reflection and frank discussion will enable her to see alternative actions that may help.

Fran's future plan may be something like this:

I will have confidence that the team will work hard and be able to change to the new system. I will show confidence in them, and in myself, and not show my anxieties through my actions. I will encourage the team to tell me if they have ideas that could help overcome difficulties. I will communicate with the team in positive ways as often as possible.

Learning from all reviews is dependent on the awareness of the individual of his or her task and personal skills, behaviours, impact and learning. So we can never be sure that any individual manager will overcome previous difficulties without further support to prompt sufficient analysis. However, through discussion, observing and talking and reflecting with others (as suggested in the awareness chapter), new insights are possible on the road to excellence. To aid critical reflection and review of actions Reeves (1994) provides four thought-provoking questions that can be used to help to facilitate new thinking:

- Did I break out of accustomed patterns and experiment with new ways of doing things?
- Did I allow invalid assumptions about situations of misplaced perceptions of people to affect what I did?
- How aware was I of my inner needs that were driving what I did, and how well did I handle them?
- Did I use my feelings constructively or allow them to block me?

The ability to question why we do certain things and in what ways we could have challenged our 'usual' ideas is an indicator of self-awareness and of movement towards excellence. Although these insights do not guarantee excellence and although excellence cannot be achieved without commitment and hard work too, excellence is achievable through the use of excellent processes.

Double-loop learning

Seibert (1999) distinguished between two types of reflection:

- 'Reflection on action' is the usual retrospective reflection or contemplation that takes place after an event and enables the process to lead to learning.

- 'Reflection in action' takes place during action and may be considered to be 'thinking on one's feet' as circumstances change.

Both of these types of reflection are important for excellence. Schon (1987) suggested that being able to 'reflect in action' was a major factor in identifying 'outstanding professionals' and that it took time to develop and is dependent on becoming aware that usual responses in situations had not led to appropriate outcomes so that a different response is required, sometimes leading to 'on-the-spot experiments'. It is, however, also important to engage in deeper learning to provide greater understanding of situations through reflection-on-action. Greater understanding of personal learning can be achieved through the activity described in the box below.

ACTIVITY

Themes and issues in learning

Use the list of questions to aid reflection (above) to review four or five important work situations that you have experienced recently so that you can recall as much detail as possible. They can be any kind of situations, whether things worked well for you in them or not.

Try to provide as much detail as possible for each question and record your feelings and opinions or beliefs, then challenge these as you try to answer the additional questions below.

What are your main findings in terms of:

- how you develop skills – what methods and approaches work for you? Which do you find difficult to use?

- your attitudes that might influence your learning, positively or negatively?

- the circumstances or people that make learning easier or more difficult for you?

- those skills you find more easy, or more difficult, to develop?

The answers should provide you with ideas about themes and issues that might influence personal and professional development and help you to identify which factors might hasten your progress toward excellence.

Action learning: an alternative methodology for excellence

Action learning (Revans, 1980) is a different approach from personal reflection and learning, and involves working with a group of colleagues. It is particularly useful to aid ongoing problem-solving in situations where each participant has responsibility for dealing with a work or personal issue and taking action on it. Reflection is facilitated through describing and evaluating the issue, with questions from the group. Each participant provides his or her own perspective on the issue and helps the problem-owner come to new understandings and define a way forward that he or she will implement. The method may be perceived, therefore, as using other people in a structured way, as described, or just as colleagues discussing work. What is essential is that the reflection leads to a better understanding not only of the task in hand but of your learning and yourself, in order to plan for future activities. Action can in this way result in change and new understanding on different levels:

- change in the learner's skills or knowledge
- understanding of a task
- personal development and increased self-awareness
- understanding the process of learning.

These outputs of action learning provide a firm basis for personal development across a wide variety of situations.

ACHIEVING EXCELLENCE: WHAT SHOULD BE REVIEWED?

We have found there is no definitive menu for items that should be reviewed. There are wide differences between individuals and no one prescription works for everyone. However, we have found that certain guidelines seem to bring the best results for the majority of reviewers. Job activities (interviewing, chairing meetings, negotiating, etc) and personal effectiveness activities (time management, goal-setting, etc) seem to be the most natural areas for managers to review. We encourage reviewers to think about standards and benchmarks for these activities. Managing relationships appears to us and to most managers we deal with a key element in improving performance and achieving excellence. Understanding the learning process is an essential part of an excellent process to lead to excellent outcomes.

These are the areas we encourage managers to explore when they are new to the review process. However, as reviewers become more experienced we suggest that there are four goals that they can pursue which we believe lead to true excellence: self-awareness, continuous learning, the use of a variety of perspectives, and understanding and using learning. These are further explored below.

Self-awareness

The more managers review their experiences, the more data they have available to make judgements about patterns of their behaviour, and whether certain behaviours are associated with certain contexts. If they have completed a personality inventory, they may come to understand how their traits and characteristics manifest themselves in situations. They may come to see which emotions accompany certain events. When this type of learning begins to happen, managers can begin to predict and anticipate situations and can build on their strengths and can use coping behaviour to mitigate the consequences of their weaknesses. With this type of review we can explore our beliefs, attitudes and values. In these types of reviews the work is more challenging but the benefits can be much greater and more extensive.

Case study

John

John was an operations manager in the NHS and was taking part in a professional development workshop as part of his personal development plan. Late in the day he was taking part in a group exercise with four other team members. One of the objectives was to complete the exercise in a specified time. John seemed to focus on this particular aspect to the exclusion of all the other objectives (associated with teamwork). This became an issue with the team, and John finished the exercise by walking away from the group complaining that the other members were not taking the exercise seriously.

At the conclusion of the workshop the participants were asked to review the activities they had taken part in, saying what they had done well and where they might have done things differently. John's group reviewed their teamwork exercise. The issue of John's focus on completion of the task to the exclusion of everything else, and his subsequent walking off, was discussed. Most people cited tiredness as the main factor – apart from one group member who also happened to be a colleague of John's. He mentioned two other occasions, back in the workplace, when a similar issue occurred. The group moved on to discuss other aspects. Later, when John was writing up the review, he began to think about this issue. His colleague had been correct: John's walkout was not a one-off. John had strong views about time, and in particular, finishing tasks on time. He knew from his personality inventory that he was a very orderly, structured person but he had never seen this in the context of his everyday behaviour. He also realised that he had some very strong beliefs about what should and should not be in relation to this issue, and if he was honest he could see that it had affected his relationships with other people.

John began to ponder whether he ought to be more flexible on occasions, although he knew that in some situations his approach was valuable. How would he know when to be more flexible? Was he able to change?

Openness to spiral learning

When we review an experience and tease out learning from it, the main benefit from the activity is that we can apply this learning to be of use in the future. To make the most of this link we need to keep repeating the reviews in an iterative manner so we can not only refine our learning over time but we can widen the learning to different situations. We can also develop new skills which along with other new skills and previously learned skills produce a synergetic effect so we make bigger and higher-quality changes in the future.

Spiral learning and interviewing

A manager might review her questioning skills during an interview for a new supervisor. In the next interview she may use better-quality questions and a greater range of questions. The next review may lead not only to better questions but also to the use of better rapport skills. Following the next review, the manager may interview a different type of candidate – eg an engineer – as well as continue to make improvements in questioning and rapport. This may then build into different types of interview such as performance review or grievance-handling as the process grows and builds from review to review.

This type of learning requires not only a competent facility with the review process but also a commitment and enthusiasm for the process and the potential of the process.

We believe that there is a fundamental distinction in attitude, not related to age or experience, between those who retain an 'openness to learn' and however experienced are aware of opportunities for developing themselves, and those who believe that they have little to learn from anyone (although often an objective view of their skills would not lead to this conclusion).

On the radio one afternoon I heard Sir Ian McKellen talking about a new role that he was preparing to play. He explained that although he was experienced and knew the part well, he 'set himself tasks to perform each night', and that this provided a challenge, continued to improve the part, in his view, and that he hoped the small improvements became an unconscious part of the whole act. This is the essence of a continued interest in learning – a lack of satisfaction with your latest performance – and requires a continual awareness of how things might be changed so that even tiny improvements continue to occur and allow us to become excellent.

Management gurus regularly say that awareness of opportunities and openness to learning or to challenge and question the way they do things (Senge, 2000) is an essential requirement for managers today – that activity and awareness to learn and try things helps to retain well-being throughout life. In this way the real benefits can be accrued and excellence pursued.

Figure 12: *The learning spiral*

Variety of perspectives

One of the most frustrating and yet enriching characteristics of the human race is that no two people have exactly the same perspective on anything. We have our own unique makeup and life history which gives each human perspective the same variability we find in our personal appearance. This is frustrating in as much as it can lead to breakdown in communication, with the consequences with which we are all too familiar in international relations, business and personal relationships. However, it is also enriching because human achievement can thrive on differences. The tensions inherent in differences can lead to major breakthroughs in commerce, scientific achievement and wherever individuals work in teams. It can create synergy as well as conflict. If individuals could harness the positive aspects of diversity rather than the negative, it would surely lead to excellence in any area where human beings need to collaborate or interact.

Young (2001), building on the work of DELOZIER and GRINDER (1987), describes four 'perceptual positions' which individuals might adopt to help enhance the benefits of and reduce the negative aspects of diversity of perspective.

- First position

  This is being yourself. It is being concerned with issues from your point of view. In this position you have a very strong sense of who you are. You see the world through your own eyes, hear the world through your own ears, and feel the world through your own body. You do not take anyone's point of view into account. You simply think, 'How does this affect *me*?'

- Second position

  This is you 'pretending' to be someone else. In this position you become the object of perception rather than the perceiver; you are experiencing not being you. In this position you appreciate another person's point of view and wonder, 'How would this appear to them?' The stronger rapport you have with someone, the easier it is to adopt their reality. You do not need to like them or agree with their point of view.

- Third position

  This position gives you the perspective of a completely independent observer. 'How would this look to someone who is not involved?' It is sometimes known as the 'fly on the wall' position. We move ourselves from the world of direct experience to a world of thought and generalisation. On this level we think about, talk about that person that we call 'me' who is engaged in everyday activities and relationships.

- Fourth position

  If we move sideways from third position we can get an objective view of the system comprising 'me' and my relationships. Fourth position can be viewed as 'we, as perceived by the system'. This position takes a view of the whole system and considers the best interest of the system.

We all spend time in these positions but most of the time they are all mixed up and we do not get a clean view of what each can tell us. We can learn more effectively if we keep these perspectives separate. They will help us to understand any situation and outcome better. We do not need other people to be physically present to use these concepts. All this can take place in the imagination, and that imagination is very real and can create strong feelings just as if other people were present. Being able to move cleanly between these four perspectives is a useful skill and one we believe is a prerequisite to excellence.

In order to use these positions think of a relationship you have in the work situation where there has been a disagreement between two of you that is still unresolved. Imagine both of you in a place you would normally meet, such as sitting across a table at work, or one of you standing and the other seated. As you move through the four positions, just imagine you and the other person discussing the problem or issue as you would do in the normal work situation. We are now going to move through the four perceptual positions in order to collect more information about your problem and your relationship.

First position

- You need to be fully present in the here and now.
- See things through your own eyes.
- Hear things through your own ears.
- Feel things through your own body.
- You have your own values and feelings about the issue.
- Say what your position on the problem is.
- Stay in this position until you feel you are beginning to open up some new insights on your relationship and problem. What have you learned from being in this position?

Second position
Before going into this position undertake some light activity to break the state of the first position. (Perhaps go over to the window and have a look at what is going on in your street.)

- Imagine yourself as the other person.
- How will he or she be positioned?
- How does he or she speak?
- What body language does he or she adopt?
- See through his or her eyes.
- Hear through his or her ears.
- Feel through his or her body.
- After a while you can believe you are that person.
- Stay in this position until you think you are beginning to get some insights into the problem/relationship from his or her perspective. What have you learned from being in this position?

Third position
Before you adopt this position, break the state with a light activity.

- Get into a position so that you observe both yourself and the other person as an observer/a 'fly on the wall'.
- Make sure the two people you are visualising are equidistant from you and of equal proportions so as not to bias one or the other in your mind.
- Make sure your voice is coming from 'an observer', not from first or second position.

- Make sure you are watching with an observer's eyes, not from the eyes of first or second position.

- Make sure your feelings are those of the objective observer and not those of either of the two parties.

- Stay in this position until you think you are beginning to get some insight into the problem/relationship from this perspective. What have you learned from this position?

Fourth position
Before you adopt this position, break the state with a light activity.

- Move to a position that enables you to see the whole system.

- What changes would benefit all the participants?

- What would be a useful intervention?

- Be as creative as you can – particularly pay attention to things different from the usual way of doing things.

Summarise the information you have got and revisit any of the positions that you feel would be useful. What new insights have you now got on the problem and on the relationship? It may seem a long process, but as you become more experienced and skilled you will become much more efficient at completing the process. If the problem is stopping you from moving on, it is worthwhile spending some time on it.

Levels of learning

In one review you may learn to ask a certain question when a candidate gives a particular prompt. In another you may learn to recognise a whole series of occasions when you need to use coping behaviour because your natural response is not an effective one. It is clear that the second type of learning is of a different order from the first. We believe that an understanding of and ability to use different levels of learning is one of the most important attributes of excellence. Learning about learning is a key aim of our more experienced reviewers. Bateson (1972, 1979) has described and explained five different levels of learning, and we believe this to be an excellent 'big picture' model for depicting the range of learning opportunities open to us:

- *Learning Level 0* is no change. It involves repetitive behaviour. There is just one reaction to a stimulus. Habits are an example of this type of behaviour. It is not subject to correction. In organisations it can frequently lead to inefficiency, resistance and complacency.

- *Learning Level 1* is gradual, incremental change. It involves making corrections through behavioural flexibility. In organisations it might mean establishing and refining new procedures and capabilities to meet the requirements of changing circumstances. At a personal level it might mean acquiring greater flexibility in rapport skills in order to match differing customer circumstances.

- *Learning Level 2* is rapid discontinuous change. It involves the instantaneous shift of response to an entirely different category or class of behaviour. In organisation terms it might happen when there is a change in policy, values or priorities. For example, Level 2 change would accompany a shift to being more service-oriented than product-oriented. This would require large-scale changes across whole areas of procedures and behaviours.

- *Learning Level 3* is evolutionary change. It is characterised by significant alterations which stretch beyond the boundaries of the current identity of the individual, group or organisation. The adoption of the Internet technologies would be an example of Level 3 change. With this type of change many organisations have been forced to move into completely new management and marketing approaches, often far beyond what they were formerly used to or comfortable with.

- *Learning Level 4* is revolutionary change. It involves change to something that is new, unique and transformative. For organisations it would involve completely new responses, technologies or capabilities that open the door to previously unknown and uncharted possibilities. This is not normally available to individuals because it has its source in the larger system or 'field' surrounding us – what Bateson describes as the 'larger mind' or 'pattern that connects'. This has sometimes been called the 'spiritual' level of learning.

This description is based on the work of Dilts (2003) and his interpretation of Bateson's model. He goes on to give a useful computer analogy to describe the five levels (Dilts, 2003).

'Data stored in a computer is like Learning Level 0. It just sits there, unchanging, to be used over and over again whatever programs are being run on the computer. Running a spellcheck program on that data would be like Learning Level 1. A spellcheck program makes corrective changes in a particular set of data.

'If the data being checked, however, is not text but numbers and financial figures that need to be updated, no amount of running the spellcheck will be able to make proper corrections. Instead, the user would have to switch to a spreadsheet or some kind of accounting software. Getting "out of the box" of one program and switching to another is like Learning Level 2.

'Sometimes the computer one is using is incapable of running the needed program and it is necessary to switch computers altogether, or change operating systems. This would be like Learning Level 3.

'To develop a completely new device, such as a programmable molecular computing machine composed of enzymes and DNA molecules instead of silicon microchips, would be like Learning Level 4.'

ACTIVITY

Think about changes you have been involved in in your current organisation and in previous organisations. Try to pick examples of Learning Levels 0, 1, 2 and 3.

Select one example from each level and write brief notes to explain the reasons you think make each a particular level for the organisation concerned.

Take each of the changes and examine the type of learning that occurred for *you personally* during the change. If the change did not have a personal impact on you, identify other people in the organisation who were affected by the change. From your observations, what was their level of learning?

Was the personal level of learning always the same as the organisational one?

What were the learning opportunities available to people in these change situations?

How was learning supported?

SUMMARY AND WAY FORWARD

Before we leave the concept of excellence it would be useful to reinforce our perspective. We believe there are two components to excellence: excellent outcomes and excellent process. We believe that excellent outcomes are achieved through excellent process. It is, however, very difficult if not impossible to define excellence in terms of outcomes because they are dependent on the activity under consideration and as such are often framed in different ways. There is also more subjectivity in judging what an excellent outcome is. One person's excellence is another person's mediocrity.

We do feel that some of these limitations apply to process as well. However, there does seem sufficient agreement in the literature to give our approach some credibility, particularly in the area, as Covey would put it, of 'sharpening the saw', as in the process of meta-cognition.

We have chosen four ideas which we believe underpin excellent process in any field, but particularly in the development of management skills – self-awareness, spiral learning, perceptual positions and understanding learning. We hope readers and practitioners will add to and build on these elements in the true spirit of continuous learning.

REFERENCES

Bagley, D. and Reese, E. (1987) *Beyond Selling: How to maximize your personal influence*. Capitola, CA: Meta Publications

Bandler, R. and Grinder, J. (1979) *Frogs into Princes*. Moab, UT: Real People Press

Bandler, R. and Grinder, J. (1975) *The Structure of Magic*, Vols 1 and 2. Palo Alto, CA: Science and Behavior Books

Bateson, G. (1979) *Mind and Nature*. New York: E. P. Dutton

Bateson, G. (1972) *Steps to an Ecology of Mind*. New York: Ballantine Books

Covey, S. (1999) *The Seven Habits of Effective People*. Cambridge (UK): Simon & Schuster

Courtney, M. (2005) 'The meaning of professional excellence for private practitioners in occupational therapy', *Australian Occupational Therapy Journal*, Vol 52, Issue 3: 211–23

Danish, S. J. and Nellen, V. C. (1997) 'New roles for sports psychologists: teaching life skills through sport to at-risk youth', cited in P. S. Miller and G. A. Kerr (2002) 'Conceptualizing excellence: past, present and future', *Journal of Applied Sport Psychology*, Vol 14, 140–53

DeLozier, J. and Grinder, J. (1987) *Turtles All the Way Down*. Santa Cruz, CA: DeLozier and Associates

Dilts, R. (2003) *From Coach to Awakener*. Capitola, CA: Meta Publications

Dilts, R. (1983) *Applications of NLP*. Capitola, CA: Meta Publications

Dilts, R. (1979) *NLP in Organisational Development*. New York: OD Network Conference Papers

Dilts, R., Epstein, T. and Dilts, R. W. (1991) *Tools for Dreamers: Strategies for creativity and the structure of innovation*. Capitola, CA: Meta Publications

Dilts, R., Grinder, J., Bandler, R. and DeLozier, J. (1980) *Neuro-Linguistic Programming: The study of the structure of subjective experience*. Capitola, CA: Meta Publications

Early, G. (1986) *Negotiations*. Holbaek, Denmark: S. M. Olsen

Gardner, H. (1993) *Frames of Mind: The theory of multiple intelligences*. New York: Basic Books

Gaster, D. (1998) *A Framework for Visionary Leadership*. Henley-on-Thames: PACE

Gobillot, E. (2007) *The Connected Leader: Creating agile organisations for people, performance and profit*. London: Kogan Page

Hermel, P. and Ramis-Pujol, J. (2003) 'An evolution of excellence: some main trends', *The TQM Magazine*, Vol 15, No 4: 230–43

Kaplan, R. S. and Norton, D. P. (2004) 'Measuring the strategic readiness of intangible assets', *Harvard Business Review*, Vol 82, No 2, Feb: 52–63

Laborde, G. (1998) *Influencing with Integrity: Management skills for communication and negotiation*. Palo Alto, CA: Syntony Inc.

Maron, D. (1979) 'Neuro-linguistic programming: the answer to change?', *Training and Development Journal*, 33 (10): 68

Marr, B. and Adams, C. (2004) 'The balanced scorecard and intangible assets: similar ideas, unaligned concepts', *Measuring Business Excellence*, Vol 8, No 3: 18–27

Miller, P. S. and Kerr, G. A. (2002) 'Conceptualizing excellence: past, present and future', *Journal of Applied Sport Psychology*, Vol 14, 140–53

Oerter, R. (2003) 'Biological and psychological correlates of exceptional performance in development', *Neurosciences and Music*, Vol 999, November: 451–60. Annals of the New York Academy of Sciences

Orlick, T. (1998) *Embracing Your Potential: Steps to self-discovery, balance and success in sports, work and life*. Champaign, IL: Human Kinetics

Peters, T. and Waterman, R. (1982) *In Search of Excellence: Lessons from America's best-run companies*. New York: Harper & Row

Pile, S. (1988) *Vision into Action: Creating a generative internal model of transformational-transactional leadership*. Master's Thesis, Pepperdine University

RAF – Red Arrows website **www.raf.mod.uk/careers** [accessed 30 April 2007]

Reeves, T. (1994) *Managing Effectively: Developing yourself through experience*. Basingstoke: The Institute of Management Foundation/Butterworth-Heinemann

Revans, R. (1980) *Action Learning: New techniques for action learning*. London: Blond & Briggs

Robson, A. and Prabhu, V. B. (2001) 'What can we learn from "leading" service practitioners about business excellence?', *Managing Service Quality*, Vol 11, No 4: 249–61. MCB University Press

Schon, D. A. (1987) *Educating the Reflective Practitioner: Toward a new design for teaching and learning in the professions*. San Francisco: Jossey-Bass

Senge, P. (2000) *The Fifth Discipline: The art and practice of the learning organization*. New York: Doubleday

Smith, S. and Hallbaum, T. (1998) *Augmenting the One Minute Manager*. Columbus, OH: The NLP Connection

Sung, J. and Ashton, D. (2005) *High Performance Work Practices: Linking strategy and skills to performance outcomes*. London: Department of Trade and Industry in association with the CIPD. **www.cipd.co.uk** [accessed 30 April 2007]

Young, P. (2001) *Understanding NLP*. Carmarthen: Crown House Publishing

Critical Variables

Experiential learning

'Here is Edward Bear coming down the stairs now, BUMP, BUMP, BUMP, on the back of his head behind Christopher Robin.

'It is, as far as he knows, the only way of coming downstairs, but sometimes he feels that there really is another way.

'If only he could stop bumping for a moment to think about it.'

A. A. Milne

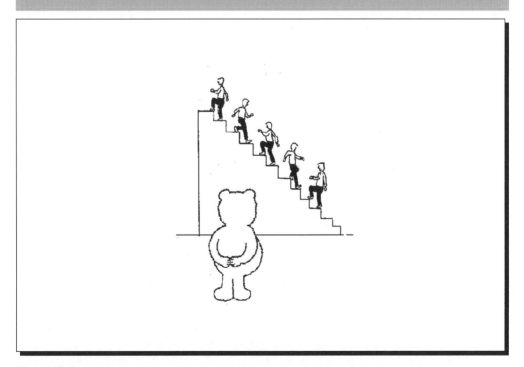

Figure 13: *Reflective learning – a bear learning how to use stairs properly*

This well-known quote has been used before to encourage us to think about what we know of the world, how we get to know these things, and how difficult it is to learn something new. The quote is initially cute, amusing, may bring back memories of childhood and playing 'pooh sticks' off a bridge and of other things that you did as a child – but re-reading it, consider how many times you have done something in the way you have always done it without questioning whether it is the most effective, efficient or pleasing way of achieving the outcome, or indeed if the outcome is exactly the one required. Although it is a childhood story, it can have important meaning for the way we behave and learn today.

INTRODUCTION

It may seem strange in a book that aims to help adults develop management and HR skill that more time has not been given to discussing the underpinning ideas of experiential learning – one of the key models used in our approach. This chapter aims to provide that discussion, although we thought it important to present and explore the range of research and ideas about experiential and related approaches to learning to examine their contribution and fit into our approach to learning using ADAX. The chapter examines factors that influence learning, particularly adult learning, due to the focus on managers. It examines experiential learning in management and HR skills, through a review of key concepts in the learning literature. ADAX is compared with other main learning models, and we provide advice for all those involved in the development of these skills either for themselves or to support the development of others.

The questions that this chapter intends to answer are:

- There are many names used to describe the links between experience and learning or 'learning by doing'; do these differ from experiential learning or are they the same?

- Is all learning experiential, or do we also learn in other ways?

- What are the shortcomings of experiential learning, and how do they influence learners?

- How does experiential learning fit with the ADAX model?

- Is experiential learning really effective – and if it is, what makes it so – and what are the limitations to its use?

- In what ways can experiential learning be used in developing skills?

- Are there alternative ways of learning skills?

DEFINING LEARNING

Before examining experiential learning in detail it will be useful to review more general meanings of learning and then to look at different approaches to learning, to contrast these with experiential learning. A well-used and simple definition of learning is that of Bass and Vaughan (1967), who said (p.68) that learning was:

'a relatively permanent change in behaviour that occurs as a result of practice or experience.'

This definition is underpinned by a number of assumptions:

- To infer learning we expect a learner to do something. The 'behaviour' may involve demonstrating what he or she has observed or explaining something. Unless the learner changes his or her behaviour, it is difficult to infer learning.

- Learning occurs through experience or practice, both implying activity and integration with previous experience.

- Learning involves more than copying, modelling someone or following instructions, although these may be a stage in the learning process. It is 'relatively permanent', so it involves some change in the learner's behaviour and understanding – a change in the internal perceptual map is involved.

- From above, therefore, learning is mediated by the learner's experience and personal characteristics, so it may be different for each learner.

Learning, then, seems to involve a number of key characteristics, related to action and understanding as well as involving a learner's experience, and one might argue – as notable writers do (Rogers, 1996; Boud *et al*, 2000) – that experience forms the basis for *all* learning. However, in education there are many learning and teaching theories that have been developed over time to address certain issues in learning, and there has been little attempt to link the main ideas together. So there remain many theories that apply in isolated conditions.

We find the categorisation of learning theories provided by Reynolds, Caley and Mason (2002) useful, their contribution to human learning distinguishing four clusters:

- learning as behaviour change or shaping

- learning as understanding (Piaget, 1950, and Festinger, 1957)

- learning as constructing knowledge

- learning as social practice.

We have found that understanding learning as knowledge construction is a particularly useful approach to aid us in helping managers to learn and develop skills. In this cluster, theorists emphasised the role of warmth and understanding in learning. Rogers (1974) is one of the main figures in the humanist movement and emphasised the potential everyone has for learning when they are understood and cared for. He advocated learner-centred learning, in which a facilitator allows learners to decide the pace of learning and values and uses their experience. Motivation and environmental factors were perceived to influence decisions about learning, with motivation being a personal driver and hence different for each learner. Humanists held experience to be the basis of all learning in which learners actively search for meaning and knowledge using reflection as the basis of the process. All learning takes place in a particular context, and usually for managers this context is a social one in which they constantly learn from other managers and employees, so that social learning and practice influence what is learned and is therefore important.

All of the above ideas include reference to the role of experience in learning, although one difficulty for many learning theories is that their main focus is on learning in an educational or controlled environment – for example, a laboratory.

The idea of learning from experience is a pervasive and powerful idea throughout the literature. In fact, it is difficult to imagine any learning taking place without some kind of experience. However, learning does not always follow from experience, as Covey (1999) points out in his influential book, *The Seven Habits of Highly Effective People.* Much of our work is to enable managers to learn within their normal everyday work. Knowles *et al* (1998) suggest that adults' experience influences their learning in four main ways:

- to create a wider range of individual differences
- to provide a rich resource for learning
- to create biases that can inhibit or shape new learning
- to provide grounding for adults' self-identity.

We have also found these factors to be important and provide ideas for using them – and overcoming the third one – throughout the book. The role of experience in learning was also emphasised by Knowles in his distinction between how adults and children learn, a distinction that is important in this book.

ADULT LEARNING

Knowles (1998) has been most influential in defining differences in the approach to learning of adults and children. This book is aimed at aiding the development of adult learners and so it is useful to review Knowles' ideas. He sees adult learners as different from children due to their greater experience, and his model of a lifelong learner expects adults to have the following skills:

- to use divergent thinking – to develop and be curious about the world around them
- to be able to formulate and, where necessary, find answers to questions about the topic they are studying
- to be able to identify and collect information about topics they are investigating
- to organise, analyse and make decisions based on data collected
- to communicate ideas and answers about a topic under study.

Adults are therefore expected to use the above skills, and teachers of adults are expected to help develop these skills where necessary. Children are to be regarded as much more dependent on a teacher to define what is learned and how it is learned and what the outcomes will be. Knowles (1989) advocates andragogy in working with adults, particularly the use of learning contracts to guide and plan learning. The key assumptions of his approach (Knowles, Holton and Swanson, 1998) are:

- Adults have to understand why they need to learn something before beginning.
- Adults need to be treated as being capable of determining their own direction.
- Adults have, and use, their experience as a source of learning, and because of their greater experience they have a larger range of individual differences.
- Adults learn as a function of need and their readiness to learn comes from being at the correct stage to learn what is required – for example, a manager will be ready to learn the Japanese language when and if he or she sees it as an appropriate development and useful for himself or herself.
- Adults are motivated to learn to solve problems or achieve tasks that they have. They learn knowledge and facts when it is shown to be important to and based in their area of experience.
- Adults respond more to internal motivation and may also be blocked by low self-esteem or self-concept; children are more externally motivated.

This set of assumptions has been challenged by a number of writers (eg Jarvis, 1992; Tennant, 2006). Some of the key challenges may be considered to be:

- that empirical studies used to support this approach ignored cultural differences in lifestyle and learning preferences, and that because the theory was developed in a Western culture it may be less appropriate for people from different cultures

- that Knowles' ideas on adult self-direction, based in humanistic clinical psychology, suggest that a change process based on self-actualisation as a state to which we should all aim, is a myth, and that there are no obvious differences from children's learning

- and finally, that the mix of humanist and behaviourist approaches in Knowles' theory is unusual because it puts together different types of learning clusters – mixing personal life development (humanistic) with specific directed achievement of objectives (behaviourism) – and that the 'individual self' might be threatened by traditional generalised teaching, whereas today we see that there are multiple views of self where each person has many different 'facets' to cope in the range of situations we experience, as demonstrated in transformative learning (King, 2005).

In our experience, it is certainly true that Knowles' assumptions do not describe all adult learners, although more effective learners are usually internally motivated, use their experience and investigate or apply their learning to help address needs or solve problems.

We have found that some learners require additional external motivation – for example, an assessment or tutor observation. They prefer not to be challenged to find answers to their own questions. Some learners are limited in their use of self-directed learning, preferring to have a tutor point out what might be learned. Interestingly, Mumford and Gold (2004) have developed some of Knowles' ideas on adult learning, when discussing management development, suggesting that adults are self-directed but have a conditioned expectation to be dependent and to be taught. This is more familiar to us in our work with adults in a higher education setting and may help to explain why some adult learners in higher education learn in ways more similar to children in Knowles' theory.

We begin sessions providing direction and more structured activities for managers, using a basic approach, with a set of questions as described later in this chapter. As we progress through weeks with managers, we develop activities that become more challenging, with fewer directed review processes and more reliance on learners to identify their learning and plan what can be applied in their work, so that whatever the content of sessions, the process we adopt encourages a move toward the first meaning of self-direction. We discuss ways in which we encourage deeper review below. Eventually we encourage managers to work in small action learning sets that support personal and professional learning on topics identified by the managers. Support comes from set colleagues and makes use of learning from all experiences.

LEARNING IN EDUCATIONAL CONTEXTS

Dixon (1994) suggests that for most people their initial experience of 'learning' is in an educational setting where a teacher provides information to learn. They therefore come to recognise that learning, in education at least, is about understanding what a teacher, or expert, tells them. They expect that there will be a known, 'correct' answer to a given problem that can be found and applied to their own situation.

Throughout education a similar approach which emphasis dependency may be adopted – for example, in higher education if one watches a class at work, one might see occasional questions provided by the tutor, or group discussions allowed when talking about a topic, but the major assumption is that the tutor is responsible for teaching so that students might learn. However, although the tutor appears to control most elements in the formal approach to teaching, there is one main essential element that is not under the control of a tutor – students' learning. This didactic approach is limiting because a student's accumulated knowledge may not be relevant in new situations or changing circumstances, which are more reminiscent of organisations today. Argyris (1991) distinguished between 'learned managers' who may have learned in a didactic way and 'learning managers' who are able to question, and who operate in changing environments. Most of the taxonomies (eg Bloom *et al*, 1956) or levels (Bateson, 2000) of learning present repetition or following a procedure as being at the lower end of learning, while understanding, synthesis, questioning and double-loop learning are at much higher levels. These higher levels of learning involve more of the learner's personal experience and, indeed, influence a learner's understanding or experience of himself or herself, and they are often experiential.

Much of the research on learning has taken place in educational, or laboratory, settings so that less is understood about how we learn from everyday experiences – for example, from discussions with colleagues, from research on the Internet, from difficult meetings with staff – and this is where the importance of a better understanding of experiential learning is essential.

EXPERIENTIAL LEARNING

Experiential learning is considered by some theorists to be distinct and more specialised than learning from experience. Usher and Soloman (1999) examined the difference and suggested that in experiential learning experience is used in a particular way to extract knowledge through reflection or similar processes.

The literature on experiential learning is extensive and different definitions of the term abound – but one that encapsulates the process is Beard and Wilson's (2006; p.2):

> **'Experiential learning is the sense-making process of active engagement between the inner world of the person and the outer world of the environment.'**

However, experiential learning through the work of Lewin (1957), Kolb (1984) and Revans (1982) has remained one of the most significant learning theories, particularly aiding our understanding of skills development. One of the most used and useful concepts to evolve from the literature on experiential learning is that of the learning cycle. Dewey (1925), Lewin (1957), Kolb (1984) and Honey and Mumford (1992) have all demonstrated how learning can be described as a cyclical process, key phases of the learning process appearing around the cycle. Kolb's learning cycle – probably the most influential of these learning cycles – is shown in Figure 14.

Kolb and Fry (1975) suggested that learning occurs through a series of stages, starting from any point on the cycle. Often the cycle begins when we do something, when we complete some action: this is a 'concrete experience'. We then have the opportunity to think about what has happened, to reflect on it or replay it in our minds. Following reflection we form 'abstract concepts and generalisations' (Kolb and Fry, 1975) making sense of what has happened and assimilating it so that we can finally test out any learning and plan in new situations.

One of the key ideas that has been made popular from the model is that we all have a preference for one, or more, of the four learning styles defined by Honey and Mumford (1986), and that we can develop other learning behaviours that enable us to learn from each situation that presents itself to us. The four learning styles (as included in Figure 14) are defined as:

- *Activist* – These people enjoy getting involved, talking and doing. They focus on doing, and may prefer to move on to a new task rather than review and understand a current one.

- *Reflector* – As the name suggests, these people prefer to watch, think and reflect on what goes on around them rather than get immediately involved in action.

- *Theorist* – This group are thinkers, preferring to ask questions about why something happens or to consider how an occurrence fits with previous experiences.

- *Pragmatist* – These people are planners and learn most when thinking about how to apply or use learning.

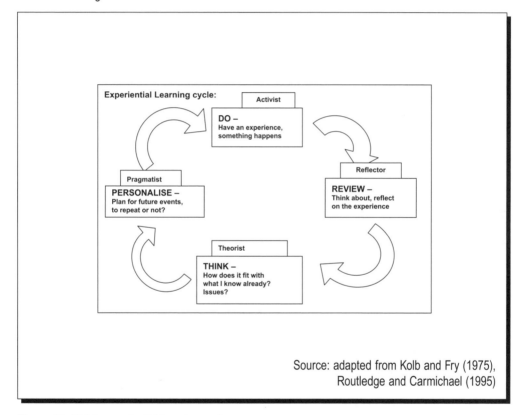

Source: adapted from Kolb and Fry (1975),
Routledge and Carmichael (1995)

Figure 14: *Kolb's experiential learning cycle*

Although these distinctions can be used to help learners examine and understand more about their learning, they are not normally considered to be stable characteristics. We often develop a different learning style when provided with different learning opportunities and different life experiences, and indeed Honey and Mumford produced publications to help with this development (Honey and Mumford, 1992). Although learning styles have been found to change over time, they are helpful in encouraging learners to think about how they learn, and this is also linked to the way we often choose to facilitate other people's learning – as in the case study below.

Case study

A clash of learning styles in induction

Many of us are involved in introducing new employees to our immediate work group and work responsibilities, even if there is a formal organisational induction. It doesn't always work out the way we expect.

Lynn is a quiet, reserved person who has worked as an HR professional in many large organisations. Her preferred learning style is through listening, reflecting and working with small groups of people to get a thorough understanding of what is required. She joined a new organisation as HR manager and her predecessor decided to stay on for a few days to 'show her the ropes and mentor her'. Unfortunately, his learning style was very activist and pragmatist, so he arranged a large meeting for her to present 'her plan' to all the staff on her first morning, to be followed by a whistle-stop tour to meet 'important people to influence' for his remaining two days with her.

At the beginning of the second day she sat down with the well-intentioned 'mentor' and explained that this was not her preferred approach, that although he believed it would be helpful it didn't fit her style, and that she wished to begin doing things her way from now on. She invited him to stay to answer any questions she had, but explained that she wanted to meet and to get to know everyone, not just those he deemed important, before announcing her priorities and way forward.

This strategy worked and he agreed to assist her, but on her terms.

How often have you been 'helped' or trained by a colleague who has made the training less effective than it could be due to a clash of approaches to learning and not considering the learner's preferences?

Think about whether there are alternative styles that would better suit a learner next time you are in a similar position training and supporting an employee.

It is important for managers to understand learning and different approaches to learning as well as to understand their own learning preferences and abilities because increasingly it is a manager who holds the responsibility for his or her own development and that of his or her staff. As coaching, mentoring and learning through work (on-the-job) grow in importance, the key to all of these initiatives is a manager's knowledge of his or her own and others' learning styles and his or her competence in presenting information and opportunities for such development.

Although Kolb's experiential learning theory is considered to be a simplistic account of learning, it is a model of learning that has remained popular and widely used to encourage a greater understanding of learning from experience, particularly in the workplace. The model intuitively seems to fit many people's experience of learning by doing if they think about learning, even though not all researchers agree with the detail of what Kolb suggested. There are other approaches to experiential learning which focus on the learner's view of situations or internal process supporting behaviour (for example, Mulligan, 2000).

ADAX and experiential learning

The ADAX process we propose is not meant as an alternative to experiential learning but an addition. It attempts to address many of the criticisms levelled at experiential learning by a variety of authors, and it does this by proposing a number of phases that address direction, motivation and ongoing development issues for adults. Several writers (Anderson, Boud and Cohen, 2000; Moon, 2004) have summarised the important characteristics of experiential learning which are further explored below.

Reflection

Reflection is regarded as an important part of experiential learning.

> 'Reflection is a form of mental processing – like a form of thinking – that we may use to fulfil a purpose or to achieve some anticipated outcome, or we may simply "be reflective" and then the outcome can be unexpected. Reflection is applied to relatively complicated, ill-structured ideas for which there is not an obvious solution, and is largely based on the further processing and understanding that we already possess.'
>
> *Moon (2004; p.82)*

Reflection involves becoming aware of an experience, representing it and integrating it into what we already know and believe; it is also involved in reorganising our learning and in developing new understandings. It probably includes what Kolb talked about as 'abstract conceptualisation', forming concepts and checking them against our past experience. Reflection is personal, and so focuses on 'I' as the main feature and includes emotional reaction which can enhance learning. One criticism of experiential learning is that not sufficient attention is paid to the nature of reflection (Boud *et al*, 1985), which does not always occur as a natural process. There are difficulties in encouraging managers to reflect because of the emphasis placed on activity rather than on time spent thinking or reviewing. We address these problems through encouraging deeper reflection which provides heightened awareness of self and others as well as skills and knowledge.

In our work with managers on professional development programmes, when we ask about how they learned to do their work many find it difficult to answer, not having really considered it before. In learning logs participants usually find it easier to describe what they have done (task information) and find it increasingly more difficult to examine and evaluate what they personally have taken from a learning task. Indeed, Mumford (1997) discovered that on management development programmes he had to ask about 'key achievements' rather than 'key learning' over a time period to get sufficient responses to examine learning in different situations. His explanation was that managers think in terms of tasks, not their learning, and to reflect on personal meaning and learning requires deeper reflection that takes time to develop.

At work most of us are monitored on our completion of work tasks, not our learning, which further diminishes its importance to us in working life. We believe this is true of most learners due to little exposure to such questions and hence a limited vocabulary relating to what and how learning occurs, even in education.

In the example below the questions encourage a reflection on different aspects of an experience:

- reflection on the content of the experience to develop skills, behaviours and knowledge and achievement or performance

- reflection on the other people and context in which the learning occurs, and how these influenced learning

- reflection on the processes of learning itself, asking yourself questions about how you learned and how effective the approach was for you

- reflection on personal awareness and skills, not specifically the subject of any development, which may also be a focus of learning – for example, how you related to, or supported, other learners during development.

Example

Experiential learning and presentation skills

On a training course for first-line managers there are usually a range of different people – some quiet and reflective, and others outgoing who enjoy socialising. These managers have a range of different educational backgrounds that may include those with a first degree, professional qualification or GCSE and 'A'-levels and different learning styles and experience. Although as trainers we cannot know everyone's personal circumstances, we begin by trying to establish overarching workshop objectives that each participant can understand, that will help them to develop personal objectives that fit their own needs, and that they can work to achieve through the workshop. These objectives usually include a mix of knowledge and skills that can add to any pre-existing experience. When running a workshop on presentation skills the workshop objectives are:

- to devise a checklist of skills and techniques of presenting, through:
    - reviewing a video on presentation skills
    - adding notes from my experience of good presentations I have seen

- to examine a presentation format aimed at meeting the needs of the whole audience, with examples

- to make a short presentation to a small group and receive feedback

- to devise a personal contract to aid the development of my presentation skills.

There are overarching objectives to be achieved in the workshop, and I expect participants to develop and review personal objectives in relation to presentations during and following the workshop.

During the workshop we feature information about presentation structures in the form of a short display, modelling presentation skills; we show a video which demonstrates presentations from the perspectives of a 'presenter' and an 'observer'. All of the information is summarised on a handout on presentations which participants receive. Participants are also expected to review their experience to add knowledge that they are aware of, and are encouraged to share their ideas about good presentations with other participants.

Skills are addressed as part of the workshop through making a presentation, observing others and providing feedback in small non-threatening groups of a size that participants feel able to cope with. They are encouraged to contract with others, following their experience at the workshop, and to work on this contract to return to a later workshop for more advanced presentations where more emphasis is put onto different techniques and interacting with the audience as well as getting feedback from a wider range of observers.

In this way we attempt, through running workshops, to address general issues and objectives but also to allow participants to work on personal objectives that take into account their current level of skill, knowledge and experience, and to expand on these, while continually monitoring their own development and learning. We provide support and encourage interaction, reviewing experience and taking part to gain experience of skills. The review questions ('Questions to aid reflection, learning and application') listed earlier in Chapter 5 are used to encourage reflection and planning for future presentations. They can be particularised for presentations (see the box below).

Questions to aid reflection, learning and application

as particularised to review (for example) presentation skills

- What did you do to prepare your presentation for the group?
- What skills did you use?
- How did you feel?
- What influenced the presentation you made?
- What went well in your presentation? What feedback did you get?
- What aspects of the presentation would you like to improve?
- What could you have done differently?
- What have you learned about presentations from watching others? How could you use this?
- What have you learned about your own presentation skills?
- What did you learn about yourself?
- What is your plan to further develop your presentation skills?

We also acknowledge that not all participants will want to review immediately, in an activist way, by discussing the event together. They may prefer to reflect alone initially and make sense of the task. But we encourage everybody to use the questions as a guideline for reflection following the session. We usually follow up the initial review at a later meeting to confirm that all learners have been able to address the questions provided.

Reviews of learning from activities may be general or focus on specific skills – for example, presentations (as in the above example) or financial or strategic decision-making, chairing meetings and planning. Even a general review of any situation is likely always to identify job-related skills that have been used and is also likely to include a review of personal skills to learn more about how they work with others. To reflect on skills for learning, the latter require deeper reflection and self-awareness.

Mike Pedler (1996) used Revans' questions, taken from action learning, which included:

- Who knows – about the problem?
- Who cares – about the problem?
- Who can... do something about the problem?

Pedler (1996) asserted that these questions were crucial to human action and suggested that in management development we focus on 'knowing' or thinking, while the other processes – feeling and willing – are essential for effective deep meaningful learning (Brockbank and McGill, 1998). Unless we become aware of our feelings about a situation and the people involved, we are unlikely to understand deep-seated beliefs or attitudes we hold that may interfere with learning or with further action.

An important part of a review is therefore being aware of feelings and understanding what things influence our behaviour, so our review questions specifically include questions to address these factors. There are additional questions (which can be added to the usual review questions) to encourage deeper reflection, recorded in the Excellence chapter (Chapter 5). These questions encourage learners to consider assumptions and biases that might influence their behaviour and constitute blockages to further development.

This deeper reflection about ourselves to provide greater self-awareness has been likened to double-loop learning (Argyris and Schon, 1974). Argyris and Schon also suggested that the difficulties we experience in questioning our personal actions and beliefs come from two different types of theory, which we each hold: espoused theory of action, which is used to explain and justify behaviour, and theory-in-use, which is the operational theory of action. Distinguishing the two types of theory, they said:

> **'The first is a set of beliefs and values people hold about how to manage their lives. The second way is the actual rules they use to manage their beliefs. We call the first their espoused theories of action; the second their theories-in-use.'**
>
> *Argyris and Schon (1974)*

> **'In working with managers we have found that they may not be aware of the underlying attitudes and beliefs that influenced their theory-in-use but due to it they were not as amenable to new learning until they were willing to test these theories and examine their theory-in-use.'**
>
> *Argyris (1991)*

Effort

Reflecting on experience in such a way to draw out learning is not an easy process and it takes effort (Moon, 2004). It is not easily hurried because it takes time to fully examine and explore behaviours, feelings and attitudes to understand personal learning.

We occasionally find in working with young managers, often from a traditional higher-educational environment where surface learning has been sufficient to achieve success at undergraduate level, that they feel the pace of personal development to be slow. Indeed, the work environment in many organisations does not encourage time for reflection, and because it does take effort, many managers prefer to 'move on' and not reflect. In one workshop related to coaching other people, a learner from one of these groups asked, 'Can we quicken up the session? I got the message of the last activity in 10 minutes, yet you allowed 20 minutes for the exercise. We could get through more material if we went quicker.' For these people there may be numerous reasons why the session seemed slow:

- It might have been poor timing on my part, although many other people were working throughout the allowed time.

- The learner might have been engaging in surface learning only. Surface learning provides knowledge and key principles that can be understood quickly, although personalising learning for future action takes longer.

- The learner might simply not have recognised any need for deeper reflection, or not felt able to engage in it at that time – and there could have been many reasons for this.

When working with a group of learners, there is often a tension – due to differences in ability and motivation to review and draw out pertinent learning – between not leaving sufficient time and leaving too much time. There is no hard-and-fast rule, but experience and a personal understanding is needed of what timing is required to draw out sufficient information in review to facilitate deep learning. It must be balanced by an ongoing monitoring of the group to apprehend the climate and energy – for every group is different and differences can occur with time of day, previous activity and group synergy. Sometimes changing approach from group review to individual contemplation or active thought-showering can influence a group's ability to put in the necessary effort. There is also the risk that going too quickly will not allow learners to capture sufficient data from the experience that is necessary for deep review – and as we noted above, for effective learning it is essential to undergo deep reflection which can lead to greater self-awareness and understanding of the learning process. It is essential, of course, that the event being reviewed is sufficiently important to the learner to encourage him or her to undertake a deeper review. We therefore provide groups of managers with tasks that involve a range of skills and roles for which they are responsible, in order to make sure that they have sufficient data for deep review.

One of the tasks we give to students is to set up a fictitious international conference on a current affairs topic, relevant to business, in a specified area of the world. This activity provides an important learning experience, involving many personal and management skills. It is completed over a number of days, ending with a presentation and brief written report covering costs and other details.

When we run this exercise with students we allocate them to groups, rather than allowing them to self-select their own groups. There are therefore a number of factors that are unknown and take learners out of their usual 'comfort zones'. The project has to be scoped, plans have to be drawn up about responsibilities for individual tasks and times, team members have to agree roles, tasks and deadlines, and research is required. Although groups have sometimes found it difficult to motivate and manage the team and the project, most become involved in the process and are willing to put in an effort to achieve the outcome.

The final presentations and reports are usually very individual and interesting – and provide a great learning experience, both in knowledge and skills.

Many of the personal reviews focus on questions related to feelings and will, or motivation, during the task, and on which skills have been particularly important to each learner. Comments are frequently along the lines of:

- 'I won't ever again make assumptions about people I have not worked with before.'

- 'I began by feeling swamped by the task and ended up proud of the achievement of the team.'

- 'I became more aware of how I influence other types of people.'

- 'I don't usually take a lead role but needed to organise how the research was conducted, so I worked with X— to ensure that the task was completed.'

These are just a small number of comments taken from reviews and underline the reflection that can be drawn out, using appropriate questions, from simulated activities with sufficient meaning and effort on the part of participants.

Timing

Most of the discussion so far has suggested that reflection comes after action. This is often the case, and what is learned from reflection is then known as *retrospective learning* (Mumford and Gold, 2004), which can occur at different times following an event to produce different learning. We can use the multiplicity of activities and perceptions of an event to reflect on it immediately after it has occurred. However, we may also revisit the event later to find new learning. In this way, for example, learning may become deepened, or may lead to identifying certain theories-in-action that a learner wishes to address. In our experience different learners require different lengths of time to make sense of learning. Some can usefully undertake deep learning immediately following an event, whereas others may need a longer time, preferring to revisit an event some time after.

Learning can also be *prospective* (Mumford and Gold, 2004), in which a learner plans and may visualise what he or she intends to do in a particular situation. For example, I may plan a particularly difficult appraisal meeting I have with a team member to encourage a greater contribution, and I can rehearse arguments to put forward, or ways to persuade him of the input he can make. This will enable greater learning again if I follow the event with retrospective learning. Using the Mumford and Gold model suggests that retrospective learning may provide ideas that can be tried out to encourage prospective learning.

Finally, there is *concurrent learning* (Beard and Wilson, 2006), in which attention to cues presented in a situation causes us to consider or change our behaviour. I may notice, as I drive down a motorway, that fog is descending, so I put on my lights and slow my speed accordingly. Although this is a simple illustration, it is learning, based on previous experience. Coaches provide cues to aid concurrent learning while a learner becomes familiar with a skill so that the learner in due course recognises the cues himself or herself. Experts are thought to be able to make use of concurrent learning – and this is one factor that distinguishes them from novices. It is an important factor in working toward excellence, and enables one to amend actions, based on circumstances and reactions to behaviour. This type of learning is similar to reflection-in-action (Schon, 1987).

To ensure that learning is effective, timing is important. We have seen, above, that learning may occur at different times after or even before an event, although we naturally hope that learning is the consequence of most situations, particularly learning and training interventions. On the other hand, if a learner has no opportunity or motivation to use or demonstrate learning, it is difficult to say with confidence that learning has genuinely happened.

Example

When managers go on update training in respect of a new disciplinary process, they generally do not behave any differently in most of their work thereafter until they need to use the new procedure. At that stage they may recall the training but usually only do things differently if their previous approach to disciplinary situations does not fit with the new requirements. So although learners may gain new knowledge from an update, it has to be integrated with their other experiences so that it is retained until it is required, or tested. It is important to encourage managers who have undertaken some training on new procedures, or who want to change their management style or skills, to personalise learning, making it real for themselves and checking it against their 'usual' approach. This personalisation may be achieved through case studies, discussing learning with colleagues, and experience in trying to keep learning 'available' to themselves so that it can be used when required.

Experience

Experience provides a basis for learning and it directs what we pay attention to in learning situations as well as influencing the way in which new material is understood. Beard and Wilson (2006) use Dewey's apt description of 'slipperiness' to describe experience, emphasising the differences that can be found in two individuals' experience of the same event, much as experiences of witness statements show. In Chapter 2 about Awareness, earlier in the book, we discussed perception and noted its very subjective nature, due to a range of factors that affect what is perceived, including previous experience and personal motivation, which focus attention in the 'perceptual set' for a learner. Any new experience is therefore reviewed to gauge its fit with the learner's conceptual map for any situation, and may be discounted if it does not match.

Learning is perceived as a process in which a learner uses previous experience and knowledge to assess external happenings. The process involves checking new experiences and information against the mental model that the learner already holds. This new information may be rejected, assimilated or accommodated, depending on the match between the learner's cognitive map and the new experience. In a new learning situation a learner may have to 'unlearn' previous information that does not fit or is detrimental before new learning can occur.

Example

On an interview panel with colleagues we asked agreed questions and listened to the candidates' answers to each and every question and probe. If I were a 'fly on the wall' observing the event, I would probably say that we all had a similar experience. However, in the discussion afterwards it often becomes apparent that what I learned about a candidate differs from what my colleagues learned. The differences are often related to our personal interpretation of the words, gestures, body language and many other non-verbal signals that we interpret, often unconsciously, based on our previous experience. Our attention leads us to focus on things that are important to us individually, from our previous experience of selecting an applicant. For example, I may judge an applicant hard-working, friendly and enthusiastic as a person to join my team, while another panel member may judge him or her as driven, loud and excitable. We both saw and listened to the same person but interpreted the speech and style differently – so who is correct? We both are, because our different experience has led us to differing interpretations of what we saw. Decisions about the applicant's appropriateness for the role also depend on how we see the role and how we generalise and make sense of the information provided anyway.

All of this is probably very familiar but provides a simple illustration that experience of the same event does not necessarily lead to common learning from a joint experience. We use panel interviews to try to increase objectivity in recruitment decisions by considering two or three panel members' perceptions of the interview, each valid but individual to one panel member, based on previous learning and experience, on cultural and social background, and on an individual understanding of the context of the interview situation. Each of these factors is likely to increase the variation in the views provided.

In any learning situation it is important to encourage all learners to value each others' contributions, not just those from more experienced learners. All viewpoints are valid and provide a different perspective for evaluation. As an opening to workshops we regularly set ground rules with groups – and the efficacy of *all* honest points of view is one of the key ground rules to include.

Within management development programmes we also believe that it is important to take time, early in sessions, to examine the experience of participants and to encourage the sharing of experiences, to aid learning, as a valid and relevant part of the workshop. We actively encourage recall and review of experiences by learners and retell our own stories to explain points throughout workshops. Even when learners do not have their own experience, hearing someone else's can be beneficial and aid learning. The approach we take in running workshops is that everyone has a valid point of view, whether experienced or not – after all, a naive learner may provide a new perspective unburdened by previous ideas. In this way we also try to overcome the criticism of not taking into account differences in culture and experiences of learners (Anderson, 1988). We cannot, however, dictate, or even guess what learning may come from any specific experience; we can only encourage an open and honest climate to facilitate understanding of different views for wide learning.

Context and learning

Any learning is linked to and understood through the situation in which it occurs, and includes information, feelings and attributions about others involved – a combination that provides a rich source for all learners who recognise this opportunity. We use the review questions ('Questions to aid reflection' above) to encourage a review of learning and to question how the context – other people, their roles, attitudes, situation and previous experience – influences learning for them.

We have occasionally encountered learners who find it difficult to learn in what they see as an artificial context, and who seem to believe that they have to be in a work environment to learn things that apply to their work. These learners find it difficult to extract learning in an educational or training context and see how it can be applied in their work. This is obviously a limiting belief and one that we challenge, because it suggests that any learning – apart from that completed in the specific circumstance it is to be used – may be perceived as artificial and not relevant. We try to make all situations as real as possible, and provide context and detail to help learners feel it is real. However, it is not always possible to 'learn on the job' if risks of making mistakes would be costly – for example, when flying a plane, or recruiting an inappropriate employee. A training event provides a safe and secure situation to allow skills to develop and time to learn. Each learner takes from the event his or her own personal learning and can then apply this within the workplace and, with further review, can shape his or her behaviour as necessary.

Understanding the context and background in any situation is likely to impact on what is learned. For example, past experience of working with an individual who a learner fears or feels uncomfortable with is likely to negatively influence the learner's willingness to take risks and try new behaviours. In our work with students on professional programmes we encourage them to work with as many different people as possible to take advantage of learning about others' organisations and ways of working, as well as seeing different skills and personal styles, even if they initially feel more comfortable working with people more like themselves.

Negative learning experiences

It is important that we realise that learning and experiences may not always be positive. In fact, many learners say they spend time more thoroughly reviewing painful learning events when things don't go according to plan. These events may stay with learners for many years and influence their subsequent behaviour. Often, this learning leads to our striving to behave differently to improve the outcome for ourselves, much as when we perform badly in an interview for a new job. Such learning causes us to work harder, prepare more carefully to improve our performance.

However, there are occasions when experiential learning can lead to detrimental learning and to negatively influencing our attitude to learning.

Example

While looking for a job, if I attend one interview and I'm unsuccessful, I am likely to consider feedback that is provided, think about what I could do differently, and work harder next time. However, if I keep attending interviews without success, it is quite likely that after a time, probably different for each learner, my self-esteem and belief in my ability at interviews will be reduced and I may begin having negative thoughts about all interviews. In this way I may learn that I do not want to continue attending interviews for fear of being rejected. In these circumstances, learning can become limiting, and I may need help to overcome negative beliefs about myself and the learning situation. Such help might come from a coach who can discuss feelings and provide options about behaviours. It might also include taking tips from experts in interview skills or self-presentation so that I can use them to improve my personal interview style.

Learning from mistakes

Learners may need support to understand the importance of learning from mistakes, particularly if the learner can understand what went wrong and therefore has options to try something different. Great inventors have been known to make many mistakes in working toward some great new invention, and in doing so learn something from each attempt. However, in business we generally do not have any such luxury, as evidenced by a well-known statement, often made in business, 'It is okay to make a mistake once, as long as you do not repeat the same mistake again.'

Although it may be difficult to manage learning for any individual learner, experiential learning is therefore still a natural and very important approach to learning. It is probably obvious, from the discussion above, that learning cannot be regarded as a simple process of working through the predetermined stages, taking account of a learner's style and then assuming that learning will be effective. Indeed, many writers have criticised the learning cycle as being too neat a cycle – not taking into account unpredictable occurrences and new knowledge acquisition (Miettinen, 2000), giving little consideration to how individuals are motivated and how they make decisions within the process (Reynolds *et al*, 2002) – and these views are valid from our experience of working with many learners. However, as demonstrated in our discussion, we attempt to overcome these criticisms through the ADAX process and by appreciating that learning is continual and must be part of the learner to be effective.

ACTIVITY

Consider your own continuing professional development (CPD) over the past six months – you may have a record that you can review or you may wish to make some brief notes from memory.

Pick out entries or events that you feel you learned a lot from, and those when you did not learn as much.

Can you identify any themes that help to explain differences in these two groups of entries?

The differences may be due to certain of the factors discussed above:

- You find deep reflection difficult and are not always able to give it the time or effort required. This may be a temporary phenomenon caused by other pressures at a particular point in time, or may be a more long-term attitudinal issue.

- You find you do not have sufficient time to review.

- You are not in a work situation that encourages reflection.

- You think you do not have opportunities to learn from.

- You believe that you are experienced and there is little development you need.

There are many reasons that people do not get full benefit from CPD, summarised in the section above.

Consider your own responses to the bullet-point factors listed above, in relation to your reflection/review.

What could you change or do differently to make the review process more effective for you?

Are you willing and able to do this?

HAVE A GO!

DIFFERENT USES OF EXPERIENTIAL LEARNING IN EDUCATION AND TRAINING

Although there is some consensus about the key components of experiential learning, and general acceptance of a model that involves doing, reviewing, making sense, and doing again, and although that consensus uses a variety of different words and emphases, there is still debate about what defines it and how to use it with learners. Boud (1989) presents what he considers to be the key dimensions of experiential education, in which each dimension can be either high or low. These dimensions are:

- the degree of learner control

- the degree of involvement of self

- the degree of correspondence of learning environment to real environment.

The dimensions help to define the range of activities that may be considered experiential learning, from personal self-development as part of work at one end to an exercise or discussion about work-related skills at the other.

It is therefore interesting to review what is done, in the name of experiential learning, on these dimensions.

Day-to-day work

Every employee has the opportunity to learn from his or her normal work activities through experiential learning, although what may actually occur is experience rather than learning, much along the lines discussed earlier in the chapter (Usher and Soloman, 1999). Most people have heard the comment that someone has 20 times one year's experience as opposed to 20 years' experience, suggesting the same point. In order for learning to occur, reflection or some similar form of review is required to make meaningful sense and hence learning out of an activity. So although employees may pick up information to help them in work, this learning might be incidental, not recognised even by the learners, or might be informal learning about organisational or group culture. It is not necessarily what an organisation wants learners to learn.

In order for learning through work to be effective, learners must be motivated to review everyday events, and personalise them in order to apply them in ways valued by the organisation. Many competence-based management development programmes, qualifications or performance review processes are designed to encourage this critical review of experience in organisations today, and to help to identify tacit knowledge and 'know-how' which are important for success. Often, development programmes provide underpinning ideas and models to help to challenge activities and behaviours, or offer a rationale for them. This form of learning is at the high end on each of Boud's dimensions – the learner having control over whether he or she wishes to learn, over what he or she learns, and over when learning occurs; the learner being wholly involved and possibly the only person involved; and because learning takes place at work, it is likely to be relevant.

Self-development

The term 'self-development' is often used when an individual decides – possibly through awareness-raising exercises or reflection – that he or she has specific development needs and sets out to address these needs. The process is self-determined and usually controlled by the learner to meet his or her own objectives. It may or may not be relevant to his or her work needs. For example, among my hobbies I enjoy sewing and needlework so I might decide that I want to undertake some self-development in quilting or embroidery – nothing to do with my current work. I may also decide to undertake some self-development in voice projection which would be very pertinent to my work, although under these conditions I would assume responsibility for selecting an appropriate method and also for finding necessary support.

Self-development involves the initial key steps of raising the awareness of the particular needs of an individual, recognising that certain development would be beneficial to the individual, and having sufficient and ongoing motivation for the development. An individual's awareness of his or her learning provides the difference between incidental learning at work day by day and active self-development, although both are controlled by the learner at work.

Work-based learning

Work-based learning has numerous meanings, including accrediting experience one has gained at work for educational purposes. However, the term is often used in education to signify a difference from traditional school or HE learning, emphasising the contribution of the real work environment and suggesting that this provides something over and above what can be provided away from work. It is true that this avoids issues of transfer of learning to work, due to its high correspondence with work.

It also has a high degree of learner involvement, and quite possibly a high degree of control, although if it is part of a development programme devised to cover certain work activities, there may be elements that are prescribed for a learner to work to complete or notice or review, so control may in fact be somewhat less with the learner than in his or her normal work. This approach provides very practical learning – many seasoned professionals learn throughout their career in this way.

Outdoor development

Although less popular now, outdoor approaches to management development were extensively used in the 1980s and 1990s and were regarded as a way of levelling all participants, providing them with common experiences outside their normal comfort zone and providing a good deal of rich data to review and learn from. Unfortunately, outdoor development got a reputation for encouraging 'macho' leadership behaviour, involving abseiling, long treks across moors, and fording rivers to find hidden treasure. This is now considered inappropriate by some organisations at a time when organisations are encouraging diversity and different ways of working, requiring different management styles. The outdoor development was costly and reviews required very careful facilitation so that the outcome was not simply how well the task was achieved, but whether it met its objective of providing rich data on personal and interpersonal style as well as leadership and teamworking. More recently, an alternative approach has been used, involving no need to go to the outdoors, with all of the accompanying risk factors and costs. Indoor activities, unrelated to usual work activities, are used to provide the same personal information about individuals that can be used to provide learning and development for managers appropriate to their own personal style. Such activities are high on individual involvement but lower on individual control because they are designed by a leader and correspond to an artificial situation, thus corresponding probably less with the work environment.

Simulation and role play

Role play and simulation is commonly used in training, in development and in education but is unpopular with some learners who feel exposed and find difficulty in establishing relevance – which means that they find the learning difficult to transfer to a work situation. However, simulations are used extensively in training individuals on expensive equipment or where the risk of incorrect action has dangerous consequences – for example, in flying planes or driving costly, oversized equipment. In these situations technology can be used to make correspondence with real life seem very close, but without the risk or cost. A learner is heavily involved in action, as himself or herself, and is usually expected to follow the procedures to be learned to achieve a given end – for example, flying and landing a plane.

It is possible for role play to be equally effective and 'real' but it relies heavily on the learner to make correspondence to life close, and to involve and learn about himself or herself through the activity. A learner may choose to make each dimension higher or lower, depending on his or her own motivation, which may be variable. Simulation and role play are usually developed by a trainer to enable practice in certain identified skills – for example, interviewing or dealing with conflict. Learners are either given a role to play or expected to 'play' themselves. Our experience suggests that many learners say that they do not like role play and are unwilling to take part. Usually, with gentle persuasion and knowing that they can take part in a role play without a large audience, doing it 'as if' they were in a role provided specifically to obtain supportive and helpful feedback, most learners find it a rewarding experience.

Games and activities

Similar to the previous interventions, games and activities are commonly used in training and education to encourage learners to get involved, usually as themselves, to complete the activity. Games may be developed to be similar to work or may be specifically devised to have low correspondence with work, allowing all participants to use their skills in a novel situation, much as outdoor development. In such exercises learners choose to become involved or not, so the dimensions of experiential learning are variable. Business games often involve a range of management and interpersonal skills along with many tasks so that learners become immersed in action often forgetting any initial reluctance. However, there can then be an important role for a facilitator to review and help to identify learning that can thereafter be used in a real work environment.

As can be seen from this brief review, there are many activities that can be used to facilitate experiential learning and they vary on Boud's dimensions identified above. What is important in facilitating learning with groups is to use variety and not repeat a similar methodology too often in designing programmes. As in all activities, it is not the activity itself that provides learning – that is only the vehicle to facilitate it. Learner motivation, active involvement and engagement are essential, and a tutor's role is crucial.

THE ROLE OF TUTOR AND LEARNER IN EXPERIENTIAL LEARNING

There has been considerable debate about what name should be used to describe someone who facilitates experiential learning, although as can be seen in the previous section the situations in which experiential learning occurs are many and the individual leading the event has a whole range of titles, from lecturer to tutor, facilitator or trainer. Boud and Miller (1996) suggest the title 'animateur' to avoid the baggage associated with other previous titles in training and development.

Although many titles may be used, it is important that people in such a role are aware of their responsibilities and the skills required within it. Due to the individual nature of experiential learning, no one can 'teach' it – but a tutor can facilitate and support the process that learners go through. It is essential that each learner gets involved and that the outcome, which may be different for each person involved, cannot be predicted.

Beard and Wilson (2006) suggest three key learning activities, based on the DEEP initiative (DEEP 1999); these learning activities are:

- relationship development to aid successful interactions with others and to facilitate review and support activities

- performance enhancement, in which a tutor may provide training and feedback on skills development for individuals and teams to aid development and help manage conflict

- consultation and intervention in which a facilitator might provide coaching or help to an individual to understand applications of learning in work.

Facilitators require a wide range of skills and understanding to be able to address the needs of different learners at the appropriate times for each learner, so wisdom and judgement are key requirements in this role.

The tasks can involve creating an appropriate climate – usually one that encourages increased independence over the time of the development, from whatever starting point any learner begins. It is important that a facilitator legitimates discussion of feelings, emotions and provides a role model for use of the process. Heron (1996) talks of using a learning cycle 'which engages the whole person construed as being of feeling and emotion, intuition and imagery, ... reflection and discrimination, intention and action'.

Because a more diverse group of individuals are involved in management, and therefore in management development, it is important to consider the different cultural expectations of groups and to meet the needs of non-dominant groups in experiential learning. Boud and Miller (1996) provide principles that help to achieve these conditions:

- Exploration of personal experience is validated.
- A holistic view is advocated.
- There is no division between the personal, the theoretical or academic.
- The creation of a safe learning climate with a non-judgemental stance on experience is important.
- Activities are designed to build self-esteem and a sense of responsibility for learning.
- Links are made between learners' experience and that of others.
- Learners are encouraged to act as animateurs.

These match the key characteristics of experiential learning discussed earlier and can be a good guide for facilitators. However, Brookfield (1996) argues that tutors in education hold a difficult role due to their holding of the assessment role which might limit their ability to encourage and support learners. We have experienced this difficulty when working on development programmes for professional qualifications that require an assessment of students. Although it may be an issue, it is not necessarily so if handled carefully. We set out clear boundaries and expectations for students and list their ground rules at the beginning of the programme. In our experience it has not been a barrier to learning for us or for student groups and should not prevent tutors from devising a challenging development programme for student groups.

SUMMARY AND WAY FORWARD

Within this chapter we have examined a range of different ideas and characteristics of learning generally, and then specifically considered the role of experience in learning. Ideas about adult learning have also been discussed and related to issues of adults' learning in a higher-education context. We have considered how to make learning as effective as possible, whether as part of work experience or training and development, and identified a range of factors that influence how learners learn.

Experiential and other learning theories have been linked with ADAX to provide a firm basis for our model, and we have defined influences on the roles of tutor and learner in experiential learning.

It is hoped that this chapter has provided anyone who is interested in facilitating learning or who wishes to understand more about his or her personal learning will leave this chapter more aware of issues and options that might further help or hinder learning.

REFERENCES

Andersen, L., Boud, D. and Cohen, R. (2000) 'Experience-based learning', in *Understanding Adult Education and Training*. Sydney: Allen & Unwin

Anderson, J. A. (1988) 'Cognitive styles and multi-cultural populations', *Journal of Teacher Education*, Vol 39 (1): 2–9

Argyris, C. (1991) 'Teaching smart people how to learn', *Harvard Business Review*, May/June: 99–109

Argyris, C. and Schon, D. A. (1974) *Theory in Practice: Increasing professional practice.* San Francisco: Jossey-Bass

Bass, B. M. and Vaughan, J. A. (1967) *Training in Industry: The management of learning.* London: Tavistock Publications

Bateson, G. (2000) 'The logical categories of learning and communication, Steps to an ecology of mind', Essay written in 1964, University of Chicago

Beard, C. and Wilson, J. P. (2006) *Experiential Learning* (2nd edition). London: Kogan Page

Beard, C. and Wilson, J. P. (2002) *The Power of Experiential Learning: A handbook for trainers and educators.* London: Kogan Page

Bloom , B. S., Krathwohl, D. R. and Masia, B. B. (1956) *Taxonomy of Educational Objectives: The classification of educational objectives, Handbook 1: Cognitive Domain.* London: Longmans, Green

Boud, D. (1989) 'Some competing traditions in experiential learning', in S. W. Weil and I. McGill (eds) *Making Sense of Experiential Learning Diversity in Theory and Practice.* Suffolk: The Society for Research into Higher Education/Open University Press

Boud, D. and Miller, N. (eds) (1996) *Working with Experience: Animating learning.* London: Routledge

Boud, D., Cohen, R. and Walker, D. (2000) 'Barriers to reflection on experience', in D. Boud, R. Cohen and D. Walker (eds) *Using Experience for Learning.* Buckingham: SRHE/Open University Press

Boud, D., Keogh, R. and Walker, D. (1985) *Reflection: Turning experience into learning.* London: Kogan Page

Brockbank, A. and McGill, I. (1998) *Facilitating Reflective Learning in Higher Education.* Milton Keynes: SR HE/Open University Press

Brookfield, S. (1996) section in D. Boud and N. Miller (eds) *Working with Experience: Animating learning.* London: Routledge

Covey, S. R. (1999) *The Seven Habits of Highly Effective People.* New York: Simon & Schuster

DEEP. (1999) *Definitions, Ethics and Exemplary Practices* (DEEP) *of Experiential Training and Development.* Cited in C. Beard and J. Wilson (2006) *Experiential Learning: A best practice handbook for educators and facilitators.* London: Kogan Page

Dewey, J. (1925) *Experience and Education.* New York: Macmillan, the Kappa Delta Pi Lecture series

Dixon, N (1994) *The Organisational Learning Cycle.* London: McGraw Hill

Festinger, L. (1957) *A Theory of Cognitive Dissonance.* Evanston, Ill.: Row, Peterson

Heron, J. (1996) 'Helping whole people learn', in D. Boud and N. Miller (eds) *Working with Experience.* London: Routledge

Honey, P. and Mumford, A. (1992) *Manual of Learning Styles.* Maidenhead: Honey Publications

Honey, P. and Mumford, A. (1986) *Using your Learning Styles.* Maidenhead: Peter Honey

Jarvis, P. (1992) *Paradoxes of Learning*. San Fransisco: Josey-Bass

King, K. (2005) *Bringing Transformative Learning to Life*. Florida: Krieger Publishing

Knowles, M., Holton, E. F. and Swanson, R. A. (1998) *The Adult Learner* (5th edition). Oxford: Butterworth-Heinemann

Kolb, D. A. (1984) *Experiential Learning*. Englewood Cliffs, NJ: Prentice Hall

Kolb, D. and Fry, R. (1975) 'Towards an applied theory of experiential learning', in C. Cooper (ed.) *Theories of Group Processes*. London: John Wiley & Sons

Lansberg, M. (1996) *The Tao of Coaching: Boost your effectiveness at work – be inspiring and developing those around you*. London: HarperCollins

Lewin, K. (1957) 'Frontiers in group dynamics', *Human Relations*, Vol 1: 5–41

Miettinen, R. (2000) 'The concept of experiential learning and John Dewey's theory of reflective thought and action', *International Journal of Lifelong Education*, Dubuque, IA: Kendall Hunt/ Association for Experiential Education

Milne, A. A. (1924) *When We Were Very Young*.

Moon, J. (2004) *A Handbook of Reflective and Experiential Learning Theory and Practice.* London: Routledge

Mulligan, J. (2000) 'Activating internal processes in experiential learning', in D. Boud, R. Cohen and D. Walker (eds) *Using Experience for Learning*. Milton Keynes: SRHE/Open University Press

Mumford, A. (1997) *Management Development Strategies for Action*, 3rd edition. London: IPD

Mumford, A. and Gold, J. (2004) *Management Development Strategies for Action*, 4th edition. London: CIPD

Pedler, M. (1996) *Action Learning for Managers*. London: Lemos & Crane

Piaget, J. (1950) *The Psychology of Intelligence.* London: Routlegde & Kegan Paul

Revans, R. W. (1982) *The Origin and Growth of Action Learning.* London: Chartwell Bratt

Rogers, A. (1996) *Teaching Adults*. Buckingham: Open University Press

Reynolds, J., Caley, L. and Mason, R. (2002) *How do People Learn?* London: CIPD

Schon, L, D. A., (1987) *Educating the Reflective Practitioner: Towards a new design for teaching and learning in the professions*. San Francisco: Jossey-Bass

Senge, P. (1990) *The Fifth Discipline: The art and practice of the learning organization.* New York: Doubleday

Skinner, B. F. (1974) *About Behaviourism*. London: Jonathan Cape

Tennant, M. (2006) *Psychology and Adult Learning*. London: Routledge

Usher, R. and Soloman, N. (1999) 'Experiential learning and the shape of subjectivity in the workplace', *Studies in Education of Adults*, 31 (2): 155–63

CHAPTER 7

The brain and skill development

It may certainly be true that managers do not need a deep understanding of neuroscience, but much of the latest brain research has provided information valuable to managers and to others about the human capacity for learning and skill development. Many of the findings are challenging formerly current paradigms about the best way to develop skills. Other findings are providing explanations for why some approaches to learning are successful and some are less so.

The literature on neuroscience and its application to learning uses a number of metaphors to explain how the brain works. Jensen (2005) describes the brain as a rain forest jungle. This seems an excellent way to portray how the brain learns most naturally.

'A rain forest jungle is active at times, quiet at times, but always teeming with life.

'The brain is similar: it is very active at times, much less so at others, but always alive and busy. The jungle has its own zones, regions and sectors: the underground, the streams, the ground cover, the low plants and shrubs, the air, the taller plants, the trees, etc. The brain has its own sectors: for thinking, sexuality, memory, survival, emotions, breathing, creativity, etc. And while the jungle changes over time, one constant remains true: the law of the jungle and no one is in charge.'

- But how does a knowledge of brain functions help us to develop management skills more effectively?
- Do we remember knowledge and skills in the same way?
- Does emotion help or hinder the development of skills?
- Does the ability to develop skills reside in the left or right side of the brain?
- Can movement and music help us develop skills?
- Can we learn management skills by reading about them or attending a lecture?

Knowledge about the brain is developing at a phenomenal rate, and in this chapter we review some of the evidence and findings of brain research that address the above questions and that have implications for the development of management skills.

The chapter begins with a brief and simplified description of the brain's architecture. This is intended to acquaint the reader with some general brain processes and some useful terminology. The chapter then continues with an exploration of the following topics and their relationship with learning and skill development:

- the brain as a parallel processer
- memory processes
- brain hemisphericity
- movement and the brain.

I have tried to keep the jargon and complexities of neuroscience to a minimum and in places I have used metaphors to explore the issues. Some readers may find this frustrating and an over simplification. There are many eminent authors who have described and evaluated our present knowledge of the structure, functions and processes of the brain (Greenfield, 2002; Ratey, 2003; LeDoux, 1998; Smith, 2004; Kotulak, 1997) and the reader can if he or she wishes refer to these and other sources for more technical information.

LEARNING AND BRAIN STRUCTURE

If you were to attend an autopsy where the brain was exposed, you would see an organ, cream in colour, weighing about 1.3 kilograms (2¾ pounds), having the consistency of a soft boiled egg with numerous folds in its surface and with two seemingly symmetrical halves. Underneath, it would also have a stem which in turn would be connected to the spinal cord. In many ways it has an unremarkable appearance for an organ which does so much. The brain regulates basic bodily functions such as blood circulation, breathing, the appetite and digestion, sexuality, fight-or-flight behaviours and simultaneously processes all our movements, emotions, senses, memories and language skills. It also enables us to think critically, to plan in the long term, to be creative and to show empathy for our fellow humans.

The brain allows us to interact with our environment (Sylwester, 1995). It communicates with the environment through our senses and governs how we choose to behave, what beliefs and attitudes we hold and how we interact with other people. Management skills are particular manifestations of these behaviours, beliefs, attitudes and interactions which lead to desired outcomes.

In order to explain the enormous learning capacity and flexibility of the brain, we must examine the function and processes of that fundamental building-block of the brain, the neuron.

The neuron

The first neuron is thought to have appeared in animals about 500 million years ago. Able to form flexible connections with other cells and to send and receive electrochemical messages, the neuron was a crucial leap in evolutionary terms. Just as DNA made life possible 3 billion years earlier, the neuron made possible complex human abilities such as language, problem-solving and creative thought (Kotulak, 1996). The power of the brain grows in direct relationship to the number of neurons. A fruit-fly has 100,000 neurons, a mouse 5 million, a monkey – man's closest relation – 10 million. The human brain, having 100 billion neurons, is in a class of its own (Rose, 1985).

Neurons perform their amazing feats by their ability to communicate with one another and function as large groupings known as neural networks. We can see how they communicate by examining their structure (Figure 15).

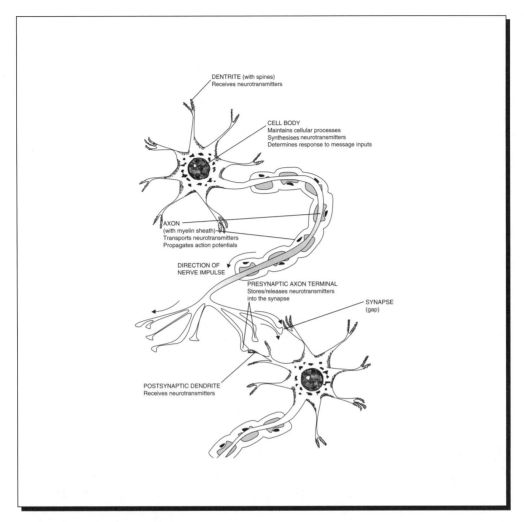

Figure 15: *Two intercommunicating neurons*

Neurons consist of three components: a cell body, dendrites, and the axon. The dendrites receive incoming electrical signals from other neurons. Electrical signals are taken to the cell body along the dendrite. The signals are passed on away from the cell body along a thin fibre, the axon. It is at the tip of the axon that one of the most enabling processes of the brain takes place. Chemical substances known as neurotransmitters are released by the axon terminal and attach themselves to the dendrites of another neuron and activate an electrical signal. In this way neurons communicate with one another by means of an electrical signal that is encoded into a chemical signal which is then decoded back into an electrical signal in the receiving neuron.

The human brain's great versatility and range of ability to deal with the wide variety of human experiences are due not to the properties of any single neuron but to the way in which large groups of neurons interact. Under appropriate sensory stimulation neurons are 'recruited' into groups all over the brain, each one connected to some specific purpose. The visual system alone may have many such groupings. We make sense of the world and then learn about the world when these neural networks communicate with one another. All our experiences and learning have representative neural networks. If we do not have a neural network corresponding to something in the environment, then it does not exist for us (Hannaford, 2006).

Learning takes place when certain patterns of thoughts, actions and emotions are repeated or habitualised. In the brain this represents a strengthening of connections between appropriate neural networks. The more we use certain skills or thought patterns, the stronger the bonds in the neural networks become. As new neural networks are activated, the communication between these groups is slow. If the networks are activated repeatedly, a substance called myelin is laid down. The more myelin is laid down, the faster is the transmission. The more practice, the faster the processing – until it becomes easy. Hannaford suggests it becomes like driving on a superhighway.

The process of neurons connecting and networking reflects our learning. As new associations are made or existing ones altered, so our learning develops. As our experience of the world develops, our system of neural networks continues to change and self-organise.

The potential of the neuronal system is mind-numbing. Taking into account the number of neurons in the brain, the number of connections is of a much higher order still. Because neurotransmitters can enhance or inhibit connections between neurons, it has been estimated that the possible combinations of messages jumping across neurons exceeds the number of known atoms in the universe (Chopra, 1989).

One of the characteristics of the brain is its plasticity. Neurons are by no means 'hard-wired': some can be 'recruited' into many different networks. Every time we learn something new, the brain remodels itself. The brain can also 'rewire' itself to compensate for losses or damage. Responsibility for a task can be shifted from one region to another. The idea that the brain inevitably decays as we grow old is not borne out by recent research (Smith, 2004). The harder you use the brain, the more it will grow. Only if you do not use it will you lose it.

Greenfield (2002) has reviewed the development of a different perspective on how the brain works which proposes the idea that the brain has specialised compartments each with its own specific function.

Phrenology

Scientific thinkers of the late eighteenth century – the most famous among whom were Franz Gall and his colleagues in Vienna – suggested that the brain could be divided up into 32 different areas, each corresponding to a particular personal quality. Not only did these include characteristics of temperament but also ethical traits. The term 'phrenology' was coined to describe this approach and the ideas embodied in it were popular at the time. Subsequent discoveries have shown phrenology to be a highly inaccurate 'science' the popularity of which was related more to the politics of religion than to its scientific contribution.

MODELS OF THE BRAIN

Various models of the brain's structure have been developed over the years to explain the growing number of observations of the characteristics of the brain. MacLean (1978) proposed a very influential model which was labelled 'the triune brain'. This suggested that the brain can be perceived as three sub-brains which are responsible for survival, emotional and rational functions of the brain. This model is easy to understand and has been widely used in advocating educational ideas associated with brain research. More recent discoveries have thrown doubt on its validity as a model that accurately explains the workings of the brain, but Cytowic (1993) suggests it is still a useful functional metaphor to explain some of the applications of brain research.

Sylwester (1995) has a different notion, developed from the idea of the triune brain. He describes two sets of brain systems one of which focuses on our internal needs and values, and the other on our interactions with the external world. The first system involves the brain stem and an educationally significant set of structures which contain the amygdala, the hippocampus, the thalamus and hypothalamus. They are together known as the 'limbic system'. These internal structures play a significant role in our survival mechanisms, digestion, sexuality, basic body cycles, fight-or-flight behaviours, emotions and memory. The second system, for external challenges, is the cerebral cortex, which represents 85% of our brain's mass and which completely wraps around the limbic area and brain stem. It comprises two hemispheres, the right and the left, which process information in different ways (we discuss the function of the two halves later). The back-to-front organisation of the cortex has a temporal dimension. The back part of the cortex combines sensory information and memories so that incoming information makes sense to us in terms of our memories. This area represents the past. The middle part of the cortex is devoted to problem-solving and dealing with current challenges, and it allows us to deal quickly with problems, giving a general response rather than an accurate one. We can then further refine our response by collecting further information. This area is associated with our intuitive process and represents the present. The very front of the cortex permits us to plan and rehearse future actions. This part of the cortex is crucial to scientific thought and because of its strong connections to the limbic system it also regulates elements of our emotional life such as empathy, compassion and altruism. The frontal cortex is vital to the development of management skills because it is involved with planning, decision-making and action. This frontal part of the cortex represents the future.

As knowledge of the brain has increased, the models of the brain have become more reductionist. The idea now is that the brain is a system of systems, many parts of the brain contributing to any single function rather than one geographical region being entirely responsible for it.

The brain as an advertising hoarding

To me the brain seems like a gigantic advertising hoarding which contains countless electric bulbs (neurons). Groups of bulbs can light up a particular section or pattern in the hoarding and each bulb may appear in many different patterns. The patterns may in turn combine with each other and make up messages, pictures and experiences which make sense to people (learning). They may be messages which give useful information by which we live our lives (brain stem). They may be rational statements or ways to solve problems (cortex). They may be images which bring us joy or frighten us (emotional systems). The more patterns appear, the more capacity the system has for producing yet more patterns. Amazingly, there is no overall controller! The brain is a true child of evolution.

SKILL DEVELOPMENT AND PARALLEL PROCESSING

Jensen (2005) reminds us that the brain evolved for survival. As a consequence, the brain learns in order to survive. To do this the brain processes the vast amount of incoming information by using parallel neural circuits. With parallel processing, conscious and unconscious actions occur simultaneously, and this involves all sorts of interconnections and feedback loops within the brain. Sylwester (1995) suggests that communication in the brain moves more in parallel patterns similar to the way a rumour spreads throughout a community (via personal contacts, phone, mass media, etc) than in a linear sequence as is the case when a letter moves through the postal service.

Hart (1983) suggests:

> **'The brain simultaneously operates on many levels, processing all at once a world of colour, movement, emotion, shape, intensity, sound, taste, weight, and more. It assembles patterns, composes meaning and sorts daily life experiences from an extraordinary number of clues.'**

We are familiar with and in many cases accepting of the fact that we do things one at a time. We get out of bed, visit the bathroom, eat our breakfast, go to work, etc, apparently in a sequence. However, this is far removed from the true operations of the brain. Biologically, physically, intellectually and emotionally we are constantly doing many things at the same time. The brain is a natural parallel processor.

This means that some training and developmental approaches which rely exclusively on a linear input to a whole group can actually inhibit learning by not taking advantage of what the brain does naturally.

With skill development there are certain approaches which use the brain's natural way of learning. Among the ones we have found useful are: whole exercises, varying sense modalities, metaphors, and in particular, allowing the learner to control most of the activity.

Giving learners complete developmental tasks, particularly in groups, encourages them to deal with a whole range of requirements such as planning, carrying out the task, feedback and evaluation, as well as the social challenges of the task and many incidental operational necessities that may crop up. Just the sort of challenge a parallel-processing brain thrives on.

The efficacy of multisensory interventions has been documented frequently (Dilts, 1994; O'Connor and Seymour, 2003; Jensen, 2005; Knight, 1999; Smith, 2004). It seems intuitively obvious that if we take in information using our eyes, ears, the sense of touch and our feelings, we will create more meaning for ourselves than if we only used one of our senses. Multisensory interventions are compatible with the brain's natural way of learning. Many people have a preferred sense modality, but their understanding is enhanced enormously when this is complemented by the other senses.

Metaphors used in learning and development operate at both a conscious and an unconscious level. The conscious mind is occupied with the actual story or activity while the unconscious mind deals with the meaning behind the story (which is the real outcome). The great benefit of metaphors is that each person creates his or her own learning from it. This will be based on the person's previous knowledge and experience, and so will be a very personal learning experience.

The last point about personal learning is reinforced by allowing learners to create their own learning. In a group of any size no two learnings will be the same, because individual experience and knowledge differs from person to person. New learnings can only make sense in light of previous learnings. If the learner is in control, his or her learning will build on his or her individual history rather than someone else's, and therefore make sense to that person. The brain is excellent at integrating new learning with old and making sense of it.

SKILL DEVELOPMENT AND MEMORY

There are four types of memory experience which appear to have implications for the development of management skills: semantic, episodic, recognition and procedural. The first two are sometimes categorised as 'declarative memories'.

- *Semantic memory* is the memory of meanings and related information, facts and figures. These memories are context-free and are useful in the development and practice of management skills – for example, remembering how a particular piece of software works or the values underpinning a mission statement. The semantic memory is rapidly retrievable if it is effectively rehearsed, unreliable when ineffectively rehearsed.

- *Episodic memories* are memories of the experience and the circumstances surrounding the experience. They are time-tagged and often very personal

Episodic and semantic memory structures are widely distributed throughout the brain but specifically involve the hippocampus, which decides on where and how the information will be stored, and the cortex, which helps package the memory into a coherent whole.

- Human beings are extremely good at *recognising places, space and faces* (Smith, 2004). Reading evolved only 80,000 years after the human brain reached its current level of evolution. During those years human beings developed a very refined capacity for visual recall. There is also evidence that the use of this visual recognition facility actually changes the structure of the brain (Maguire *et al*, 2001).

- *Procedural memories* are automatic skill sequences, such as reading, touch-typing, juggling, riding a bicycle and swimming. They are hard to learn and forget (we can ride a bicycle after years of not doing it), inflexible and thoroughly reliable. They involve two brain structures which control movement: the basal ganglia and the cerebellum.

What are recognised as management skills in the literature are not the province of any one memory experience. There is no one correct prescription for a skill such as delegation. The process of delegating may well vary between managers with differing degrees of success. Managers personalise their own skill. Some of the elements may be common but the process will be put together differently for individual managers.

Delegation and memory experience

The process of delegation may start with a manager remembering a role model and his or her approach to delegation. This memory may be in the form of a story from the past (*episodic memory*). If it is recalled often enough over time and proves to be successful, it may well form an attitude to delegation. The manager may then assemble together a number of facts, tasks and instructions that will form the substance of the delegation (*semantic memory*). The manager will then have to pass on his or her instructions to the subordinate. To accomplish this, he or she will have to use the skills of articulating ideas, rapport, questioning, and body language. It is likely that these aspects have been so well rehearsed that they become automatic (*procedural memory*). Subsequently, the manager may want to check that the delegated tasks and actions have been successfully carried out. To do this he or she may use familiar faces and places as a reminder of different aspects of the delegation and the need to check these out (*recognition memory*).

The reliability of memory experience

Forgetting

From a practical point of view the quality of management skills will correspond to a significant extent on the reliability and efficacy of the memory experience the manager is drawing on. Before we examine this in terms of the four types of memory experience, it is useful to remind ourselves that forgetting is not always a negative concept. Smith (2004) argues that our memories are far from perfect and that this is so for a reason. He asks us to imagine what it would be like if we could remember everything. There is so much stimulation in our environments that we would be overwhelmed if there were not processes and mechanisms which only selected certain stimuli.

'In truth each memory is an act of reconstitution. The process of recall is influenced by many variables including emotional state, physiological condition, context and how this memory may connect with others. The same event can never be remembered exactly as it was. Every recall is a reconstitution and so plays its part in slightly distorting the original.

'In some cases we cannot remember because the memory was not encoded properly in the first place. We fail to give our memories serious significance. Some scientists believe that many memories are simply put out of reach to stop confusing clutter. This process is known as inhibition.'

Episodic

So how reliable and effective are our memory experiences? We referred above to episodic memory, which is the capacity to place facts and events in time and to refer to them freely. It allows us to examine both the past and the future and gives us the widely used process of storytelling. It is the most plastic of the memory experiences, and Smith (2004) describes above how it is easily distorted. If we are to use episodes from the past as part of our management skills, we must constantly demonstrate that our memories are relevant to new situations – otherwise, they become unreliable. Stories do not necessarily need to be 'true' to be useful as a basis for management skills, but they do need to be relevant.

Semantic

Semantic memories are detached from personal experience. Semantic memory allows us to retain facts, everyday functions, categories of events, objects, symbolic description and names. Our capacity for semantic memory is limited, whereas our capacity for episodic memory seems unlimited. Unless effectively rehearsed, semantic memory is unreliable – so if it is to be used as part of our management skills, we must make sure that we can access the information as and when we want it.

Procedural

As mentioned above, procedural memories involve the recall of habits and skills which once learned do not have to be consciously accessed. A great deal of our everyday functioning and learning and, indeed, of what developing management skills involves is the result of turning semantic memories into procedural memories. In developing questioning skills, at first we have to think about what type of question is appropriate during a conversation. As we master the skill, we no longer have to actively remember what to do. We just do it. Brain scans actually show the location of the memory in the brain changes as it becomes explicit. The problem for practising management skills is not the accessing of the memory but whether the skill laid down flexibly is embedded sufficiently to cope with the range of situations encountered. So, for example, does a manager have the flexibility in rapport skills to deal with someone on the one hand who is cool and impersonal, and someone on the other hand who is warm and friendly? The implications of this for developing management skills are significant.

Recognition

In the delegation example above, recognition memory was given as an example to show it might be used as a prompt for checking that tasks had been carried out. Recognition memory tends to be excellent. So we should have no problem remembering the prompt. The main problem is remembering how the prompt is linked to the tasks to be checked. We need to establish a strong anchor between the prompt and the information to be remembered. We pursue how this might be done in the next section.

Figure 16: *Some memories are better than others*

THE ROLE OF EMOTION IN MEMORY

Pert (1999) argues that if the brain is not to be overwhelmed by the amount of sensory information presented to it, there must be some sort of filtering system that enables us to pay attention to what our body/mind deems the most important information and to ignore the rest. It is our emotions that perform this task.

Ratey (2003), commenting on the work of Damasio (1994), states that the amygdala (part of the limbic system of the brain) attaches emotional significance to sensory information. In turn its emotional evaluation is passed on to the hippocampus (that part of the brain which organises the information and integrates it with previous memories of similar sensory details). The greater the emotional significance assigned by the amygdala, the more permanently is the memory recorded by the hippocampus.

The way our brains are wired shows that in order to learn and remember something, there must be sensory input and a personal emotional connection. As we experience the world, our images and our responding actions are all run through an emotional filtering system in the limbic system of the brain. This determines the value, meaning and survival potential of the experience in light of past experiences. Emotions interpret our experience and help us organise our view of the world and our place in it.

This must have enormous implications for how we design learning situations and develop management skills. Knowing how to utilise emotions gives us a vital tool in facilitating learning and developing management skills. In skill development workshops music and drama can be and have been used to 'emotionally mark' learning experiences. Body language and particularly our voice can generate and convey emotion. Humour can be a most effective device in generating emotion and anchoring learning. Physical movement can be used to generate and change emotions. (The role of movement is examined more fully later in this chapter.) Teamwork exercises and role-play have enormous potential for 'emotional marking', and this is why they can be so effective in developing management skills.

IMPROVING MEMORY

Most techniques for improving memory are aimed at improving **semantic** memory. Most techniques are based on the following procedure:

1   Give the information emotional significance.

This is mainly about the importance of the information to us. If it is not important, the odds are you will not remember it. We need to clearly establish why the information is important. Who is involved? What are the consequences of remembering or forgetting, etc?

2   Organise and encode it.

Smith (2004) cites a memorable mnemonic to describe a process for encoding information: SPECS: See the information, Personalise it, Exaggerate it, Connect it, Share it. This enhances the likelihood of remembering the information.

See it
Personalise it
Exaggerate it
Connect it
Share it

3   Practise.

I believe this is the most important phase of the process. Experience and research suggests that practice should be 'little and often'.

4   Finally, test your recall.

Improving the **procedural** memory is about moving items from the semantic memory to the procedural memory. Once this is done, the memory is very reliable. The way to accomplish it is by having an effective methodology for the skill, breaking it down into manageable chunks, and then practise, practise, practise. The chunks should blend together and the skill in time will become automatic.

As far as improving **recognition** memory such as the memory of a journey, evidence from the study of London taxi drivers (Maguire *et al*, 2001) would suggest that this is best done through practice and undertaking the journey. This is a multisensory experience and people learn through picking up visual, auditory and kinaesthetic clues from undertaking the journey. This appears to be the best way of improving this type of recognition memory.

BRAIN HEMISPHERICITY

If you were to stand in front of a full-length mirror and look at yourself, your first impressions would be that we are symmetrical about a vertical line that runs down the centre of our bodies. However, this is not the case. We are almost completely asymmetrical. We have a dominant hand, eye, foot and ear, and if you carry out the procedures in the box below, you can determine your profile of dominance for these four body parts.

A self-assessment method for determining, hand, eye, ear, foot and brain dominance

Hand
Whichever hand you currently write with. You can assist other people to determine their dominant hand by offering them a pencil at their body's midpoint (at waist level, in the middle part of their torso). Whichever hand they reach out with to take the pencil will be their current dominant hand.

Eye
Make a 'window' by overlapping the two hands so there is a small opening between thumb and forefinger of both hands. Hold the window at arm's length. With both eyes focusing on the window, line up an object (another person's face or a picture). Without moving either the window or your head, close one eye, then open it and close the other eye. Whichever eye holds the image is the dominant eye.

Ear
Pretend there are people on the other side of a wall across the room who are talking about you. Walk to the wall and put your ear close so that you can listen to what they are saying. Which ear did you put against the wall? This is your dominant ear.

Foot
Step onto a chair or step and notice which foot you used first. Or kick a ball and notice which foot you used.

Or lean forward until you are about to fall with feet together. Which foot do you step out with to stop you falling? A better reading is given by having someone push you in the back when you are not expecting it. (Obviously, be cautious with this suggestion.)

Brain hemisphere
Use the Logic (left) and Gestalt (right) lists in Table 4 below to decide which hemisphere you currently access most. A better test would be to recognise how you would initially respond during a highly stressful situation. During stress you rely more on your dominant brain hemisphere.

- If you are logic-dominant: when under stress your first response is to analyse the situation. You would tend to write or talk about it and look for specific reasons behind it. Your focus will be on the details, with a strong need to understand each aspect of the situation.

- If you are Gestalt-dominant: when under stress your first response is to see the whole situation and feel the emotion. You may be unable to decipher the details. You will have difficulty in breaking the whole situation down into the pieces of language to express it. Language is not an initial response. Often you feel a strong need to physically move or express emotion.

The human brain looks like two identical halves but it too is asymmetrical. The left and right halves are responsible for different functions. Differences in the functions of the two halves have been detected in infants as young as two days old, and it is suspected that this asymmetry probably begins to develop in the womb. The difference between the two halves is most noticeable in the way they control opposite parts of the body. The right brain controls sensory movements on the left-hand side of the body and the left brain controls sensory movements on the right-hand side of the body. The left brain tends to deal with detail first and processes information sequentially. The right brain tends to deal with the whole picture first and processes information simultaneously. Table 4 gives a more comprehensive list of the characteristics of the two methods of processing. It is based on Hannaford's (2003) summary of several authors.

Logic	Gestalt
Processes from pieces to whole	Processes from whole to pieces
Parts of language	Language comprehension
Syntax, semantics	Image, emotion, meaning
Letters, printing, spelling	Rhythm, dialect, application
Numbers	Estimation, application
Techniques (sports, music, arts)	Flow and movement
Analysis, logic	Intuition, faith
Looks for differences	Looks for similarities
Controls feelings	Is free with feelings
Language-oriented	Prefers drawing, manipulation
Planned, structured	Spontaneous, fluid
Sequential thinking	Simultaneous thinking
Future-oriented	Present-oriented
Time-conscious	Less time sense
Structure-oriented	People-oriented

Table 4: *Left- and right-brain functions and responsibilities*

Although the lateral specialisation of the brain is generally highly specific, the brain is a very plastic organ and this specialisation is subject to the following conditions for the function of language:

- Language tends to be located in the left hemisphere for most humans.

- In a significant population of humans language occurs in both left and right hemispheres without any apparent loss of function.

- The left hemisphere suppresses the right hemisphere's speech potential.

- When the left hemisphere has been removed or badly damaged, the right hemisphere takes over the language function.

When the different modes of processing were discovered by Sperry (1968), a good deal of analysis and comment appeared in the popular books and journals and was often characterised by a pejorative view over 'right-brain' and 'left-brain' learning. Fortunately, this unhelpful and inaccurate view has largely died out. For effective processing we need both hemispheres to act together. The following example illustrates this issue in connection with creativity.

Example

Right-brain logic and left-brain creativity

There has been a tendency to think that one side of the brain (the right) is the source of creativity in human thinking whereas the other side (the left) is not creative. This view is now being superseded by a more balanced holistic view. We can be very creative using logical options, patterns and sequences. The work of Debono and Buzan remind us that we can use left-brain processing to be creative.

It was once thought that music was a right-brain creative activity. Researchers using instruments to map blood flow and electrical activity in the brain found that non-musicians tend to process more in the right hemisphere whereas musicians are more likely to process music in the left hemisphere. Research by Clynes (1982) suggests that harmonic structure, interval quality, timbre and the special temporal long-term patterns are recognised by our right hemisphere. Short-term signatures, like rapidly varying volume, rapid and accurate pitch trajectory, pacing and words are recognised by the logic hemisphere. Clynes research suggests that music is a 'whole-brain' activity. Other artists such as painters and photographers (usually thought of as right-brain individuals) show bilateral activity in their work.

All of us have a certain degree of hemispheric dominance. Individuals do exhibit a preference for one method of processing over the other, particularly in times of stress. However, more and more evidence points to the fact that the differences are relative. To be optimally efficient in any activity we need access to both hemispheres.

The two hemispheres are connected by the corpus callosum, which allows processing between the two hemispheres. The more both hemispheres are activated by use, the more dendritic connections occur across the corpus callosum and the more myelination occurs and the faster the processing becomes between the two hemispheres.

The brain and individual learning styles

Dennison and Dennison (1984) and Hannaford (2003, 2006) report a fascinating method to gauge and characterise individual learning styles. Dennison's approach is to determine dominance profiles based on a person's lateral dominance of eyes, ears, hands and feet in relation to his or her dominant brain hemisphere. Dennison argues that this assessment gives a deep insight into how individuals process information and experience their environment. Dennison also states that not only do the dominance profiles give information about learning styles but they also provide us with an understanding of how we act in moments of stress.

In less stressful situations the learning style associated with our dominance profiles are more flexible, and as we meet changing situations we depart from our preferred learning style and adapt to more appropriate ones. Under stress, however, we react by returning to our preferred learning style that is associated with our basal dominance profile. Under stress, only our dominant brain hemisphere is efficiently functioning and we have less effective use of the senses that do not feed into or are expressed through that dominant hemisphere.

Smith (2004) states that the evidence for this link between learning style and lateral dominance is less than substantial because he maintains that it is difficult to assess hemispheric dominance meaningfully. He also suggests that it is difficult to get clean evidence of hemispheric dominance without cultural or lifestyle influences, and that the quantification of learning style preference is in itself not secure.

Despite these reservations, the results obtained using these concepts (Hannaford, 2003) with schoolchildren in the United States suggest that this is a line of research worth pursuing.

So what are the implications of left and right brain in the development of skills and for learning in general? The overriding conclusion is that the two halves of the brain do not operate independently. There are not solely right-brain activities or left-brain activities. Both sides are involved in learning and development. However, they are not identical in the way they process information, but the differences are relative rather than absolute. They do differ in the way they process language. They deal with spatial relationships differently. The right brain processes more holistically and simultaneously whereas the left brain processes in more detail and sequentially. The right brain appears to have more neurotransmitters associated with emotional arousal and inhibition. The important point is that for optimal understanding and performance *both sides work together*.

In developing and learning new skills not everyone starts from the same point or finishes at the same point or completes an outcome in exactly the same way. If learners are working in groups, allowance should be made for differences. Not everyone can use identical methods for the same duration or achieve outcomes to the same standard.

Switches should be made between holistic and detailed. Constantly search for connections in skill development. Use different sense modalities. Deliberately include cross-lateral learning using the differences creatively. Mix small-chunk skills with large-chunk. (Focus on developing rapport skills but allow learners to see how this can be used in negotiating.) In light of the fact that learners probably have dominant eyes, ears, etc, think about where you are positioned in a learning event.

Finally, remember that the brain is a wonderful parallel processor: using right and left simultaneously is what comes naturally to the brain.

MOVEMENT AND THE BRAIN

It would seem that only organisms that move require a brain. Movement is fundamental to the existence of the brain. Plants turn their faces to the sun through cell growth, not by moving their location, and they do not need a brain. There is a small sea squirt that initially has a brain because it swims around like a tadpole, but once it permanently attaches itself to a rock its brain is gradually absorbed and digested (Ratey, 2003).

In spite of facts like this, the power of movement was always considered inferior and separate from cognitive abilities. This view is now changing. Much of this is due to Gardner (1999), who has delineated the bodily kinaesthetic intelligence and demonstrated its equal and complementary role to other manifestations of intelligence.

When we develop physical skills, we do so by the movement of our muscles. When we learn to swim or juggle or ride a bike, we do so through a series of movements which we learn from modelling other people. Once we have practised the movements sufficiently and the firing patterns of the neurons which underpin these movements become established, the behaviours become automatic. They no longer need conscious attention. That is why once you have learned to juggle you can pick it up again almost immediately even if you have not juggled for months. The skills last a lifetime. These automatic behaviours form in the frontal cortex of the brain. During this period many neighbouring neurons are recruited to assist in the process of establishing this new learning. It is very expensive in terms of neuronal activity. In developing a skill such as juggling we develop numerous repertoires of automatic actions. These are then stored in a different part of the brain until they are required and the neurons used in their formation are freed up and become available for new learning. If we did not have this automatic process, acquiring complex skills would soon overwhelm us. Just to get out of bed in the morning takes numerous sequences of these automatic behaviours.

Hannaford (2006) argues that the same process holds true for cognitive skills used in education and in managing people in organisations. She goes on to argue that thoughts must be brought into being through movement. It is the movement inherent in speaking or writing that gives substance to thoughts and builds nerve networks in the brain.

Talking is very much a sensory-motor skill, requiring fine motor co-ordination of millions of facial, tongue, vocal fold and eye muscles as well as many other associated muscles. Talking allows us to organise and elaborate our thoughts. When we talk about what we have learned, the physical movements internalise and solidify it in nerve networks. A neurotransmitter is released across the synapses of activated neurons. This stimulates muscle function during talking. Increased and consistent release of the neurotransmitter at these nerve endings stimulates and attracts dendritic growth in these areas thus encouraging nerve networks (Hannaford, 2006).

It seems to me that learning can be strengthened by encouraging learners to share experiences and discuss how training activities can be personalised. I also believe that this is something effective teachers/trainers have always done as part of their normal routine.

Many people report that they have a distinct tendency to think more effectively when engaged on a low-level routine task. Some people find making a cup of tea helps them to think more freely and resolve a problem. Other people apparently use walking, running, knitting or equally physical tasks to do the same. Although this may be just hearsay, there is no doubt that movement seems to stimulate dendritic growth, as Hannaford outlines above.

Perhaps this relationship between cognitive functions and movement functions is not that surprising in view of the fact that it is the prefrontal cortex part of the brain that handles both motor and cognitive functions

(Ratey, 2003). The frontal cortex learns, routinises and processes motor and mental functions in parallel. Movement becomes inextricably linked to cognition. The mental and cognitive processes share common neurons. The more routinised and automatic processes are stored in the lower part of the brain (brain stem and cerebellum). Actions and cognition that are more complex or new are dealt with further up the brain towards the frontal cortex. More brain regions are involved in the process and offer more input. This allows more neurons to readjust and produce a more precise final action or cognitive process.

The motor system allows us to shift back and forth between deliberate and automatic movements and deliberate and automatic cognition. This allows us to perform many different skills and tasks which involve movement and mental components at the same time.

There is increasing evidence that physical activity has a beneficial effect on cognitive activities. Hannaford (2006) reports on two pieces of research. The first describes 500 Canadian children among whom those who spent more time exercising performed better in class than less active children. The second examined 13 different studies on the exercise/brainpower link and found that exercise stimulated developing brains and prevented deterioration of older brains. Smith (2004) reports that the Exeter Fit to Succeed Project disclosed a positive link between hard physical exercise and performance in maths.

Given the evidence of the link between movement and learning and skill development, it would seem beneficial to build some movement into skill development programmes. I do not think this can be quantified but the following guidelines might be indicative. Frequent change of activity will build movement naturally into skill development programmes. Where possible it is a good idea to use activities which by their very nature are characterised by movement. Role plays and simulations both present opportunities for physical movement. Certain types of icebreaker do as well. Learner-centred activities such as teamwork exercises and projects not only allow learners plenty of opportunities to move but also allow them to control the amount of movement.

Sometimes because of the nature of the learning event, the opportunity for movement will be limited. I have been on programmes where a routine of exercises has been built in. Recent research suggests cross-lateral movement is beneficial in these cases because it creates connections between the left and right side of the brain. This type of exercise encourages both logic and intuitive thinking. Brain Gym is a collection of such exercises that have been put together by Paul and Gail Dennison (1984). Such exercises can be done at the start of a programme and at several times throughout the day. The exercises are simple and need take no more than five to 10 minutes per session.

SUMMARY

In the last two decades the growth in knowledge about the brain and the way it functions has been phenomenal. More and more of this knowledge is now being applied to the field of learning, education and skill development. We are now developing plausible explanations for why some learning strategies and approaches are more successful than others. At last learning and development has a credible body of knowledge to underpin it. Certainly, the idea that learning environments should be brain-compatible is becoming irresistible.

In this chapter we have examined some of the pertinent findings that are influencing the direction of learning and skill development.

We began by giving a general description of the brain's architecture and how theories of the brain have developed.

Secondly, we examined the brain's capacity as a parallel processor and examined how this property can be used in the field of skill development and learning generally.

Thirdly, we explored the memory functions of the brain and considered how the different memory experiences could be used in skill development.

Fourthly, we looked into the hemispherical differences in the brain and considered the implications of them for learning and skill development.

Finally, we considered the relationship between movement and the brain and how these effects can be exploited in learning.

We would exhort our readers to consider their learning styles, approaches and environments and examine their compatibility with the findings we have discussed. Learning is more effective if we work with the brain's processes than if we work against them.

REFERENCES

Chopra, D. (1989) *Quantum Healing: Exploring the frontiers of mind/body medicine*. New York: Bantam

Clynes, M. (ed.) (1982) *Music, Mind and Brain*. New York, NY: Plenum Press

Cytowic, R. E. (1993) *The Man who Tasted Shapes*. New York: G. P. Putnam

Damasio, A. (1994) *Descartes' Error*. New York, NY: Putnam & Sons

Dennison, P. E. and Dennison, G. E. (1984) *Personalised Whole Brain Integration*. Ventura, CA: Edu-Kinesthetics, Inc.

Dilts, R. (1994) *Effective Presentation Skills*. Capitolia, CA: Meta Publications

Gardner, H. (1999) *Intelligence Reframed*. New York: Basic Books

Greenfield, S. A. (2002) *The Private Life of the Brain*. Penguin Press Science

Hannaford, C. (2006). *Smart Moves*. Arlington, VA: Great Ocean

Hannaford, C. (2003) *The Dominance Factor*. Arlington, VA: Great Ocean

Hart, L. (1983) *The Human Brain and Human Learning*. White Plains, NY: Longman Publishing

Jensen, E. (2005) *Teaching with the Brain in Mind*. San Diego, CA: Brain Store

Knight, S. (1999) *NLP Solutions*. London: Nicholas Brealey

Kotulak, R. (1997) *Inside the Brain*. Kansas City, Missouri: Andrews McMeel

LeDoux, J. (1998) *The Emotional Brain*. New York: Weidenfeld & Nicolson

MacLean, P. (1990) *The Triune Brain in Education*. New York: Plenum Press

Maguire, E. A., Gadian, D. G., Johnsrude, I. S., Good, C. D., Ashburner, J., Frackowiak, R. S. J. and Frith, C. D. (2001) 'Navigation related structural change in the hippocampi of taxi drivers', *Proceedings of the National Academy of Science, US*, 97 (8): 4398–403

O'Connor, J. and Seymour, J. (2003) *Introducing Neuro-linguistic Programming*. London: Aquarian Press

Pert, C. B. (1999) *Molecules of Emotion*. New York: Touchstone

Ratey, J. J. (2003) *A User's Guide to the Brain*. New York: Random House

Rose, C. (1985) *Accelerated Learning.* Aston Clinton, Bucks.: Accelerated Learning Systems Ltd

Smith, A. (2004) *The Brain's Behind It.* Stafford: Network Educational Press

Sperry, R. (1968) 'Hemisphere disconnection and unity in conscious awareness', *American Psychologist*, 23, 723–33

Sylwester, R. (1995) *A Celebration of Neurons.* Alexandria, VA: ASCD Publications

State: a prerequisite for skill development

When I was in the top year at my primary school, many years ago, I was taught by two teachers, Mr Smith and Mr Jones. These names are fictitious but the teachers were real.

Mr Smith was a disciplinarian. When he walked in the room you could hear a pin drop. He taught mainly by rote. He used sarcasm and threats as tools in his teaching strategy. He also resorted to corporal punishment more often than any other teacher. Parents admired him. No gain without pain. Children feared him.

Mr Jones was a famed storyteller. In the days before television and computers were commonplace in schools, he would describe areas of the world that we never could have imagined. He made history come alive. He had few teaching aids other than his voice, but he instilled in all of us a sense of wonder of the world around us. Above all, he developed in all his students a love of stories. Children loved him. Parents thought his teaching was more like play and not as effective as Mr Smith's style.

Both these teachers created strong learning states. Their classes were surrounded by atmosphere. I know which I preferred. Looking back all those years I am struck by two things. I remember how quickly Mr Jones's classes seemed to pass, whereas Mr Smith's classes dragged on agonisingly slowly. Secondly, I cannot remember one specific thing I learned in Mr Smith's classes (although I am sure I did learn many things). However, even after all these years, I can still vividly recall many of the stories and descriptions from Mr Jones's classes which laid the foundations of my interest in geography, history and the natural world.

I am sure you will be able to recall a positive learning state and a negative learning state that you have experienced. Take a moment to do that.

I believe that all effective teachers and trainers have always known, explicitly or intuitively, how important learning states are to meaningful learning.

Whatever activity we engage in – whether it is sport, our job, socialising with friends or taking part in a learning event – we are aware that sometimes we feel much more 'up for it' than at other times. These changes in how we feel, or our 'state' as it has become known, can have a major effect on how productive we are in the above activities and on the very quality of our lives.

- What do we know about our state?
- What exactly is it?
- What role does it have in learning and skill development?
- Is there any pattern to the appearance of our states, or do they occur randomly?
- People report feeling in a positive state when they listen to music or exercise. Is there evidence to support this – and what else might affect our state?
- Is there any way we can control our state and call up positive states when we need them?

This chapter attempts to answer these and other questions.

The first section explores different explanations of state, and in particular how it relates to learning and the idea that there may be an ultimate learning state.

The second section discusses biorhythms and how they affect our states. It also examines the link between state and variables such as music, metaphors, the human voice and movement.

The final section investigates the proposition that we can control and change our states. We invite the reader to try out a routine for doing just that, and demonstrate how this valuable resource can support the development of management skills.

STATE – WHAT IS IT?

Intuitively, we all recognise a productive learning state, whether we are learning on our own or in a group being facilitated by a trainer. Likewise, we all recognise an unproductive learning state. However, it is not so easy to define or describe just what a state is. When I have posed that question to groups of learners, I get responses such as 'a feeling of well-being', 'mental alertness', and 'a feeling of preparedness'.

O'Connor and Seymour (2003) describe state as all the thoughts, emotions and physiology that we express at one moment. Because mind and body are interconnected, so our thoughts influence our physiology and emotions, and vice versa. Hall (1996) describes state as the total mind-body linguistic-semantic-neurological phenomenon. He further explains that the state you experience at any given time has components of thought, internal representation, neurology, physiology, emotion, and so on. These can function in a way that you find resourceful or limiting, productive or sabotaging, positive or negative, pleasant or painful, empowering or disempowering.

Kenyon (1994) has suggested that the variation in electrical activity seems to be linked to variation in states. Every time a neuron is stimulated, it transduces energy. The biochemical reactions at the tips of the dendrites fire off electrical activity. If enough neurons fire off simultaneously, there is an electrical surge in the brain which can be detected and measured. Neuroscientists use electroencephalographs (EEGs) to measure such activity. The resulting measurements are called electroencephalograms and correspond to a record of brain waves. Marshal (1989) suggests that states in the brain occur when the electrical activity becomes coherent throughout the brain. This is based on the principles of quantum mechanics.

Bolstad and Hamblett (1998) describe the effect in terms of an analogy.

> **'The simplest way to understand this idea is to think of an ordinary electric light, which can light up your room, and a laser which can beam to the moon or burn through solid objects. The difference is that the light waves coming from a normal light are disorganised; in a laser they are arranged in a coherent beam. They all move in the same wavelength in the same direction.'**

It seems that states in the brain are the result of a similar process. This consistent vibration results in a coherent state emerging out of thousands of different impulses processed by the brain at any given time.

Learning states

Jensen (1995) suggests that certain states are positively correlated with learning. He reports on studies which demonstrate that relaxed states and emotionally charged states are useful for memory retention. A state of uncertainty is linked to high levels of learner involvement. Jensen also reports on a number of studies that have described the phenomenon of state-dependent learning, whereby each emotional state 'binds' information as if a memory record can only be retrieved in the state in which it was originally stored.

Kenyon (1994) suggests that certain learning activities are related to certain brain states. Table 5 shows the range of brain states measured (as waves, with frequencies) by EEG.

Delta brain wave patterns are associated with sleep. At the lowest levels of delta there are no mental images and no awareness of the physical body. Although most individuals experience sleep in delta states, these states have been found in people who are in deep trance but fully conscious.

Theta is the state we go into immediately before going to sleep or waking up. This state has been found useful for certain accelerated learning techniques. It has also been found to be useful for the association of creative ideas. Possibly this is why we get some of our best ideas lying in bed at night.

Brain state	Frequency range (Hertz)
Super-high beta	35–150 Hz
K complex	33–35 Hz
High beta	16–32 Hz
Beta	12–16 Hz
Alpha	8–12 Hz
Theta	4–8 Hz
Delta	0.5–4 Hz

Table 5: *Brain waves/states and their frequencies*

The alpha state is a relaxed attentive state. It is appropriate for listening and watching. It is the state for listening to a speaker or watching a demonstration. It is the state sought in stress management training. It is neurophysiologically difficult to experience states of agitation or stress in the alpha state.

The beta state is our normal waking state. It is good for asking questions and problem-solving.

High beta is a more alert intense state, suitable for activities such as debates, role play and presentations.

K complex state occurs only in short bursts. It is speculated that this might be characteristic of the 'A-ha' experiences of high creativity.

As yet no learning applications have been associated with super-high beta states.

It has been suggested that there is an optimal learning state. Csikszsentmihalyi (1997) describes the ideal conditions under which learning takes place:

- A person faces high challenges, uses high skill and is intrinsically motivated.
- He or she has clear goals with relevant and immediate feedback.
- The environment is generally relaxed/low stress.

■ The participant is immersed in the task with his or her attention on doing and learning. There is no self-consciousness or self-evaluation.

Csikszentmihalyi describes this as a 'flow' state. Flow tends to occur when a person's skills are fully involved in overcoming a challenge that is just about manageable. Optimal experiences usually involve a fine balance between one's ability to act and the available opportunities for action. If challenges are too high, one gets frustrated, then anxious, and eventually seriously worried. If challenges are too low relative to one's skill, one becomes relaxed, then bored, and finally apathetic.

When high challenges are matched with high skills, the deep involvement that is characteristic of flow is likely to occur. See Figure 17.

When a person is in flow, attention becomes ordered and fully invested. Because of the demand on psychic energy, a person in flow is completely focused. There is no space in consciousness for distracting thoughts and irrelevant feelings. Self-consciousness disappears, yet one feels stronger than usual. The sense of time is distorted – hours seem to pass in minutes. When a person's entire being is stretched in the full functioning of mind and body, whatever one does becomes worth doing for its own sake.

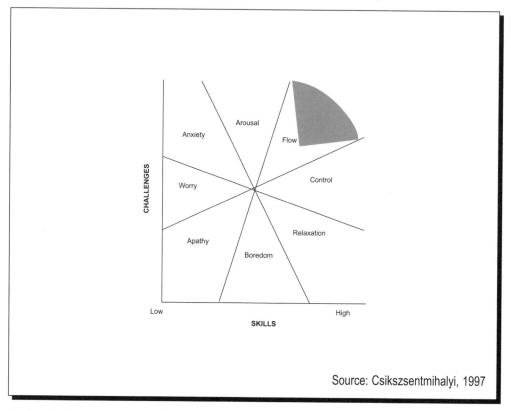

Source: Csikszsentmihalyi, 1997

Figure 17: *Flow, and the optimal learning state*

The idea of flow has been expressed in the more popular literature as being 'in the zone'. This has more often been used in the context of sport and has a distinct physical aspect to it. Mulry (1995) has used the idea of the mind/body system to demonstrate that the concept of the 'zone' can be used equally well for both cognitive and physical skills or a mixture of both. He describes four key elements for achieving this state as relaxation, balance, flexibility and focus.

Mulry's four key elements of energy efficiency

Mulry (1995) maintains that when the body and mind are working in relaxed, balanced, flexible and focused unison, you have approached the peak of energy efficiency and have put yourself 'into the zone'. This applies to any dimension of our lives: physically, socially, intellectually and professionally. He asserts that through physical training you can bring your mind to a state of calm, centred and creative concentration that is crucial to mastery of any activity.

Relaxation

Relaxation is an alert state of mind, variously described as inner stillness, clarity of consciousness, sense of readiness, and keenness of perception. Our senses are alive and we are prepared for effective action. We are calm yet fully able to deal with ongoing circumstances. We are separate from, yet in touch with, things around us. We are open to multiple alternatives. We feel hopeful and experience a general sense of well-being.

Balance

All balance requires a pivotal point. In this case the pivotal point is within you. Locating, recognising and using your centre is a crucial first step. When you function from your centre mentally, your actions are grounded in deeply held personal values. When you function from your centre physically, your actions are are balanced around your body's centre of gravity. In a fully balanced person, these two processes are ongoing and interrelated.

Flexibility

Flexibility is key to problem-solving and effective interpersonal relationships. Breakthroughs in relationships and in professional life do not always arise by trying harder with the same means and plans. Progress, innovations, solutions and resolutions require flexibility to some degree. Freedom of movement and the ability to take alternative courses of action is essential to a state of readiness. Flexibility, when integrated with relaxation and balance skills, facilitates our readiness for action.

Focus

The power to focus, to bring ourselves entirely into our situation or task at any given moment, is what distinguishes a high-level performance from an erratic, unreliable one. Many people use this power in specific and highly specialised fields of activity. The surgeon, artist or manager must concentrate all his or her precise skills and trained judgement in real-time action. Any activity where success or failure depends on the extent to which you are 'all there' requires the ability to focus.

FACTORS THAT INFLUENCE A CHANGE IN STATE
Biorhythms

Rhythms of living things are known as biorhythms. These are patterns of physiological or psychological processes which are repeated over periods of time. Human beings possess them and are affected by them. There are a number of different cycles that are defined by how frequently they occur or how long they last:

- *circadian* are cycles are based on a 24-/25-hour period
- *ultradian* are cycles based on less than 24 hours
- *infradian* are cycles based on between 24 hours and 12 months
- *circannual* are cycles of about 1 year's duration.

The most basic of the circadian cycles is the sleep/wake pattern. There is evidence to suggest that this cycle is actually 24.9 hours rather than 24 hours (Bentley, 2000). Most people seem to need about 8 hours' sleep per night, but there are wide variations. Some individuals need as little as 4 hours' sleep per night. It would appear that we can tolerate small variations in sleep patterns but research suggests that sleep is essential for normal cognitive performance and behaviour.

Our metabolic rate is on a 24-hour cycle. Colquhoun (1970) found that the rate peaked at about 4pm and dipped 12 hours later. This rhythm correlates with many cognitive functions such as memory and attention. Core body temperature also varies on a 24-hour cycle. This is thought to be a byproduct of the metabolic rate because temperature is related to energy use.

As far as learning is concerned, the ultradian cycles appear to be most significant. Klein and Armitage (1979) found ultradian rhythms in cognitive vigilance – namely, a 96-minute cycle in participants' performance on verbal and spatial tasks. This was named the 'basic rest-activity cycle'. Carlson (1986) suggests that there are numerous cycles such as these with a periodicity of 90 minutes all linked to a biological clock in the medulla. Hobson (1989) asserts that the ability to maintain learning attentiveness is affected by these natural cycles. The fluctuations vary across the 24-hour day. At night we experience periods of deep sleep (rapid-eye-movement, or REM, sleep) and light sleep. During the day these cycles continue but at a level of greater awareness. The brain seems to have a natural learning pattern of a pulse. Learning is best when focused, then diffused, focused, then diffused. Constantly focused learning becomes increasingly wasted over time. Learning should consist of a focused period followed by a diffusion activity such as a different form of learning, a complete break or some breathing or physical relaxation.

Oakhill (1988) found that we seem to favour literal memory in the morning and inferential memory in the afternoon. In the morning we are better at learning facts, and in the afternoon we are better at integrating knowledge with what we know. Brewer and Campbell (1991) found that certain types of activity seem to be suited to certain parts of the day. 9am to 12 noon is best for rote learning, spelling, problem-solving, maths, theory and science. Noon to 2pm is best for movement-oriented tasks, paperwork, music, singing and art. 2 to 5pm is best for literature and history, sports, music, theatre and manual dexterity tasks. Because some of us are morning people and some of us are night people, there is a 2- to 4-hour variance among learners for optimal timing.

The menstrual cycle is the most common of the infradian cycles. This affects 50% of the population for a large part of their lives. There is considerable scientific and anecdotal evidence of the impact of this cycle on both cognitive performance and behaviour. There have been suggestions that the lunar cycle may be linked to mental disorders. However, this may be little more than superstition. It is known that lunar cycles do play a part in some animal behaviour, hinting that there may be some neural clock linked to the cycles of the moon.

Circannual cycles have a periodicity of about one year. Migration and hibernation are examples of these cycles in animals. The most reported cycle of this type in humans is seasonal affective disorder (SAD). Some brain neurotransmitters are thought to be seasonal in their action. Melatonin – a neurotransmitter and hormone produced by the pineal gland in the forebrain – varies with the quantity of natural light, and so its concentration varies with the seasons. People who are particularly sensitive to their levels of melatonin can suffer in winter from a low-melatonin type of depression (SAD).

Human voice

The human voice is perhaps the most readily accessible of methods for changing one's state. Someone who is skilled in using such characteristics of his or her voice as volume, tone, rhythm, pitch, tempo, etc, can make his or her words come alive. We listen on two levels, one for meaning/words (auditory digital) and one for how things sound (auditory tonal). It is the auditory tonal, which is processed mainly by the right brain, that appears to stimulate emotional states within the brain. Some individuals appear to be more influenced by the auditory tonal component of the voice, and for them the state generated could be more intense. We can affect other people's state by the use of our voice, and in turn our own state can be affected by other people's voices.

Metaphors, stories and quotations

Parkin (1998) suggests that metaphorical speech is becoming more widely accepted and recognised as a way of helping people to acquire new knowledge, and helping them to transfer learning from what is well known to what is less well known in a vivid and memorable way.

She observes that much of our learning is taken in at an unconscious level. It is the slower brain waves (alpha and theta) that trigger the unconscious mind and produce a relaxed awareness. It is in this state that we experience feelings of heightened concentration and are very receptive to learning. Parkin maintains that storytelling is a natural method of reducing the brain's activity. In a learning context it is a non-threatening way of relaxing people and making them receptive to learning. She concludes that the power of storytelling lies in the fact that listening to the content, our conscious mind is occupied, leaving the unconscious mind open to directly receive the underlying message.

Example

Metaphors and skill development programmes

Metaphors, stories and quotations can be very useful in skill development programmes. I have used them frequently on such programmes. I cannot describe all the situations where they might be useful, but two examples demonstrate where they are particularly appropriate.

Beginnings and endings are times in a programme where metaphors are natural and effective. Stories can be an entertaining and memorable way of introducing themes or describing what is to come. In a similar manner, metaphors lend themselves to summarising important issues, content and key messages at the end of a programme.

In terms of learning outcomes I have found metaphors are a subtle way of dealing with issues surrounding attitudes and beliefs. I found the quotation below very effective on a management skills programme for general managers. One of the key issues to be addressed at the beginning of the programme was the nature of the learning process. Who is responsible for the learning? What is the trainer's role? What is the participant's role?

Learning is finding out what you already know. Doing is demonstrating that you know it. Teaching is reminding others that they know just as well as you. We are all learners, doers and teachers.

Richard Bach (1970)

Music

It is not difficult for most people to accept that music can change your state. Who has not relaxed to their own brand of popular music or been motivated to dance by their favourite rock band? Who has not been inspired by a great symphony or concerto or felt sadness because a melody reminds them of a sad event? However, examples are often anecdotal or subjective, and the media have the tendency to glamorise and generalise particular findings.

Nowhere has that been the case so much as in the 'Mozart effect'.

Rauscher, Shaw and Ky (1993) found that undergraduates in a control group undertaking mathematical tests involving spatial and rotational symmetry showed significant performance improvements when played a Mozart piano sonata for 10 minutes prior to the task. Smith (2002) later described how such findings can be corrupted and generalised by the popular press.

However, there is accumulating evidence of the beneficial effect of music.

Smith (2002), quoting Professor Shaw of the above study, maintains that 'training a child in music at three or four years of age improves the way his or her brain recognises patterns in space and time.' Weinberger and McKenna (1998) suggest that 'millions of neurons can be activated by a single musical experience. Music has an uncanny manner of activating neurons for purposes of relaxing muscle tension, changing pulse and producing long-term memories which are directly related to the number of neurons activated in the experience.'

Smith (2002) summarises: 'Music offers educators the possibility of energising or relaxing students, carrying content information, priming certain types of cognitive performance and enhancing phonological awareness.'

Kenyon (1994) reports two studies as evidence for music changing an individual's state.

Example

Kenyon's two studies of the food of love

The first study concerned a group of premature babies who were played a stringed version of Brahms's *Lullaby* several times a day. Their progress was compared to a control group who did not listen to the Brahms music. In every other respect the babies were treated identically. It transpired that the 'Brahms babies' had fewer complications, gained weight faster and were released from hospital an average of one week earlier than the control group.

In the second example, Kenyon reports a story about Alfred Tomatis, the French music and acoustic pioneer. Tomatis was called to a Benedictine monastery outside Paris, where most of the monks had become severely depressed, listless and uninterested in eating. On investigating the circumstances surrounding the sudden outbreak of communal depression, Tomatis discovered that the monastery had recently acquired a new abbot. The new head of the monastery had progressive views and considered Gregorian chant to be too 'medieval'. He therefore stopped all chanting shortly after his arrival. Unfortunately, chanting was about the only form of auditory stimulation the monks received. When Tomatis had the abbot restore the chanting, the depression miraculously lifted.

Kenyon suggested that the rhythms, tones and patterns inherent in a piece of music directly affect the brain's electrical activity. Kenyon (1994) has identified seven such brain states (discussed earlier in this chapter). Each of these different levels of activity has been found to be associated with certain learning states. It is thought that the music induced a relaxed alpha state in the case of the Brahms babies and the French monks.

Movement

In the chapter on the brain (Chapter 7) we examined evidence which suggested that movement was closely associated with cognitive activity in the brain and explored the idea of the mind/body system. In particular, we discussed how activity on a low-level task such as going for a walk or making a cup of tea could often free up a state of 'stuckness' and lead an individual into a state of 'problem-solving'. It seems appropriate to include a reference to movement in this discussion of factors which influence state change.

MANAGING STATES

Emotional states can have a profound effect on our thinking, behaviour and performance. In terms of skills it is sometimes the key factor in a successful outcome. Have you ever used a particular skill on one day and everything just fell into place and went really well – and the next time you used that skill the opposite happened, nothing seemed to go right? When you looked back over these two occasions it was difficult to tell what you had done differently. Often the difference is in our state. Positive states drive successful outcomes.

Imagine what your life would be like if we could switch on appropriate states at will – become confident when giving a speech, energise ourselves when we face a difficult challenge, be creative when we have a problem to solve, relax at the end of a stressful day and put our worries out of mind.

All of us at some time in our lives have experienced a wide variety of positive and empowering states. What we need to re-experience them is a trigger that will bring those original feelings to the present. We all use triggers or anchors to bring past feelings to the present: it is a natural human process. Music can be a very strong anchor for many people. When they hear a particular piece it invokes a pleasant memory, and repeated use of the association seems to strengthen it. Smells, voices, elements of the weather and favourite places can all be naturally occurring positive anchors.

The word 'anchor' is the terminology used in neurolinguistic programming (NLP) for these association triggers, and anchors occur in all three senses.

Visual anchors are widespread in our society. How do you behave or feel when you see a red traffic light or the sun symbol on a weather forecast?

What emotions do you feel when you hear a police emergency siren, or hear the dawn chorus on a late May morning or the cry of a newborn baby? These are examples of auditory anchors.

How do you feel when you experience kinaesthetic anchors such as the smell of newly baked bread or freshly made coffee, the feel of warm water in the shower or the comfort of sitting in your favourite chair at the end of a tiring day?

Anchors are personal things: their meaning is different to different people, and how individuals react to them is equally different. However, there are similarities in the way anchors are created and work. Firstly, anchors can be created through repetition. If we felt anxious when we heard the sound of a police siren and this was repeated a number of times, an association between this sound and anxiety would be set up. So every time we hear a police siren we will feel anxious. Secondly, if the emotional state is strong and personal and the timing of the feeling and the anchor are well synchronised, the association can be set up instantaneously with no repetition. The less emotionally involved you are, the more need there is for repetition.

Steps for anchoring a positive resource

1   Identify a resource state that would help you improve your skill performance (eg determination, creativity, energy, relaxation, motivation, etc).

2   Find something to use as an anchor to trigger that resource. (Initially it may be more effective to use three anchors, one in each sense modality – eg a mental picture, a key word that expresses the essence of the state, and a physical gesture.)

3   Remember a time when you experienced the resource state strongly.

4   Put yourself back into that resourceful experience. Use all your senses – see what you saw, hear what you heard, and feel what you felt, as vividly as possible.

5   Connect the memory of this experience to your anchors by shifting your attention to your anchors as you feel your memory reaching its most vivid. The timing of this can be critical.

6   Clear your mind for a moment by thinking of something else. Try looking out of the window.

7   Put your attention back on the anchors. You should get the resourceful feeling.

This routine is a skill, and like any other skill it needs practice to become proficient. I also found when I first started to use this resource that you must believe it can happen. One thing that helped me in this belief was the understanding that our physiology works just as well mentally as it does in the original context. The exact same physiological connections in the brain are made as when you had the original experience.

As you become more practised in the routine, you can shortcut the use of three anchors down to one – usually the kinaesthetic gesture.

An example of this process is presented below. One of the first resources I developed was for an energy state and I hope my experience will encourage you to develop a proficiency in resource anchoring because I have found it to be a most empowering process which is completely free and readily available.

Example

The development of an energy state through resource anchoring

When I first began to experiment with the resource anchoring process I found difficulty in finding a good example of a clean state. I think sometimes you can be too cautious. A good rule is 'Just do it.' At least you then have a benchmark to improve against. I came upon my example rather by accident. I was and still am a runner. One day after a particularly hard run I was showering and noticed I had what is known as a 'jogger's high'. This is a very energised feeling that is accompanied by a general feeling of well-being. It is caused by the effect of endorphins which are brain opiates. These can be released into the bloodstream after hard exercise. I had found an example of a clean state.

I decided I would anchor this feeling after my next run. I thought about the process and the context it would take place. I was going to anchor the state while it was actually taking place so I would not have to recall the event. I chose three anchors. The visual anchor was the shower nozzle which delivers the water. The auditory anchor is the sound of the water spraying onto my body as well as the sounds I make clearing my mouth and nose of water. The kinaesthetic anchor was a gesture I make with my fist (hiding my thumb underneath the four fingers of the same hand).

After my next run I began to shower and waited for the endorphins to act. When the feeling reached its peak I momentarily switched my focus to the three anchors to establish the association. About half an hour after I had showered I tried firing (simultaneously using all) the anchors. It worked – but only to a limited extent. The feeling was not very strong. This was possibly because the original feeling had not been strong or I had not synchronised the anchors well enough with the experience. I repeated the routine every time I went for a run for a period of a month. After this time the anchor was well established.

In time I began to use the resource to aid my running. Near the end of my run there is a rather steep hill and it is a daunting prospect. I decided to fire the anchors just before the hill. This made a tremendous difference, for I received a great boost in energy. At the end of the run I was still exhausted, because you cannot create energy from nowhere. It was as if I was borrowing it to get over a local difficulty. In time the hill itself became an anchor and I got the boost in energy as I approached the hill without having to fire my original anchors.

I am sure many people discover a process similar to this unconsciously, but I find it much more reassuring to have a process I can manage and manipulate. My number one piece of advice is to experiment. Everyone is different. Do not be put off if things do not appear to work perfectly after the first try. It takes practice. If you are easily put off, perhaps you should try to anchor perseverance!

No one would question a sportsperson for practising at their chosen sport, for keeping their body and mind in shape to deal with the physical and cognitive demands of their particular sport. In fact, just the opposite – people would wonder how a sportsperson could remain competitive if they did not practise. Recently – particularly in sport but also in other spheres of endeavour – coaches and mentors have suggested that people need to be mentally fit to succeed at their particular activity, that winning is as much a mind game as a body game. I believe these 'mind games' are about being in the appropriate emotional state, and the practice that people do in this sphere is about anchoring appropriate states. Whatever type of activity you take part in, you need to develop the appropriate physical and/or mental skills and be in the appropriate emotional state in order to achieve optimum performance.

Figure 18: *Managing your state*

Before we leave this chapter on state, I invite the reader to try out a little experiment just in case he or she is not fully convinced of his or her ability to change his or her state. We mentioned earlier in the chapter that both music and movement were activities that could influence/change our state. I would like you to combine these two activities to show that changing state is within our control.

EXERCISE

Changing your state

Below is a song you may recognise.

> *My **b**onnie lies over the ocean,*
> *My **b**onnie lies over the sea,*
> *My **b**onnie lies over the ocean,*
> *Oh **b**ring **b**ack my **b**onnie to me.*
> ***B**ring **b**ack, **b**ring **b**ack, oh **b**ring **b**ack my **b**onnie to me, to me.*
> ***B**ring **b**ack, **b**ring **b**ack, oh **b**ring **b**ack my **b**onnie to me.*

Firstly sing through the song, on your own or in a group, to remind yourself that you are familiar with it. Then you or the group should sit on a chair. A dining-room-type chair is best. Sing the song again and every time you sing a word with a 'b' in it, if you are sitting down, stand up; if you are standing up, sit down. Complete the song with the appropriate movements.

I think you will notice a change in your state.

(With thanks to Lara Ewing of NLP Comprehensive who demonstrated this routine with 60–70 course participants early one Sunday morning in Colorado.)

SUMMARY

The reason we have devoted a chapter to the topic of state is because we believe that effective learning has to be underpinned by an appropriate state. The two factors go hand in glove. This chapter has explored a number of ideas. Firstly, we have examined what state is, and in particular the nature of learning states. Secondly, we have explored the factors that influence states. And finally, we have examined the proposition that we can manage our states and outlined a routine for doing just that.

We would encourage readers to try out two things.

Firstly, attempt to track your states across a day. Are there particular states that occur at certain times? Are they positive or negative? If you find out about your states, you can then choose to change them if you feel it would be to your benefit.

Secondly, try out the routine to manage your states. Identify which state would be useful and where. Think how useful it would be to have that state when you wanted it. YOU CAN!

REFERENCES

Bach, R. (1970) *Jonathan Livingston Seagull*. Avon Books

Bentley, E. (2000) *Awareness: Biorhythms, sleep and dreaming*. London: Routledge

Bolstad, R. and Hamblett, M. (1998) *Transforming Communication*. Auckland: Longman

Brewer, C. and Campbell, D. (1991) *Rhythms of Learning.* Tuscon, AZ: Zephyr Press

Carlson, N. R. (1986) *Physiology of Behaviour.* Boston: Alleyn & Bacon

Colquhoun, W. P. (1970) 'Circadian rhythms, mental efficiency and shiftwork', *Ergonomics*, 13 (5): 558–60

Csikszsentmihalyi, M. (1997) *Finding Flow.* New York: Basic Books

Hall, L. M. (1996) *The Spirit of NLP.* Carmarthen, Wales: Anglo-American Book Company

Hobson, J. A. (1989) *Sleep.* New York: Scientific American Library

Jensen, E. (1995) *Brain-Based Learning and Teaching.* Del Mar, California: Turning Point

Kenyon, T. (1994) *Brain States.* Naples, FL: U.S. Publishing

Klein, R. and Armitage, R. (1979) 'Rhythms in human performance: 1.5-hour oscillations in cognitive style', *Science*, 204: 1236–7

Marshal, I. (1989) 'Consciousness and Bose-Einstein condensates', *New Ideas in Psychology*, 7: 73–83

Mulry, R. (1995) *In the Zone.* Arlington, Virginia: Great Ocean

Oakhill, J. (1988) 'Time of day affects aspects of memory', *Applied Cognitive Psychology*, 2: 203–12

O'Connor, J. and Seymour, J. (2003) *Introducing Neuro-linguistic Programming.* London: Aquarian Press

Parkin, M. (1998) *Tales for Trainers.* London: Kogan Page

Rauscher, F. H., Shaw, G. L. and Ky, K. N. (1993) 'Listening to Mozart enhances spatial temporal reasoning: toward a neurophysiological basis', *Neuroscience Letters*, 185: 4–7

Smith, A. (2002) *The Brain's Behind It.* Stafford: Network Educational Press

Weinberger, N. M. and McKenna, T. M. (1998) 'The sensitivity of single neurons in auditory cortex to contour', *Music Perception*, 5

The role of the senses in skill development

'In the work, *The Republic*, Plato describes a group of people who have been chained within a cave in a manner that prevented them from looking out, and forced them to look inward to the cave's back wall. A large fire burned outside the mouth of the cave, and when anything passed between the fire and the cave, it created flickering shadows on the back wall, shadows that provided the cave dwellers with information from the otherwise unseen world.

'The cave's information system reduced the outside world's complex, colourful, three-dimensional visual reality to simple two-dimensional black and white shadow representations of whatever happened to pass between the fire and the cave. It wasn't much, but the cave dwellers watched the wall with great interest, since it was their only access to the outside world. Over time, they became quite adept at interpreting these shadows, and at ascribing deeper meanings to the limited representations they could observe. Their chains, however, left them helpless to directly experience the outside world.'

Sylwester, *A Celebration of Neurons* (1995)

This allegory is an excellent example of the problem faced by our brain in interacting with the outside world, and trying to give meaning to it. If we imagine Plato's cave to be our skull and the fire at the mouth of the cave to be our sense organs, sending shadowy representations of the outside world onto the back of the cave (our sensory receptors), we can think of the cave dwellers as our brain's neural networks trying to interpret the limited representations of reality set by our sense organs and figure out what is happening out in the real world.

In this chapter we develop some of the ideas we introduced in the chapter dealing with the *action* element of the ADAX process (Chapter 4). Some of the questions we consider are:

■ What are the main abilities and capacities of our senses?

- How do these abilities feed through to management skills?
- Can we tell how someone is using his or her senses internally, how someone is thinking?
- Does everyone have the same sensory abilities?
- How do senses influence skill strategies?

In the first part of the chapter we provide some general information about the function of our senses and how they work and their characteristics. This information is necessary to understand how our senses enable us to produce an amazing range of skill strategies.

The second part describes and explores the different indicators of how someone might be thinking – that is, using their senses internally. We explore posture, eye movements and language as indicators of thinking. This can increase our ability to detect and interpret someone's body language.

In the final part we examine how the senses form skill strategies and explore how differences in individuals' sensory discriminations can determine the differences people can exhibit in deploying management skills.

Learning and skill development arise from experience. All our sensory experiences provide us with information and build the neural networks that enable us to understand the world and to act purposefully in it. A major part of the experience of our environment comes from our senses – our eyes, ears, taste buds, nose and skin – and from our bodies via nerve receptors on each muscle and organ.

Our body is well designed as a sensory receptor for collecting information. The sensory organs that pick up distant signals (eyes, ears and nose) are set at the top of the body, which acts as a stable bipod. Our parabolic ears reflect sound waves into the ear canals. Our eyes work in focused and peripheral vision, and our nose detects minute chemical messengers in the air. Taste buds monitor dissolved chemicals immediately before they enter the body. Every square inch of skin has receptors which detect touch, pressure, cold and pain. Internally, every movement we make sends messages to the brain to keep it informed of all changes in position and our orientation in space. All these sensations provide material from which learning and skill development emerge.

Interestingly, our sense receptors detect changes over quite small ranges. They can only detect a range of 72 degrees Celsius/130 degrees Fahrenheit in temperature, about 30 odour-related molecules, 10 octaves in sound pitch, four food tastes, and the narrow band of visible light in the broad electromagnetic spectrum (Sylwester, 1995). Our genetic sensory system is quite limited. However, limitations are entirely logical in that our brain could not possibly process all the information that the surrounding molecules and vibrations carry.

THE FUNCTION OF OUR SENSES

In Chapter 4 we discussed five senses – seeing, hearing, kinaesthetic (touch and feeling), taste and smell – and how these senses combine to form learning strategies. However, Hannaford (2006) suggests that to understand how our five senses contribute to skill development and learning we must consider two other 'internal senses'. The vestibular system and proprioception play a significant role in our ability to understand and learn. The vestibular system controls our sense of movement and balance and allows our bodies to maintain equilibrium under the influence of gravity. The system allows us to maintain our body position when we are standing still or when we are walking and running. Proprioception is the body's sense of itself in space. All of our muscles have prioceptive receptors which sense the degree of stretch in the muscle. These receptors provide us with both feedback about our physical position and information which enables us to move and maintain our balance. They allow us to understand the environment through our muscle sense. A sophisticated proprioceptive system is constantly aligning every part of the body giving us the ability to execute successful and complex movements.

Sylwester (1995) suggests that we can sequence our sense organs according to their reach for information, from those that gather and process information inside our bodies to those that reach out well beyond our bodies. So after the vestibular and proprioceptive senses, our next sense in terms of reach for information is our sense of taste, our gustatory sense. This sense is a contact sense and it can be seen as a final check on food before it enters the digestive system. Taste receptors on our tongue monitor four taste sensations: salty, sweet, sour and bitter. Other sensory receptors in the mouth and on the tongue and teeth provide information on temperature, texture and hardness of the food we eat.

Our kinaesthetic sense has two components: touch and internal sensations. Our sense of touch arises from the great array of sensors in our skin. The mantle of skin which surrounds our bodies is the largest organ of a person's body. The sensors in the skin can detect five elements: temperature, pressure, texture, moisture and pain. We are also aware of internal sensations which arise from a number of internal systems in our bodies such as our musculo-skeletal system, our cardiovascular system, our digestive system and our autonomic nervous system. These internal sensations are extremely important in learning. We learn to interpret these sensations and recognise them because they are often physical signs of our emotional systems.

In order to taste or touch something, you have to be in contact with it. This is not the case for our sense of smell. This sense alerts us to nearby objects through molecules they release into the air. Our sense of smell is one of the most powerful senses. People can detect odours at concentrations of several parts per million. Whereas all other sensations are mediated through the cerebral cortex, smell has a direct connection to the nervous system. This gives smell a critical role in animal survival.

Although our sense of smell may tell us that the source of the odour is nearby, it will not tell us the precise location. It will not tell us anything about the size and shape of the object. Our visual and auditory senses permit our brain to locate objects at a distance. The doubling of eyes and ears adds sensory perspective, enhancing our brain's ability to create an external impression of the object at its location. This is a significant sensory advantage. Vision and hearing are the only two senses that allow our brain to psychologically leave its skull. We see and hear the object or event at its location, not inside our brain where all sensory perception really takes place.

THE DEVELOPMENT OF SKILLS THROUGH OUR SENSES

When we use skills we act on the world through our senses. We use our sight, our hearing, our sense of touch and feeling, our senses of smell and taste, as well as our sense of balance (vestibular system) and our muscle system (proprioceptive system) to construct our thoughts and actions which in turn develop these skills. In Chapter 4 (*Action*) we described this process. We now consider some of the characteristics of our senses which give rise to such a flexible and varied process. In order to simplify this account we limit our discussion to the visual, auditory and kinaesthetic senses. Emotions, the vestibular system and the proprioceptive system are considered part of the kinaesthetic sensory system.

The visual sense

The visual sense is about making pictures. People can view the world externally or make pictures in their minds. *Visual acuity* is about the effectiveness of people's vision. It is not just about how far we can see or how well we can read small print but about all sorts of capacities. It was said that Babe Ruth could read numbers off licence plates so far away that other people could not even make out the colour of the plate. Some people can detect up to 500 different colours in the spectrum whereas others may only be able to detect a few. Some people can estimate distances, sizes, degrees of brightness, contrast and focus to a high degree. There are many different types of measurable visual variables and people have different abilities to detect these parameters.

The eyes have two ways of seeing: *detailed vision* and *contextual vision*. Imagine you are walking through a large crowd of people in a large open space. In this type of situation your eyes will operate in contextual mode, sometimes known as peripheral vision. You are not looking at anything in particular; you are just generally scanning the world around you. Suddenly a face appears in your visual field that is very familiar and you completely focus on that face to the exclusion of everything else. Your vision is now in a different mode: detailed vision.

Detailed vision is good when you want to know a lot about a little. In contrast, contextual vision roves and sees nothing in particular. It is good for detecting relationships as well as motion and movement. We observe body language in peripheral vision. Normally, people are preferentially disposed to detailed or contextual seeing. We can learn to see in both and be able to move from one form to the other when appropriate. This ability gives us much greater flexibility in the way we deploy skills.

People have the ability to remember in pictures. Not all people remember the pictures in the same way. People will remember either in a detailed mode or in a contextual mode, depending on how they saw the event in the first place. So some people may not remember the details of an event but remember the general context, whereas other people will remember details of a particular event but not the entire event or its context. Have you ever been to a party with your partner and discussed the event at a later date only to wonder whether you both attended the same party?

People vary in the ability they have to think in pictures. Some people claim to completely lack this ability. It has been suggested that an individual's ability to remember pictures is a function of two parameters: the *degree of clarity* of the image and the *stability* of the image – ie how well a person can maintain the image. Some people may have a very low ability to maintain a stable image, which may give the impression of an inability to form pictures at all.

Individuals may remember in two modes, associated and dissociated. *Associated memories* are those in which we remember things through our own eyes, so we do not appear in the memory. *Dissociated memories* are ones in which we can see ourselves in the picture so the perspective is from somewhere outside ourselves. We cannot produce associated memories of an experience where we were dissociated in the first place, and vice versa. Again it seems that individuals are predisposed to one mode or the other. Some people may live their lives in dissociated states and wonder why they cannot access associated memories. This again will have implications for the way they deploy skills.

As well as remembering pictures, we can also construct them. Take a moment and imagine a blue circle inside a green triangle. You have just accessed what we call a visual construct. If I had asked you to think of an everyday object – eg an elephant – you would have accessed a visual memory. However, with the circle and the triangle you create something new to you in your mind's eye. The visual construct ability is an extremely important faculty in science and engineering. Some of the greatest of our scientists – Einstein, for example, in his putting together the theory of relativity – owe their genius to this faculty. Reading also involves visual construction. Often, a large part of teaching reading is concerned with pronunciation. However, the basic skill in reading is in scanning the words and making pictures in our heads which make sense of those words.

Summary

The visual sense can represent a tremendous amount of information immediately and simultane-ously. The saying that 'a picture is worth a thousand words' really is true. We can get more information from a picture than any other representational system. The visual sense is the realm of space, whereas the auditory sense is the realm of time – and it is the auditory sense that we discuss next.

The auditory sense

Unlike our use of the visual sense, when we represent things for other people to hear we can only represent them sequentially in time. Auditory distinctions are concerned with differences between one instant in time and another. People vary enormously in their ability to make these distinctions.

In order to appreciate how the auditory sense works it is important to understand and distinguish two components of the sense: tonal and digital. *Auditory tonal* describes an ability to hear and distinguish between sounds. People with a facility for the auditory tonal are able to distinguish between different aspects of sounds – volumes, tones, rhythms, pitches, tempos and locations. These people are good at knowing whether something sounds right. *Auditory digital* mainly describes vocalised words and whether they make sense together. Understanding and making sense of conversation is an auditory digital ability. Another aspect of the auditory digital is our internal dialogue. This can be a very useful process or a very destructive one. People who cannot dissociate from their internal dialogue have no awareness that they are having an internal dialogue and it becomes them – their conscious awareness *is* their internal dialogue. However, people who can dissociate from their internal dialogue can monitor it and redirect it as appropriate. The ability to dissociate from internal dialogue is a critical factor affecting self-awareness.

Most people use tonal and digital in tandem, and both are necessary to fully understand the many conversations we have every day.

As with the visual sense, we hear in a *detailed* mode and a *contextual* mode.

Detailed people want to listen to one sound or one conversation at a time. They process sounds linearly. They do not like distractions. They can listen to the radio or hold a conversation but not at the same time. Detailed managers often ask their secretaries to 'hold all calls'. They tend to figure out what to say before they talk. For them, content of conversation is what is important, not context.

Contextual people appear to thrive on chaos. These are the types who can listen to the radio, work on the Internet, hold a conversation and take a mobile phone call all at the same time. They simply extract the basic content from it all without bothering with the details. They leave their doors open for people to drop in, like phone calls and generally perform many functions at the same time. They are good at recognising tone or mood, and they speak before they think. Context, not content, is important. Talk does not have to be focused or directed. Conversation helps in determining the context or mood.

It takes discipline and skill to develop an ability to use both forms of listening.

There are two dimensions to remembering sounds: *auditory tonal remembered* describes a memory of what something sounds like, whereas *auditory digital remembered* describes some previously heard words such as a poem or a speech.

A facility in remembering the auditory tonal is usually well developed in musicians. They remember how a note sounds to tune their instruments to. They remember sequence of notes and the timing between notes. In learning a foreign language it is necessary to remember what a word means, what it sounds like, and how it is pronounced. People who speak several languages usually store and speak each language in a different tone and tempo. When they speak each language, they remember the tone and tempo. This stops them from confusing the different languages. When they switch from one language to another, they shift into a different physiology and speak in a different tone and at a different rate.

The ability to create *auditory tonal constructs* is most common amongst musicians, poets and speechwriters. Musical composers are able to hear in their minds what a composition will sound like. Poets construct combinations of words that not only make sense but that also sound right. Speechmakers construct speeches that inspire people through sounds as well as words. Anyone who matches his or her voice to a situation is forming an auditory tonal construct. Our educational system is geared to training students to respond with *auditory digital constructs*, and their progress is measured on their ability to carry that out. This of course is our examination system.

Summary

An auditory tonal ability is valuable for adding emphasis and for enriching 'raw data'. Two people can say the same thing and yet have two totally different impacts. As every good speaker knows, an effective speech is more than just delivering words. Whenever a manager wishes to influence or persuade, he or she will find a facility in the auditory tonal essential. The auditory digital is valuable for keeping track of our memories and experiences. It is also important for planning and setting direction – two very common components of management skills. It is also valuable for summarising, drawing conclusions, reasoning and analysis – common components of cognitive skills for managers.

The kinaesthetic sense

The kinaesthetic sense is a more complex sense to understand because it deals not only with the tactile sense of feeling but also with the emotional aspect of feeling as well as the vestibular system (the sense of equilibrium) and the proprioceptive system (muscle sense).

As noted in Chapter 3, we have sensors in our skin to detect temperature, pressure, texture, moisture and pain. People vary in their ability to detect changes in these tactile parameters. When people can remember and access these sensations, they can use these memories to help them understand physical operations and environments. This faculty can be extremely useful in certain types of management jobs. Managers who can use this faculty may be described as having a 'hands-on' approach, and it will influence how they deploy their skills.

Touch
Touch is an essential requirement for effective learning. There is a greater array of receptors for touch around the mouth and hands than in any other area of the body (Penfield and Jasper, 1954). Babies love to put things in their mouths, not to eat them but to touch and fully sense them with their mouths and hands. Throughout our lives, using 'hands-on' experience during the learning process greatly increases learning efficiency Whenever touch is combined with the other senses, much more of the brain is activated, thus building more complex nerve networks and tapping into more learning potential.

Internal feelings, emotions
Internal feelings or emotions are the most common ways in which people make evaluations about the world. This makes this internal sense extremely important in decision-making. People often go along with

a proposition if it looks right, sounds right or feels right. The feeling sense is often the one which unconsciously is the most influential. We sometimes refer to it as our 'sixth sense' or our intuition because it is not often transparent or easy to explain.

In Chapter 8 we examined how people might manage their state, and in particular a technique in which we could use 'anchors' to engage a remembered feeling. So, for example, we might experience a feeling of relaxation when we sit in our garden under a blossoming tree. At times in the future when we think about our garden and the sounds associated with it, we can re-experience the feeling of relaxation. This technique uses our ability to recall past feelings. A facility to recall past feelings and manage our state is a prerequisite for the effective deployment of many management skills.

Memory of internal sensations

The memory of internal sensations plays a major role in human performance. It enables us to remember the feelings associated with maintaining body equilibrium (the vestibular system), and the messages our muscles send us to tell us how and when we should move our limbs and orientate our bodies to perform a certain physical function (the proprioceptive system). It is an essential requirement for any athletic feat – for instance, knowing how much force is required to propel a football and at what angle. Mulry (1995) emphasises the link between four physical characteristics of our bodies – relaxation, balance, flexibility and focus – and the four similar characteristics of our mind. To achieve these four states we must be alert to the internal sensations in our bodies. Mulry argues that relaxation, balance, flexibility and focus are the bases for deploying all management skills with efficiency and elegance.

Summary

Our kinaesthetic sense is less well understood because it is dependent on what senses you categorise as kinaesthetic. Our sense of touch is very important in learning, particularly in conjunction with our visual sense. Our internal feelings (emotions) are intimately linked to how we evaluate and make decisions. Our muscle sense and our sense of balance are essential to the development of any physical skill.

ACTIVITY

Questionnaires: What is your preferred sense?

The sense modality someone is using can often be inferred from the particular sensory language he or she employs. Your responses to the statements in the first part of this double questionnaire should suggest which sense modality you prefer.

Tick against each statement you agree with.

1	I pay attention to what I see.	☐		
2	I let things rattle around in my head.		☐	
3	I often reflect on my physical sensations.			☐
4	I see things in my mind.	☐		
5	I like it when things click into place for me.		☐	
6	I churn things over in my stomach.			☐
7	I make up pictures in my head.	☐		

#	Statement	Visual	Auditory	Kinaesthetic
8	I enjoy listening to music.		☐	
9	I pay a great deal of attention to my emotions.			☐
10	I sometimes ask people to draw me a picture.	☐		
11	I talk with myself, either aloud or silently.		☐	
12	When I sit, I feel the chair.			☐
13	I try to get a mental picture of things.	☐		
14	I often imagine hearing a dialogue in my head.		☐	
15	It is important for me to feel physically comfortable.			☐
16	I look for the big picture.	☐		
17	I maintain attention at lectures and speeches.		☐	
18	I trust my gut impressions.			☐
19	I hate it when people block my view.	☐		
20	I like a good conversation.		☐	
21	I like physical touch.			☐
22	I tend to write things down.	☐		
23	I prefer a boss to explain things to me verbally.		☐	
24	I like hands-on involvement with problems.			☐
25	I look at the person who is speaking to me.	☐		
26	I pay more attention to what people say than how they look.		☐	
27	I like to touch people when I am talking to them.			☐

Now count up the number of boxes you have ticked in each of the three columns. The left column represents visual statements, the middle column auditory statements, and the right column kinaesthetic statements. The column with the most ticks corresponds to your preferred sense; the column with the fewest to your least preferred.

The sense modality someone likes best may alternatively be inferred from how easy or difficult he or she finds it to think in one or other particular modality. Your responses to the statements in the second part of this double questionnaire should also suggest which sense modality you prefer. Indicate on the scale how difficult (4) or easy (1) you find imagining each of the listed tasks. Use whole-number scores only.

		Easy			Difficult
1	Remembering the face of a teacher from when you were at school.	1	2	3	4
2	Recalling hearing which of your friends has the quietest voice.	1	2	3	4
3	Listening to the sound your voice makes under water.	1	2	3	4
4	What it feels like to roll a car wheel down the road.	1	2	3	4
5	What it feels like to put your left hand in very cold water.	1	2	3	4
6	Hearing a favourite tune in your head.	1	2	3	4

		Easy			Difficult
7	Visualising the largest book in your house.	1	2	3	4
8	What it feels like to hold a smooth glass paperweight in both hands.	1	2	3	4
9	Seeing a favourite entertainer on your TV screen wearing a top hat.	1	2	3	4
10	Picturing which of your friends or relations has the longest hair.	1	2	3	4
11	Thinking what it would feel like to stroke a cat or dog.	1	2	3	4
12	Listening to church bells ringing in the distance.	1	2	3	4
13	Thinking how it would feel to put on a pair of wet socks.	1	2	3	4
14	Recall hearing the voice of a childhood friend.	1	2	3	4
15	Seeing the colour of the front door where you live or work.	1	2	3	4
16	Hearing a car engine starting on a cold morning.	1	2	3	4
17	Visualising the stripes on a tiger.	1	2	3	4
18	What it feels like to jump off a 1.2-metre-/4-foot–high wall.	1	2	3	4

Now copy your scores onto this triple grid:

Question 1		Question 2		Question 4	
Question 7		Question 3		Question 5	
Question 9		Question 6		Question 8	
Question 10		Question 12		Question 11	
Question 15		Question 14		Question 13	
Question 17		Question 16		Question 18	
TOTAL		TOTAL		TOTAL	

The left-hand grid represents visual imagination, the middle grid auditory imagination, and the right-hand grid kinaesthetic imagination. The lowest total score corresponds to your preferred sense; the highest total score to your least preferred sense.

These two inventories are only rough guides to your preferred sense. To confirm them, notice your behaviours over a period of time and ask other people who are familiar with the indicators to tell you what they think is your preferred sense, along with the reasons why.

More than one sense

Individuals often have a preferred sense. My own preferred sense is visual. Although I do use the other two, I tend to use visual language predominantly, and I rely and trust what I see and I tend to think by forming pictures in my head more often than sounds or feelings. Some people have a joint preferred sense – eg visual *and* auditory. I once heard Nick Faldo's coach on the radio explaining that Nick seems to have an equal faculty for all three sense systems. When he hit a shot he could tell whether it was good by seeing how the ball moved through the air, by the sound of the club on the ball and by the feeling in his body.

Sometimes people may have a *lead representational system*. Mine is the same as my preferred system – visual. Some of my colleagues have a different lead system. For instance, one colleague when recalling a memory such as a holiday will always start with a picture in her head. She will then move to her preferred system, kinaesthetic, and it is feelings which mainly dominate the rest of her thoughts about the holiday.

So we can take in information in one sense and represent it internally in another. Sometimes this process is immediate and unconscious. We call these links between the senses 'synaesthesia patterns'. Some are common to many people but others are peculiar to individuals. They can be so strong and consistent that they act as if they are hard-wired. The most common synaesthesia patterns are see–feel and hear–feel. Some people feel faint when they see a hypodermic needle. I always feel a sense of kinship when I hear an accent from near my home town, Preston. Many people associate colours with mood – red with anger, blue with peace. Between 30 and 40 synaesthesia patterns have been identified (Woodsmall, 1999). There are many skills where the ability to perform them effectively depends on the development of highly refined synaesthesia patterns.

If we think in just one representational system, we limit ourselves to just one perspective. If we have a decision to make, we can gather a good deal more information about the problem by thinking in all the representation systems. Multisensory thinking is at the basis of effective skill deployment, particularly in the realm of decision-making.

Figure 19: *Multisensory learning*

Below is an exercise for groups of three people to practise the faculty of multisensory thinking.

GROUP EXERCISE

Practising multisensory thinking

In groups of three, person number 1 tells a short story using just one sensory language, visual. The second person retells the story just changing the sensory language to auditory. The third person then retells the story using the third sensory language, kinaesthetic.

The group perform this exercise three times, using the different sensory languages in the following order.

Round 1:	visual	auditory	kinaesthetic
Round 2:	kinaesthetic	visual	auditory
Round 3:	auditory	kinaesthetic	visual

After the three rounds the group should discuss the issues and problems involved in the exercise.

CAN WE DETECT HOW SOMEONE IS THINKING?

When people think or speak in a particular sense modality there are certain physical and behavioural characteristics that we can detect. The ability to spot these characteristics is a very useful skill in the management of people. A large part of the management of people is influencing, and being in rapport with people is a prerequisite of influencing. The ability to match someone's sensory preference is a useful tool in creating rapport (James and Shepard, 2001).

- *Visual people* tend to have an upright, erect posture. They stand tall with their head up and shoulders back. They tend to move quickly, with tight, jerky movements, and their eyes may be flicking from object to object. Their breathing tends to be shallow and high up in their chest. They speak quickly because they see pictures which contain a lot of information and they need to speak quickly to get everything out. People accessing visually tend to look up so the elevation of their eyeline is often up, albeit momentarily.

- *Kinaesthetic people* tend to have a looseness to their movements and be quite flowing in the way they move. They breathe down in their belly and their voice seems to come from down there too. They appear to have more breath to work with, giving their voice an airy quality. They tend to speak slowly, because feelings have more momentum and do not move as quickly as pictures. Someone accessing kinaesthetically will look down to their right and describe how they feel by speaking more slowly, using fewer words and taking more time.

- *Auditory people* tend to have a more variable posture. They may tilt their head to one side in the telephone posture. When talking to auditory people they may not look straight at you but turn their dominant ear to you so that they can hear you more clearly. Their breathing ranges from high up in the shoulders to down in their belly, and this means that their tonality varies considerably. Highly auditory people will have a rich manner of speaking, almost like singing a song. They are very melodic and rhythmical. When people process auditorily, their eyes move from side to side.

- *Auditory digital people* are concerned with the meaning of the words they use. They often stand erect with their arms folded. This can also signal someone who is cutting themselves off from you. With an auditory digital person it is a sign that he or she is interested in what you are saying. So the clue itself is unreliable and you must seek other evidence in order to have confidence in its meaning. Another typical pose is 'the thinker' – one arm folded across the chest and the other bent with the hand on the chin.

  There tends to be some rigidity around the neck and shoulder area. They often have their jaw clenched. You may see their jaw muscles moving as they grind their teeth or talk to themselves in their head. As a result of this tension, breathing is quite restricted. For auditory digital people tonality is irrelevant. The voice is just a means of communication. Their voices can have an even tonality or sometimes a monotone. Their gaze tends to be down to their left. Sometimes they may appear to be looking through you, but it is not that they are not interested – they are just processing the words you have spoken.

These general clues are not infallible but they should enable you to take an educated guess at the way people are processing at any particular moment when you first meet them.

Pattern	Visual	Kinaesthetic	Auditory (tonal)	Auditory (digital)
Words and expressions that predicate a representational system	See, look, vision, bright, focus, perspective, scan, colourful	Feel, grasp, touch, firm, warm, cool, get a handle on, get hold of	Hear, listen, loud, rings like a bell, sounds like, harmonious, playing our tune	Statistically speaking, know, reasonable, logical, understand
Posture	Straight, upright, head and shoulders up	Curved, bowed, head and shoulders down	'Telephone' posture, head tilted to one side	Arms folded, erect, head up, one hand on chin
Breathing	High up in the chest	Low in abdomen	Full range from high in chest to low in abdomen	Restricted, tight
Voice, tonality, speed and volume	High, clear, fast and loud, coming from throat area	Low, airy, slow and soft, coming from abdomen	Melodic, rhythmic, variable, from throat to abdomen	Monotone, clipped, consistent
Eye elevation in relation to others	Above others, looking up across the top	Below others, looking down, quite often to their right	Level, moving from side to side, often diverted down or away to listen	Gazing over others' heads, appearing detached and dissociated

Table 6: *Clues to other people's representational systems*

Table 6 is based on a summary of information in James and Shepard (2001).

Eye movements associated with sensory accessing

Our eyes move in a systematic way depending on how we are thinking. Studies have shown that different types of eye movement are associated with activating different parts of the brain (Luria, 1966; Day, 1964; Dilts *etal*, 1980; Butler, 1998; DeVore, 1982). There is a neurological connection between eye movements and our representational systems. When we remember something, our eyes tend to move up and to the left. When constructing a picture in our minds, our eyes tend to move up and to the right. The eyes move across and to the left for remembered sound and to the right for constructed sounds. When accessing feelings, our eyes typically go down to our right. When talking to ourselves (internal dialogue), our eyes go down to the left. Defocusing the eyes and staring straight ahead can also be a sign of internal visualising. Most right-handed people have eye movements as shown in Figure 20. This pattern may be reversed for left-handed people, who may look right for remembered images and sounds, and left for constructed images and sounds.

Eye movement detection is a skill and not simply a matter of being aware of the above rules. There are always anomalies and the degree of movement varies widely between individuals. The answer is not just in applying generalisations but in calibrating the movements with the activities the person is involved in.

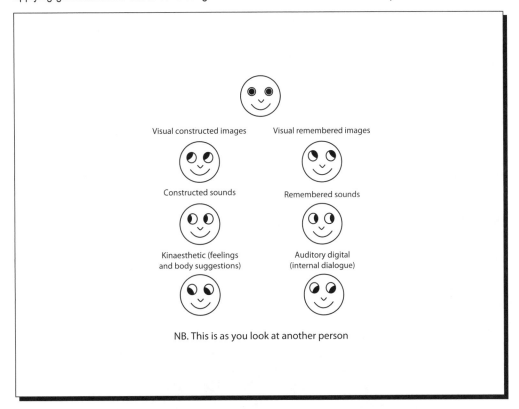

Figure 20: *Eye movements and their general interpretation (for right-handed people)*

Thinking and sensory language

It has been suggested that internal thinking processes are reflected in the sensory language that a person uses. When a person is creating pictures internally, therefore, he or she may use correspondingly visual language when in conversation with another person. This also means that when you are in conversation with a visual person, you are much more likely to achieve rapport with him or her by choosing sensory words which match the sensory words he or she is using. Table 7 contains lists of words and expressions that would match each of the four sensory types described. It is based on tabular information in James and Shepard (2001).

Visual	Auditory (tonal)	Kinaesthetic	Auditory (digital)
see	hear	feel	basic
colourful	tone	grasp	knowledge
reflect	call	get hold of	principle
look	say	touch	specific
scan	rhythm	heavy	random
murky	clash	slimy	usual
hazy	speak	gritty	understand
gaze	screech	contact	enhanced
go blank	ring	wobble	compatible
observe	shrill	tight	idea
brilliant	quiet	sharp	variable
scene	shout	hit	reciprocal
flash	loud	uptight	learning
highlight	cadence	tickle	value-added
opaque	echo	dig	concept
snapshot	babble	impact	logical

Table 7: *Words and expressions that generally correspond to representational systems*

Sensory acuity just about pervades all management skills, so the development of this faculty is critical in the deployment of management skills. Below is an exercise that can be carried out, unobtrusively, to improve sensory acuity.

EXERCISE

Improving sensory acuity

Write down your answers to the following questions. But let no one else see them.

1 Can you think of colleagues or members of staff who are visual?

2 Can you think of any colleagues or members of staff who are auditory?

3 Can you think of any colleagues or members of staff who are kinaesthetic?

4 What have you noticed about these people in terms of their behaviours and postures, their eye movements and the sensory language they use? Make these observations support or negate what you think is their preferred sense.

5 How have you worked with these people in the past?

6 How might you work with them in the future?

SKILL STRATEGIES

It was mentioned in Chapter 4 that management skills, or for that matter any skill, could be represented as a series of sensory accesses and that the effectiveness of the skill was dependent on two factors. Firstly, there are the sense modalities chosen and the sequence in which they are deployed. Secondly, there are abilities or the distinctions that each individual can make within each of the sense modalities.

Spelling Strategy

In order to demonstrate this we can examine a common successful strategy: the spelling strategy (O'Connor and Seymour, 2003; Woodsmall, 1999). The most effective strategy for spelling is a visual one.

Firstly, the individual thinks of something pleasant and familiar so that he or she can recognise a sense of familiarity. He or she then registers the word he or she is going to spell (Ade). Then he or she visualises the word internally (Vi). He or she then accesses an internal feeling of familiarity which tells him or her if it is the right or wrong spelling (Ki). When this feels right he or she can spell the word orally (Ade). Rather than doing this routine orally it can be done by writing the word down.

So the steps in developing a successful spelling strategy are as follows:

- Firstly, think of something that feels familiar and pleasant. This will help you recognise your personal feeling of familiarity (Ki).

- Secondly, look at the word you want to spell for a few seconds. Access the feeling of familiarity while you are looking at the word. Say it out loud. This helps to register the word for yourself or anyone listening (Ve, Ki, Ade).

- Thirdly, look up to your left (right, if you are left-handed) and visualise the word. You should be able to see the word in your mind's eye (Vi).

- Fourthly, quickly look down to your right. Do you get the feeling of familiarity? If not, repeat the first three stages until you do (Ki).

- Fifthly, spell the word either orally or by writing it down (Ade)

- Sixthly, a good way to check if you have really mastered the strategy is to spell the word backwards. A visual strategy allows you to spell backwards just as easily as forwards.

Individuals who read a lot become familiar with the spelling of a vast number of words and hence tend to be good spellers. The sequence of sensory accesses for this strategy would be:

Ki, Ve, Ki, Ade, Vi, Ki, Ade

There is another strategy for spelling: an auditory/phonetic approach. In the phonetic approach people try to remember what the word sounds like. This is a less effective strategy because of the eccentricities of the English language in which words that have a similar spelling may be pronounced in several different ways. Think of words that contain the letters 'ou'. We might come up with *tough*, *route* and *doubt*, all of which have the 'ou' combination of vowels.

Just sequencing the sensory accesses in a particular order is not sufficient to produce an effective and elegant strategy for deploying a particular skill. Much of the variability in the efficacy and elegance of skill deployment is concerned with what abilities each individual possesses within the way he or she uses the senses. Some people can make highly refined distinctions within their sense modalities which enables them to perform much more effectively than people who lack these distinctions.

For instance, I personally am limited in my ability to carry out the spelling visual strategy because I have difficulty making the image of a word stable. Certainly, this makes it difficult for me to read the word as easily backwards as forwards. People who have no difficulty with this strategy can form clear and stable images and simply read off the letters backwards or forwards. I seem to be able to spell more effectively forwards than backwards, and I guess an element of auditory strategy accompanies my mainly visual strategy. This allows me to compensate for the instability of my mental images.

Some people can manipulate the characteristics of their visual sense to help them perform the strategy more effectively. Some individuals can alter the size of the letters, the font style, colour or shape of the letters to enable them to read the letters more readily and easily. This is something we can all train ourselves to do to some extent.

Auditory multi-tracking (or how to listen to more than one conversation at a time)

A good example of an effective strategy and the ability to make sensory distinctions arose during a recent skills development programme I was running. The group I was training was examining strategies people used to listen to more than one conversation at a time.

We are often in situations where we are tempted or would find it useful to listen to more than one conversation at a time. Different people use different abilities to do it. The simple routine described below examines three situations in which someone can demonstrate what strategies he or she uses to achieve it. The routine requires three people working as a group; if there are multiple groups, the results are more useful because it is then possible to explore a wider variety of strategies.

Routine for auditory multi-tracking

One person sits on a chair and the other two people walk around the chair, one in a clockwise direction and one in an anti-clockwise direction. As the two people walk around the person on the chair, they read a series of descriptive adjectives of two different characters – eg:

Male	Dark brown hair
Black shoes	Light fawn skirt
5ft 8ins	Female
Gold wristwatch	Brown shoes
Brown belt	5ft 9ins
Ponytail	Silver wristwatch
Dark blue pullover	Pageboy haircut
Light brown hair	Black belt

The persons walking round read the lists at the same pace with words alternating from each list. After the groups complete their lists the person in the chair is required to recite back the two lists keeping the two descriptions separate. The tutor then debriefs the group asking them what strategy they used for completing the task. It is best to ask who remembered the most items correctly, and start with that person. (Note that the items can be in any order – the only requirement is that the two lists are kept separate.)

The most effective strategy to emerge from the exercise (highest number of items recalled from two separate lists) was:

1   Ability to recognise tone of voice (distinguishing between lists) – auditory tonal

2   Ability to hear and remember the words – auditory digital

3   Ability to form an internal picture of two people in two different locations and dress them – visual internal

which may thus be transcribed as: Ae, Adi, Vi.

This strategy was repeated until both the fictitious characters were fully described. Although this was the best strategy, there were many variations and distinctions which were used by different people. Some people used tailor's dummies locating one to their upper left and one to the upper right at a distance of about 12 inches from their eyes. Some people used their relations and dressed them – eg partner, parent, sibling or child. This seemed to be a good strategy for keeping the lists separate. The most amazing distinctions were made by one person who used dummies to dress. He would add an item of clothing or two to one of the dummies and then, in his head, move that dummy around to the back and bring the other one into play and dress that for a while. Then he would swap them over, move the second one around the back and bring the other one round to the front. The astonishing thing was that when they were out of sight he did not need to remember what they were wearing because they reappeared just how he had left them. In fact, he revealed later that this was a really easy task for him since he could have worked on up to eight 'screens' at a time. His mind was like a TV producer's studio, and he could work independently on eight different visual operations in his head.

There were other strategies, such as auditory ones by which people tried rote memory to bring back the two lists – but these were nothing like as successful as the visual strategies.

In two other versions of the same routine that our group exercised with, one of them used two stories rather than two lists, and the other used one list and one story.

The delegates were then given 15 minutes to think about their strategies, and we then finished with a plenary session examining the variety of strategies used.

Those final two rounds produced some interesting results – but it was the first round that produced the greatest variety in sensory characteristics used and demonstrated both the remarkable number of individual strategies there are for achieving the same result and the incredible distinctions people can make within their sense modalities.

SUMMARY

This chapter has built on the ideas introduced in Chapter 4 (*Action*). In the first part of the chapter we discussed the function of the senses and some of the ways in which they work. Because our senses are so intimately linked to the deployment of skill strategies, it is necessary to be familiar with how our senses work. This knowledge gives us an appreciation of the nature of skill strategies and how they may vary from one person to another.

The second part of the chapter explored some of the indicators that tell us which sense a person is using while he or she thinks. These indicators manifest themselves as part of a person's body language.

Finally, we described two examples of how individuals use their senses to build skills: spelling strategy and the skill of multi-tracking (listening to more than one conversation at a time). These examples are illustrative of how senses contribute to skill strategies.

If you find someone who does something very well, what strategy is he or she using? Try adopting other people's strategies. You may suddenly find you can do something you did not know you could.

Examining our sense modalities is a very useful lens/perspective through which to examine aspects of skill development. As our knowledge of neuroscience grows we are learning more about the complex mechanisms that link the operations in the brain, our senses and the way they interact to enable us to use all the cognitive, behavioural and linguistic skills we deploy as managers and professionals.

In particular, the study of the senses throws light on the reasons for the wide variety of strategies people employ in deploying skills which on the surface appear to be the same. It also reveals the incredible capacities that we can enjoy through our senses and how amenable they are to development in the important context of management and skill development.

REFERENCES

Bolstad, R. and Hamblett, M. (1999) 'Visual digital: modality of the future?', *NLP World*. Vol 6, No 1

Butler, B. (1998) 'The lesser used perceptual systems', *Anchor Point*, Sept.: 37–40

Day, M. (1964) 'An eye movement phenomenon relating to attention, thoughts and anxiety', *Perceptual Motor Skills*, Oct., 19: 443–6

DeVore, S. (1982) *The Neuropsychology of Achievement Study Guide.* San Francisco: SyberVision Systems

Dilts, R., Grinder, J., Bandler, R. and DeLozier, J. (1980) *Neuro-Linguistic Programming: Vol. 1. The Study of the Structure of Subjective Experience. Cupertino, California: Meta Publications*

Hannaford, C. (2006) *Smart Moves.* Arlington, Virginia: Great Ocean

James, T. and Shepard, D. (2001) *Presenting Magically.* Carmarthen, Wales: Crown House

Luria, A. R. (1966) *Higher Cortical Functions in Man.* New York: Basic Books

Mulry, R. (1995) *In the Zone.* Arlington, Virginia: Great Ocean

O'Connor, J. and Seymour, J. (2003) *Introduction to Neuro-Linguistic Programming.* London: HarperCollins.

Penfield, W. and Jasper, H. H. (1954) *Epilepsy and the Functional Anatomy of the Human Brain.* Boston: Little Brown

Sylwester, R. (1995) *A Celebration of Neurons.* Danvers, MA: ASCD

Woodsmall, W. (1999) *Strategies.* Course notes accompanying a programme on Behaviour Modelling.

Personal characteristics and learning

> **'If a man does not keep pace with his companions, perhaps it is because he hears a different drummer.'**
>
> *Henry David Thoreau (1854)*

INTRODUCTION

To say we are all different is a cliché. 'Difference' is a concept that has been used in many types of management jargon – for example:

- 'Doing things differently' in strategy and change
- 'Accepting' or 'Working with difference' in equal opportunities
- 'Difference as strength' and 'Embracing difference' in diversity
- 'Working through differences' in conflict resolution.

There are many more topical slogans that extol the virtues of difference. It is true that we are all different. Unless you are a twin, it is unlikely that you will meet anyone who is exactly like you, whether in looks, personality, attitudes, beliefs, likes and dislikes or any of many more characteristics.

EXERCISE

Difference

Make a list of the following groups of people:

- List all the people you meet or contact in one hour at work.
- Now add to the list five to 10 close friends.
- Finally, add members of your immediate family.

You will probably have quite a long list of names.

From what you know about them for each person on the list briefly answer the following two questions:

- In what ways is this person like me?
- In what ways is this person different from me?

When I do the above exercise with a group and we review what is included on the lists, a number of comments can usually be made:

- There are usually at least as many differences as similarities, often more, because we all like to think of ourselves as individuals and differentiate ourselves from other people.
- We often recognise more similarities to ourselves with people we like.
- There are myriad ways in which you can differentiate yourself from others.
- The characteristics that you have chosen, in all categories of difference, are likely to be those that are important to you.

This is an interesting exercise to do and it can suggest some interesting findings. It encourages you to identify the people on the list and define your own terms of difference, so that even if you initially use some well-known categories the list is personal to you.

In this chapter we briefly define and review the key personal characteristics that lead to personal differences:

- What models can be used to describe these differences?
- What are the key stable personal differences and what is their impact on our life?
- How important are those differences in learning and development?
- How do the differences influence how people learn, particularly in experiential situations?
- What are the implications of difference for each person's learning, and how can we use this information in personal and skill development?

The questions above have helped to structure this chapter, which we believe provides an important means of understanding and valuing differences that are often found when individuals work together on self-development. We all find certain people, or types of people, more difficult or easy to work with. In many circumstances we probably do not stop to ask why. However, in a work situation, or project team, we sometimes find that certain individuals are difficult and we realise that it is because they do not work or think in the same way that we do or because they see things from a different perspective.

When I work with groups of managers for a period of time, I strongly encourage them to work with as many different members of the group as possible and to actively try to understand the differences that they find, through using the models presented in this chapter. These models provide explanations of differences and encourage each of us to engage with people who are similar or different from us with understanding on which to base learning and to try out different behaviours.

This chapter does not intend to provide a comprehensive account of every factor or characteristic that might account for individual differences, but it collects together theories and applications of difference that have been found to specifically influence learning from experience and to suggest ways in which difference may be of practical significance.

THE CAUSES OF PERSONAL DIFFERENCES

Psychologists and other social scientists have long-running debates about the causes of difference, particularly the contribution of genetics as opposed to environment in explaining our make-up – the so-called 'nature-versus-nurture debate' (see for example Huczynski and Buchanan, 2004). There are many arguments for an emphasis on either environment or inheritance to explain differences, and similarities. However, there seems to be some agreement that it is probably a combination of our genetic inheritance, which provides certain predispositions and potentialities, together with environmental influences that actually determines what each one of us becomes. We can see the influence of genetic inheritance within families on height, on bodily and facial features and on other personal characteristics. Yet the influence of the environment is obvious, too, in the way we do many things, our speech patterns, our accent, our religion and our choice of friends and lifestyle.

We might therefore expect each of us to be different from everyone else due to the unique nature of the combination of our genetic and environmental experience, and still also have certain characteristics that are similar if not the same as others'. You may even find if you compare your list from the first exercise with other people's lists that you have selected similar types of construct – for example, related to personality, physical characteristics or certain behaviours.

UNDERSTANDING DIFFERENCE

In trying to understand and make sense of difference we can identify consistencies of difference that are relevant to everyone, so that each person can be placed somewhere on a dimension that is relevant to them – for example, height, weight, hair colour, all of which can be assessed easily. The main categories of difference that are commonly used include physical differences, intellectual differences, gender, psychological and personality differences, personal style, interests, nationality and religious and cultural differences. Some of these differences are physical and therefore obvious, as discussed above. However, there are certain differences – for example, ability or personality characteristics – that can only be inferred through observing someone's behaviour. So on an informal level we make judgements of others' personality and style, using cues we pick up when we meet them, although these judgements may change as we gather personal experience of them and get to know more about them. Making judgements about others is important to us so that we in turn know how to respond to them. We use our implicit personality theory to make these judgements based on consistencies that we believe to exist from our experience. There are many techniques used to help determine what constructs we use to interpret our implicit personality theory and how we assess other people. Probably the best-known is the repertory grid ('rep grid') technique (Fransella and Bannister, 1977), which is used in both psychological and management research.

The tasks for psychologists and those interested in understanding difference is to identify and define constructs that are stable over time, that are relevant to everyone and that can be assessed. There are many different characteristics that have been thought to fulfil these criteria, particularly related to intelligence and personality and often assessed through inventories.

The use of inventories to assess these characteristics relies on the belief that there is consistency in a person's behaviour over time, and that it is therefore important to assess deep-seated characteristics thought to underpin the consistency in what we do. Most people expect people to behave in much the same way over time and in different situations – otherwise, it makes living and working with others a risky and uncertain experience. There is likely to be some variation, of course, taking account of situational variations, although we expect general consistency.

ACTIVITY

Think about friends or colleagues at work.

How did they behave last time you saw them?

Unless there are unusual circumstances, you will surely expect them to behave in a similar way when you next meet.

If your nearest work colleague is usually quiet, thoughtful and well-organised, you probably expect that this approach will continue on most days and also be evident at home or in other situations too. If one day he or she behaves in a loud, argumentative way, you will probably assume that something is wrong, and might ask him or her about it.

Think about what the world would be like if you had no idea of a friend's likely reaction or behaviour each time you meet. We expect consistency from people we know, although we may be more tolerant of apparently inconsistent behaviour in strangers.

Key differences important in learning

Although it is interesting to review all types of personal difference, there are certain key differences that are most closely related to learning – and these are the ones that are the main focus of the remainder of the chapter.

The key differences important to learning can be identified by considering what is involved in learning. All learning must involve:

- a learner's personality characteristics – the *personality*
- intellectual capacity – *intelligence*, and
- preferences for perceiving and interpreting – a *cognitive style*.

It is thought that these three are key factors that account for differences in learning (Riding and Rayner, 1998). Riding and Rayner researched and developed a model of cognitive style that is discussed below. Intelligence and personality are thought to be the deepest and most stable factors underpinning learning, and to interact with cognitive style, which is perceived as an independent construct defined (Riding and Rayner, 1998; p.7) as:

'a relatively fixed aspect of learning performance [that] influences a person's general attainment or achievement in learning situations.'

We thus consider an individual's personality, intelligence and cognitive style as factors that might be the major influence on learning. Each of the constructs has a variety of measures, as we shall see, although there seem to be general physical and psychological features that underpin them. They are thought to be developed very early in life, probably prior to birth, and then are 'cemented' during our early years, through experience.

PERSONALITY

Ever since the ancient Greeks identified four 'humours' the different combinations of which in the composition of humans determined mental and physical characteristics, people have been interested in personality differences. Although such ideas proved to be an inaccurate account of personality, the search for explanations of personal differences and for a comprehensive framework to describe the range of different personalities continued. One of the most enduring models of personality has been the Myers-Briggs Type Indicator (MBTI), which was developed from Jung's work on type (Myers, 1980) and which has been widely researched and used internationally. It is interesting that the MBTI dimensions are similar in interpretation to four of the 'Big Five' personality dimensions (Costa and McCrea, 1992), which were defined through a meta-analysis of many previous personality measures. They suggest that the Big Five are the basic traits from which most other measures are formed, so confirming the comprehensive nature of the MBTI measure.

The MBTI is well known and used extensively in personal development, team-building and management development, and the dimensions are described in many books on this subject.

The four dimensions identified in the MBTI are:

- extraversion–introversion   (E-I)

- sensing–intuiting   (S-N)

- thinking–feeling   (T-F)

- judging–perceiving   (J-P).

Identifying type usually requires completion of an inventory (effectively a questionnaire), from which each person receives a score on the dimensions. These scores sort people into types, signified by four of the letters shown above (one from each pair), making 16 different possible combinations – so everyone is fitted into one of 16 types.

Assessing type

There is not space here to provide a full description of every aspect of the type dimensions, and if readers wish to know their own type they must complete the MBTI inventory, which is professionally interpreted. This will provide the reader with a thorough analysis of his or her type and the connections between separate dimensions. It is also possible to find similar inventories that can be completed via the Internet, and although the analysis and dimensions are not so stable, it provides a starting point to understand one's type. There are also checklists provided within some of the books in the reference list, which can help in a self-analysis.

Summary

Descriptions of the MBTI dimensions

Extraversion–Introversion (E-I)
This is the first dimension and it concerns how we prefer to live our lives. Those with a preference for extraversion get energy from and focus their energy on the outside world, so they prefer to have many people around and to have a lively environment, making decisions through talking to others and speak before thinking about all the implications of what they say. Introverts are the opposite, usually more quiet, and they tend to consider issues before speaking about them. They prefer a quiet environment to allow for concentration, and they focus their attention and get energy from within themselves, and so need little external stimulation to work.

Sensing–Intuiting (S-N)
This dimension looks at our preference for gathering information about our world and for decisions. Those with a sensing preference rely on and believe their five senses, and so live in a very practical 'here-and-now' world, not being concerned about what might be but rather what is. 'Sensing preference' people like procedures and knowing what is, whereas those with a preference for intuition prefer change and usually focus ahead on what might be. Intuiters are less good at dealing with detail but better at seeing connections and patterns than those whose preference is sensing.

Thinking–Feeling (T-F)
The third dimension tells where and on what we focus attention when making decisions. Those who have a preference for thinking make decisions based on truth, logic and principle, whereas those with a preference for feeling make decisions based on values and the impact of a decision on people. People who prefer 'thinking' value impersonal decisions and are often described as 'business-like' in dealing with others. However, people who have the 'feeling' preference in decision-making usually value harmony, preferring to avoid conflict and behave in a personal way toward others, seeing everyone as a unique individual.

Judging–Perceiving (J-P)
The final pair of preferences relate to how we each prefer to live our lives. The judging preference is about those who prefer to be organised in whatever they do – planning and time schedules are very important to these people. They usually work with a very well-developed plan of action, often listing jobs to be completed, and they focus on finishing the list in the allocated time. Conversely, those with a preference for perceiving live their life in a spontaneous way and are unlikely to have a well-defined plan, or any plan at all. They prefer to live life as it comes and to focus on what is important at any time, rather than on completing a plan. Perceivers cope with unexpected happenings, whereas those with a preference for judging often find the unplanned upsetting and difficult to manage.

Type and learning

Although the MBTI model of personality presented above is based on preferences linked to how we gather, use and understand information and how we prefer to live, because it assesses very basic preferences a type profile explains how we do many things – eg manage and influence and lead others, work in teams, cope with life and work, and coach and learn. These traits are pervasive and long-lasting, providing an explanation of differences in behaviour and found to be influential in explaining similarities and differences in the way each of us uses many management skills and in how we learn. The MBTI model has a very developmental focus and so we might expect it to be closely linked with learning. We do not expect anyone to learn in the same way all of the time, and preferences have been found to influence our learning style in numerous studies researched by Lawrence (1993). Most of the studies undertaken have been on classroom learning and teaching

Each of the dimensions has some influence on learning from a different perspective.

The E-I dimension tells about where we get and focus our energy, where our motivation for learning comes from. Those with an E preference are motivated by activity external to themselves, and enjoy learning with and talking to others to form ideas, using trial and error and getting involved in whatever is happening. Those with an I preference choose to learn alone, letting internal ideas direct their thoughts – although sometimes they discuss thoughts with someone they trust. They look inward for resources, listen to others and reflect, producing considered ideas before vocalising them, and need time to think before answering questions.

The S-N dimension is the key one associated with basic learning style because it indicates what types of information we trust. Those with an S preference believe practical data from their senses and current facts and figures. They therefore prefer to learn step by step, moving in their own time from what they know to what is unfamiliar. They like to know what is expected of them, to handle materials practically and to link new learning to their current experience. People with an N preference prefer to focus on concepts and general principles rather than on detailed facts. They use imagination to generate possibilities, looking for connections between ideas, often jumping from idea to concept in an unstructured way. They enjoy finding their own way through work using books and ideas, preferring to work on their own.

The two remaining dimensions influence the first two in terms of learning.

The T-F dimension relates to our focus in decision-making. T-preference people value logical analysis, naturally critiquing ideas in an objective way. Logical organisation is important to this group of learners so that they have clear objectives to achieve and for whom people and relationships are not the main feature. Feedback provided for this group must be specific and related to objectives. Learners with an F preference maintain a focus on people and relationships, being aware of the personal issues in learning. They work best in a harmonious environment, helping others to learn, and prefer to study subjects that are important to them. Feedback to this group is most effective if it appreciates their needs and offers suggestions.

The J-P dimension tells about work and learning habits. Those with a J preference like a clear work plan that is known at the beginning, which they can complete without unexpected interruption while knowing what the specific criteria for assessment are. They like to know what has to be achieved at the end point and at intermediate points along the way. Those with a P preference learn in a spontaneous way, responding to what they find interesting and keeping options open for more and new information. Perceivers often work better when they can input to the agreed outcome and will work intermittently throughout a project, spending time on topics that are new and so interesting to them.

Type combinations and learning

The descriptions of each dimension are useful although they also interact with each other to produce what are called the temperaments (Keirsey and Bates, 1978), which effectively relate to combinations of type dimensions. Keirsey and Bates believed that the J-P dimension influenced people with a sensing (S) preference, and that the T-F dimension influenced those with an intuiting (N) preference. The main combinations considered were therefore:

- SP, thought to enjoy excitement, flexibility and respond to predicaments

- SJ, held to be responsible and to plan carefully, preferring what has gone before to new ideas

- NT, said to enjoy developing and criticising models and achievement

- NF, regarded as preferring self-development and to support others in learning.

Lawrence (1993) provides an interesting account of 'four minds' based on the combinations of our preference for gathering information (through S or N) and for making decisions (T or F). The groupings are slightly different from the temperaments of Keirsey but the outcome is similar. The concept of four groupings to give different 'minds' came from the work of Osmond, Siegler and Smoke (1977) in which the names for each mind were developed:

- ST is the *structural mind* in which good clean data, from the senses, is logically organised and categorised for 'filing' so that it is available for future reference. Although this has to be a simplified account of reality, the structural mind prefers to work in this way.

- NF, the *oceanic mind*, works in a very different way by focusing on the 'unique, subtle, personal and ambiguous features of experience' (Lawrence, 1993; p.190). For the oceanic mind categorisation is limiting, so this group prefer to store as much experience as possible, often apparently chaotically and unconsciously, relying on connections and memory to pull together relevant information when they are faced with a new problem.

- NT is the *ethereal mind*, which has a partiality for intuition in common with NF preferences so using 'big picture' thinking, although the ethereal mind constructs and develops mental models and concepts. NTs prefer objective data but do not categorise and store facts as STs do – instead, they prefer to use the facts to test and develop models still further. The NT's world is abstract: NTs use frameworks and meanings to survive everyday life.

- SF is the *'experial' mind* which has the 'S' in common with ST, resulting in a practical down-to-earth view of life, but it also has the 'F' in common with NF, which means that SFs treat experience individually and personally. The word 'experial' was coined by Osmond and colleagues to suggest that everything was 'validated in personal, practical daily experience' (Lawrence, 1993; p.191). For this group every experience is considered, not analysed, and individual meaning attached.

What does type mean for developing skills?

There are a number of ways in which information about type can be used in selecting techniques and approaches to developing skills that suit the type, or in knowing what to avoid. It is also useful to develop greater self-awareness through understanding the strengths and potential blind spots associated with our own type in learning, and then to address any identified weaknesses through personal development. This information can also be helpful in training others, whether individuals or large groups.

Example

I am an INFP in Myers-Briggs terms, so I prefer to learn through reading, sitting listening or working through something myself, rather than get involved in a large group discussion before I have worked through learning for myself. I enjoy playing with ideas and working when I feel ready to do so, and I am aware that I can get distracted by other partly related thoughts while working. When I set objectives for my development, I prefer to have broad and general ones so that I don't limit myself too much and miss a possible new interest that comes along. I am obviously saying this from an INFP perspective, and it feels quite comfortable to me, although I am aware that if you happen to be a completely opposite type – say, ESTJ – reading this, you are probably thinking 'What about being specific in what you want to achieve? How can you waste time just day-dreaming when you have a particular piece of information to learn?', and that I should set a timetable to work to and focus more to allow no distractions! Well, that is possibly your way of learning – and it is probably successful for you – and in fact if I have a specific test to pass, I will probably adopt your approach to learning with timetables, specific information, practice in timed tests of facts, etc. The point is that some learning situations are more appropriate and so effective for certain preferences. It is, however, helpful to understand what your own preferences mean for you and how you can adapt what you do to help match your needs.

It is through exploring different situations and being aware of what we enjoy and avoid that we are able to develop greater self-awareness, usually through using review questions related to learning models and theories, and thereby come to understand more about our own learning style and preferences. Unless some emphasis is placed on examining learning preferences and also shortcomings, many people are not encouraged to understand what influences their learning during the learning process or how they might be able to make use of their preferences in learning or deal with potential blind spots.

In the above example I know the ways I prefer to learn and contrasted this approach with the ST structural mind. I can recognise the parts of the process that I might overlook or avoid so I can plan learning to maximise the positive aspects of my preferences or, through understanding how opposite types learn, I can try to adopt those strategies and so ensure effective coverage if I need to learn in ways that do not fit my preferences. Another example will help to explain different preferences for each type of mind.

Example

Consider a situation in which I am to be trained on a new IT system along with three colleagues, each with a different preference, following a step-by-step procedure with an instructor monitoring each action to ensure that each person follows the procedure to complete each action.

This type of learning is most likely to suit the ST mind because it utilises a clear, organised, step-by-step approach, providing a procedure that can be used for future reference. It is real and detailed, and there is no decision-making required – just do as the instructor says.

How would the other two groups deal with it?

The tutor reads out instructions and expects each of us to follow her lead and press buttons in turn as instructed. The NT ethereal mind is likely to enjoy the practical, factual nature of the approach but will probably want to know how the instruction fits into the systemic operation, and will want an overarching system model. The NT may well become frustrated by having to keep following instructions once a mental model of what is required has been formed in the mind.

The SF temperament in this group will probably enjoy the practical, real-time task and follow the factual instructions with ability. However, the SF's learning is likely to be influenced by the relationship with the tutor and other learners, and the SF is especially likely to want to please the tutor.

I, an NF learner, find this approach difficult and frustrating. My preference with a new system is to test it out, trying to work out what to do just by having a go. I am keen not to annoy anyone and to maintain harmony, but I find my mind (and fingers) wander when I'm told to follow a procedure and I'm not told why and what if.

As can be seen from the example above, it would be fairly easy to include activities that would help to meet the needs of each type and to make the learning more effective for all.

There has been concern since the 1970s that education is biased toward introvert and intuitive types, with an emphasis on individual reading, understanding concepts and seeing connections (Lawrence, 1993). Those who have opposite preferences (E and S) are at a disadvantage in traditional educational settings although they may perform well in the step-by-step IT training described above, as long as they are able to see relevance and application from the training. In particular, the sensing preference requires support to help to see meaning in education or training. It is the intuitive (N) preference that helps to see patterns and links between one context and another for learning. Sensing students do not naturally link together ideas or work confidently with abstract meanings due to their preference for checking ideas against facts and dealing with matter-of-fact information rather than imagination. Our experience of working with groups of managers is that those with a sensing preference find more difficulty in trying to see a reason and meaning for certain workshop-based activities, often complaining that it is 'not like the real world'. This is an example of the above problem and requires careful handling to try to aid their application of concepts to their work and to find 'real' applied examples of theories. Of course, these students also are encouraged to work to find meaning for themselves and to develop skills in linking the theoretical and conceptual to applied actual data.

In a paper reviewing international executive development as distinct from didactic education (Harris and Kumra, 2000), tutors used the Myers-Briggs dimensions to form a 'learning diamond' to ensure that learning was effective for each type combination (NT, NF, ST, SF). A range of interventions was therefore used, including experiential activities to address emotion and ideas for NF; intellectual and theoretical models to address logic and ideas for NT; problem and case examples with checklists to address the logic and data needs of ST; and discussion to share actual problems to address the personal and factual needs of SF types. This example puts experiential learning into a wider development programme aimed at meeting the learning preferences for all types.

In a recent article, cognitive style as defined by the MBTI dimensions was found to influence managers' strategic decision-making. The author concluded that an understanding of different ways of using information could aid the effectiveness of strategic thought and implementation (Gallén, 2006).

As a tutor it is important to try to provide an assortment of training techniques, resources and activities to fit the learning styles of all groups while being aware of one's own preferences so that learning is effective for all, even if the tutor does not know the types of all the learners. In training it is important to recognise that usually we train in ways that suit our own personal preferences, so that a teacher with an NT preference will tend to teach in ways that suit NT students, although such ways are less appropriate for other groups. In such a case, a teacher is likely to provide a global overview with structured well-organised lessons, delivered in an objective, impersonal way, and featuring theoretical models. However, this is likely to lack relevance and practicality for S types and enthusiasm and personal meaning for F types.

Type and ADAX

Much of the research on learning has focused on the classroom although learning from experience is important, particularly in relation to skills development. It is likely, from the discussion above, that type will influence what we attend to and the way in which we evaluate experience. In respect of each stage in the ADAX process we can see the differences that might occur.

The initial element of *becoming aware* of what we need is likely to rely on how we gather and interpret information, so S or N preference will be relevant, providing information that is either practical, detailed and specific to the context in which it occurred (S type). An N type is likely to identify needs in more global, less specific terms, and more related to what to change and what that will mean.

At the *decision* stage, STs will produce specific plans, with clear objectives and with a time-frame, whereas an NF type is likely to produce more general plans based on personal feelings and with consideration for the effect on others.

In the *action* phase, E-preference people are likely to jump in and have a go with little forethought, whereas I types will be slower to get involved, being preoccupied with thinking through options and likely effects. Review is likely to be influenced by S-N and T-F preferences, and moving toward excellence and creating self-awareness will be influenced by E-I and J-P dimensions as well as the context in which behaviour occurs.

It is apparent, then, that the particular preferences that each individual has are likely to influence each element of ADAX, providing a different experience for learners of different types. We recommend that learners try to collect perspectives from different people, some of whom will have different preferences, so that however unusual or out-of-normal experience the perspective of a colleague might be, it may be held to be a valid perspective, to be considered and understood, and may provide new views of ourselves or options to be considered.

DIFFERENT TYPES OF INTELLIGENCE

Level of intelligence was thought to be important in providing explanations of why some people seemed to be more effective or quicker than others. Although people vary in tests that measure intelligence and specific abilities, there would seem to be evidence that most people have a sufficient level of intelligence (an IQ within the average range of 85 to 115) to undertake most training activities and learn from them. Specific abilities may influence learning – for example, a high level of spatial ability is likely to make the learning of tasks involving judgement on the positioning and rotation of shapes easier. Research suggests that intelligence is not one-dimensional and that there may be at least two types of intelligence (Horn and Cattell, 1996) or possibly three components to intelligence (Sternberg, 1988). Although there is not space here to consider the merits or all of the implications of each theory, there is a general finding that is of importance in learning. It seems that throughout life adults use different facets of intelligence to compensate for failings in other facets. For example, Sternberg suggests that the three components he identified – the meta-component (the key monitoring and controlling element), the performance component (to implement higher-order instructions) and the knowledge-acquisition component (that gathers information and helps solve problems) – work together to support one another, allowing adults to continue learning through experience. It seems, then, that experience is vital for continued learning and may have an increasing influence on what new information is noticed and used.

Gardner's (1993) work on multiple intelligences identifies different aspects of intelligence which might influence learning ability in different circumstances. For example, those with a high level of interpersonal intelligence may pick up signals from others that help them identify the appropriate response quickly. Education, until recently, has not focused on the range of intelligences identified by Gardner but has concentrated instead on mathematical-logical and verbal-linguistic intelligence. There is a great deal of work on accelerated learning which attempts to enrich learning, both in the classroom and experientially, using many of the intelligences identified by Gardner. Training specialists have used combinations of intelligences to support learning and increase its effectiveness.

Areas of multiple intelligence identified to address in learning include (after Gardner, 1993):

- mathematical–logical
- naturalistic
- creative
- moral
- spiritual
- intrapersonal
- verbal–linguistic
- interpersonal
- bodily–kinaesthetic
- visual–spatial.

Emotional intelligence (Goleman, 1998) also influences what and how effectively we become aware of ourselves and our understanding of others. We can all therefore make our learning more effective by becoming more aware of our own thoughts, feelings and motivations (our EQ) and those of other people, as discussed in the chapter on awareness (Chapter 2).

Goleman's broad definition of emotional intelligence has found general agreement amongst researchers; Goleman (1998) declares that emotional intelligence is:

- knowing what you are feeling, and being able to handle those feelings without them swamping you
- being able to motivate yourself to get jobs done, to be creative and to perform at your peak
- sensing what others are feeling, and handling relationships effectively.

It is, of course, important to keep in mind that all of the elements of emotional intelligence are personal to any individual, so that combinations of different EQ competencies result in different behaviour. In addition, in an organisational context an individual's behaviour is influenced by the organisation's culture.

No one is expected to be equally skilled in all of the 25 identified dimensions – we all have strengths and areas to develop. Goleman's book *Working with Emotional Intelligence* (1998) provides a detailed analysis of each competence within the framework. The dimension of self-awareness/self-regulation and the competence of understanding others are obviously important in gaining awareness of our development needs and many of the dimensions are important in respect of developing skills.

COGNITIVE STYLES

Although many different labels have been used to assess the dimensions of cognitive style, Riding and Cheema (1991) identified two principal dimensions that account for style. These dimensions are defined (Riding and Rayner, 1998) as:

■ the holistic-analytical dimension that indicates whether a person *organises* information as a whole (holistically) or in parts (in detail)

■ the verbal-imagery dimension that indicates how a person is likely to *represent* information, whether in pictures or words.

Together these two dimensions produce a four-quadrant model (see Figure 21) in which the dimensions are believed to be independent.

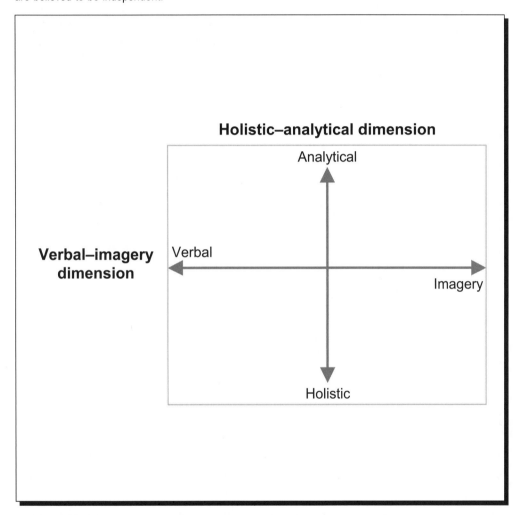

Figure 21: *Riding and Rayner's (1998) two-dimensional model of cognitive style*

The model in Figure 21, from Riding and Rayner (1998), suggests an interaction between the two dimensions. These two dimensions seem to influence our approach to learning in the following ways:

■ Holistic versus Analytical

The holistic-analytical dimension is similar in interpretation to the S-N dimension on the MBTI, although it also includes field-dependency (McKenna, 1983) and divergent-convergent thinking (Grierenko and Sternberg, 1995), so it is somewhat less focused in meaning.

Example

Analytical and holistic focus

The influence of this dimension seems to be fairly consistent for most people throughout their lives, and influences what they become aware of in terms of their personal development. I have a preference for intuition, so I see and understand any situation through a frame of reference that corresponds to trying to understand and interpreting what happens. Alternatively, a colleague of mine has a sensing preference. He therefore sees detail, without making inferences, much as one might require in an eyewitness account. We were both part of a team which was asked to undertake a large new piece of work for a new client, and our different approach and focus typifies the two opposite ends of a dimension:

	Me (Big picture)	**Colleague (Detail)**
Focus	Impact; project outputs and links to other work; future work opportunities	Project plan, dates, times, deadlines; current work requirements
Questions	What does this mean for us, the team, the university? Why? How? Fit with strategy?	What information do we have, what do we need? What must be done now?
Actions	Outline sketch of impact and links to current and future activities – the future work to be done	Detailed plan of what specific actions are needed now, cost, time

As can be seen from the table above the actions and focus are very different, and in fact both important for success in this, or any project. However each results in our becoming aware of different development needs due to our differing perceptions of how to undertake the work. Mine are about overall fit of the work to our current strategy and needs in managing a different client group and the future, whilst his are around breaking his inputs into specific pieces of work to meet whatever current requirements may be. Therefore, wherever you are on the 'big picture' to 'detail' dimension will affect what you focus on in any context, so resulting in raised awareness of different issues.

- Verbal versus Imagery

    Verbal and imagery dimensions suggest the ways that we most easily represent information, either in words or pictures.

Much of the research to develop the model shown in Figure 21 was undertaken in an educational context and concentrated on didactic learning.

It seems probable that cognitive style is a deep-rooted preference for dealing with information, and its influence in experiential learning will be evident. There will be a detailed focus on specific, real activities for S types, or the broader attention of N types, who will look ahead and work with the meaning of events – and hence in planning these two types will differ also.

Learners choose how to record and review learning events, and there are inevitable differences therefore between types in the focus of such reflection. The verbal-visual dimension in experiential learning is likely to cause many such people to record learning perhaps in the form of a log, or on tape, or in any event involving detailed reflection which uses a verbal description to help to reach conclusions and plan, while many others instead use imagery to 'replay events in their minds' or may prefer to use a structured sheet with a clear section placed on a page to represent different review questions and to link information.

In a group of people each one's approach to review, reflection, planning and recording outcomes will be influenced by the above range of factors and result in a unique log of development. No two reviews will be standard because each will see and interpret information differently depending on both personal and contextual differences.

LEARNING STYLES

Learning styles are thought to be broader than cognitive style and include preferences for learning situations. There are numerous models of learning styles, including Kolb (1984) and Honey and Mumford (2000), both of which are based on the experiential learning cycle, and although both have limited empirical support, they are regularly supported by trainers and seem to have face validity. Riding and Rayner (1998) have suggested that this is due to their being drawn up to represent stages in a process, rather than denoting more stable individual differences, as the model on which cognitive style is based. In a more recent review of learning styles (Reynolds, Caley and Mason, 2002), the writers classify and describe a range of styles and include all of the personal and cognitive dimensions previously mentioned, along with additional ones relating to inductive or deductive learning and active or reflective learning (Felder, 1996). They contend that it is less important which model is used than to recognise the range of different styles and to be aware of the strengths and weaknesses of a preferred style. Then a learner can develop learning strategies to overcome the weaknesses in any one style. As the range of learning opportunities increases, we will all need strategies that enable learning to be as effective as possible. Torrance and Rockstein (1988; p.278) have suggested that:

> **'A learning style may become a learning disability if cultivated at the expense of other ways of learning.'**

We have therefore endeavoured to provide managers with a range of different models so that over time they may try to encompass as many different options as necessary and consider where they are on all dimensions – which mean most to optimise for their own strengths and which they should use to promote their own and others' personal development.

Activities to develop different learning preferences

Although we have discussed a range of personal differences within this chapter, it is useful to have a full view of how such differences intervene in learning and how use can be made of them in developing both yourself and others. At all times, in devising and utilising activities to help in developing management skills, it is essential to take into account the wide range of different personal characteristics and preferences.

Example

How we use and allow for personal differences in teamwork

One of the key skills that we frequently work on with groups of managers is teamwork. This is a poorly defined skill and has a multitude of meanings at work so it may include assertiveness, rapport-building, persuading or motivating colleagues, communication, monitoring and managing others, setting objectives, dealing with conflict, and decision-making, to name but a few. Working on this range of skills is a challenge for a number of reasons:

- Many people believe themselves to be good teamworkers.
- Many 'fat' skills are involved.
- The skills vary greatly with context and role.

To develop teamwork skills we begin by asking managers to assess themselves on teamwork, to justify their rating to a colleague, and then to tease out the skills they think are the key ones involved. From this activity learners can develop objectives to work toward in future activities, so aiding planning in a form most appropriate to them.

We provide a number of theoretical and practical models or team roles, skills and processes. Among the models provided is Myers-Briggs, which is used to examine and understand differences and how to value difference in personal and management style. Another important element of process is that we provide a range of personal models and tools that individuals can use to understand themselves and others – for example, the Johari Window (Luft, 1970) in giving and receiving feedback.

We use a number of situations in which we focus on team skills – from beginning with decision-making in convergent and divergent problems, to completing a self-managed group project over a number of weeks, and many situations between. We also include activities where the focus is on other key management skills but in which there is also a teamwork element – for example, gathering and analysing data to present it. There are additionally a range of contexts with a more or less obvious teamwork element, in which participants are encouraged to work with a wide range of people and for some of which tutor feedback or assessment is provided.

Following each activity participants are encouraged to review the situation, both in teams and individually, so that they receive feedback from many people, gaining multiple perspectives.

This range of activities is designed to meet the needs of most learning styles:

- E or I types by allowing managers to select roles within the team, also addressing the active and reflective learning styles
- S and N types by providing detailed activity briefs, as realistic as possible, while providing the initial and ongoing global view of teamwork
- concrete learners have activity to ground experience, and abstract learners are given models and concepts to support reviews
- deductive learners have theories and models to use to plan action, while inductive learners are encouraged to record and explain events.

Although personal objectives may not all be achieved through providing so many different opportunities, most learners are able to address the skills that are particularly relevant to them and all develop greater self-awareness.

What do differences in personal characteristics mean for skills development?

Throughout series of skills development workshops we introduce different models to examine personal differences at intervals. These may be models like MBTI, which is very thoroughly researched and its use is controlled, to models that can be found on the Internet and are freely available. It is important that any models used are understood and that an explanation is provided for learners outlining links with experiential learning.

Individual differences are so pervasive that their influence is felt in learning in many ways and they provide both a challenge and fascination for learning facilitators. The challenge comes from an acknowledgement that if each of us learns in different ways, it is difficult to generalise about presenting concepts because everyone is unique and so all approaches – even common ones – must be tailored to individual circumstances.

There is also a fascination in working with a variety of personal characteristics and style to better understand the contribution that these differences make to everyone's learning and to find ways that effectively use the differences to make learning more effective.

SUMMARY AND WAY FORWARD

A greater understanding of personal differences helps us to work with other people and provides increased self-awareness. We believe that this is an important factor in understanding how and why managers develop skills and which skills they develop. We therefore cannot expect any two managers to take the same learning from any session, and we must use strategies and processes that allow for individual learning and development, within an overarching aim for development.

We must also remember that this is only one factor that might be used to account for our behaviour and that of others. Each organisation has a culture that influences the behaviour of employees and managers, an acceptance of what is expected and what will be tolerated.

Individuals are also influenced by the behaviour and perceived intentions of others who are part of each situation. Each of us has a long history and experience that we bring to every encounter.

We may be unconscious of many of these factors sometimes, but we hope that by having a greater understanding of differences each manager is encouraged to develop greater awareness of others which will provide options that can be used to aid skills development.

All of the above models of different characteristics have been found to influence our learning and can help us to understand how we develop skills. There are a number of questions below that can be used to aid in the reflection of experiences and greatly contribute to deeper self-awareness:

- How do you see yourself as different from other people?
- Can you identify where, on each type-dimension, you fit?
- How would you describe your personal learning style, using the dimensions discussed?
- What can you do to further develop less-preferred characteristics? How might that be beneficial?

REFERENCES AND FURTHER READING

Bayne, R. (1995) *The Myers-Briggs Type Indicator: A critical review and practical guide*. London: Chapman & Hall

Costa, P. T. and McCrea, R. R. (1992) 'Normal personality assessment in clinical practice: the NEO Personality Inventory', *Psychological Assessment*, 4 (1), 407–23

Felder, R. (1996) cited in R. Reynolds, L. Caley and R. Mason (2002) *How do People Learn?* London: CIPD

Fransella, F. and Bannister, D. (1977) *A Manual for the Repertory Grid Technique*. London: Academic Press

Gallén, T. (2006) 'Managers and strategic decisions: does cognitive style matter?', *Journal of Management Development*, Vol. 25, No. 2, 118–33

Gardner, H. (1993) *Frames of Mind: The theory of multiple intelligences*, 2nd edition. New York: Basic Books

Grierenko, E. L. and Sternberg, R. J. (1995) 'Thinking styles', in Saklofske, D. H. and Zeinder, M. (eds) *International Handbook of Personality and Intelligence*. New York: Plenum Press.

Goleman, D. (1998) *Working with Emotional Intelligence*. New York: Bantam Books

Harris, H. and Kumra, S. (2000) 'International manager development: cross-cultural training in highly diverse environments', *Journal of Management Development*, Vol. 19, No. 7. 602–14

Hirsh, S. K. (1991) *Using the Myers-Briggs Type Indicator in Organizations*. Palo Alto, CA: Consulting Psychologists Press

Honey, P. and Mumford, A. (2000) *The Learning Styles Helpers' Guide*. Maidenhead: Honey Publications

Honey, P. and Mumford, A. (1992) *Manual of Learning Styles*. Maidenhead: Honey Publications

Horne, J. L. and Cattell, R. B. (1996) 'Refinement of the test of the theory of fluid and crystallized intelligence', *Journal of Educational Psychology*, 57, 253–70

Huczynski, A. and Buchanan, D. (2004) *Organizational Behaviour: An introductory text*. London: Financial Times/Prentice Hall.

Keirsey, D. and Bates, M. (1978) *Please Understand Me*, 3rd edition. Del Mar, CA: Prometheus Nemesis

Kroeger, O. and Theusen, J. (1992) *Type Talk at Work*. New York: Delacortre Press

Lawrence, G. (1993) *People Types and Tiger Stripes*, 3rd edition. Gainesville, Florida: Centre for Application of Psychological Type, Inc.

Luft, J. (1970) 'Johari's Window: an experience in self-disclosure and feedback', in Pfeiffer, J. W. and Jones, J. E. (eds) *A Handbook of Structured Experience for Human Relations Training*. University Associates

McKenna, F. P. (1983) 'Field dependence and personality: a re-examination', *Social Behaviour and Personality*, 11, 51–5

Myers, I. B. (1980) *Gifts Differing*. Palo Alto, CA: Consulting Psychologists Press

Osmond, H., Siegler, M. and Smoke, R. (1977) 'Typology revisited: a new perspective', cited in G. Lawrence, *People Types and Tiger Stripes*, 3rd edition. Gainesville, Florida: Centre for Application of Psychological Type, Inc.

Reynolds, R., Caley L. and Mason, R. (2002) *How do People Learn?* London: CIPD

Riding, R. J. and Cheema, I. (1991) 'Cognitive styles: an overview and integration', *Educational Psychology*, 11, 193–215

Riding, R. J. and Rayner, S. (1998) *Cognitive Styles and Learning Strategies: Understanding style differences in learning and behaviour.* London: David Fulton Publishers

Sternberg, R. J. (1988) 'The concept of intelligence and its role in lifelong learning and success', *American Psychologist*, 52, 1030–7

Torrance, E. P. and Rockstein, Z. (1988) 'Styles of thinking and creativity', in R. R. Schmeck (ed.) *Learning Strategies and Learning Styles.* New York: Plenum Press

Summary and conclusion

In this final section we:

- summarise our main ideas and the themes developed in this book
- reflect on the implications of some of these ideas and themes
- provide suggestions about how the ideas in the book might be taken forward.

SUMMARY

In the Introduction we described our 15-year journey which led to the ideas embodied in this book. Every journey begins with the first step and ours was to embrace the ideas of experiential learning to meet the challenges of continuous professional development and the development of management skills. In particular, we operationalised the ideas of Kolb and Honey and Mumford to enable practitioners to review and improve their work performance by enhancing their skill development.

Out of this beginning we developed our ADAX process. This describes an approach to developing skills. Individuals move from awareness to excellence. In short, they develop a perceptual map of their skill needs, decide to pursue and commit to these skills, actively practise these skills and embark on a quest for continuous improvement.

We also have developed and borrowed many exercises, cases and stories, a number of which we have included in the book. This emphasises the experiential approach we have adopted to develop the model. In Part 2 we introduced a number of theoretical themes and ideas which we believe give greater insight and understanding into the skill development process. *Neuroscience* is providing us with explanations of the learning processes. *Experiential learning* is the fundamental basis to our approach. *Personal differences* are one of the greatest challenges for skill development. *State*, we believe, is a key prerequisite for developing skills. The *senses* are our ways of connecting and impacting on the outside world and hence determine the way we deploy skills.

REFLECTIONS

As we approach the end of the book we would like to leave you with a number of ideas to reflect on.

You can reap most benefit from our process by using it so that it becomes a habit. Pick a skill you know is important to you and you want to improve. *Then just have a go!* Every habit starts with the first try. Then reflect, understand and personalise it. Enjoy successes – they help turn the process into a habit. Look upon your failures as prerequisites of success.

To benefit from the process you do not have to start at the beginning (awareness) and finish at the end (excellence). It is not a linear process. Access it where it makes most sense to you. You may want to work on your beliefs or motivation. You may be very competent at a particular skill and want to start by pursuing excellence. You may just want to get some 'hands-on' experience of a skill. You choose. People may recognise that they are already partly through the process for certain skills. You are more likely to adopt a process if you are in control of it and can use it to suit your purposes.

From a personal point of view our model and book was developed using the ADAX process. When you read about a model or process it often appears more neat and tidy than it is in practice. Our process is no different. We mentioned in the book that it is more like a jungle than a neat, tidy English garden. Enlightenment often seems to follow confusion!

Throughout the book we have often referred to our process as a journey. There is a slight difference with our journey in that it does not have an end. The pursuit of skill and excellence in an ever-changing world is a never-ending journey. Some people may find this frustrating, others challenging, but the history of work organisations suggests that the pace of change is increasing and this means ways of working and management skills become obsolete. Continuous professional development no longer seems an option but a necessity.

In the same way excellence is best viewed as a process and not as an outcome. Yesterday's excellence can soon become today's mediocrity if we believe excellence is a state we achieve. It is our contention that excellence in process goes hand in glove with excellent outcomes.

The final point we would make about the development of management skills is that no two people use them in exactly the same way. Everyone brings something of themselves, something unique, to the way they deploy a particular skill. This is one of the most exciting and challenging characteristics of facilitating skill development. On the one hand there are routines and skills suggested by 'best practice' – but these skills are only brought to life by individuals' investing something personal in the skill. If everyone used skills in an identical manner, we would find the whole process very bland. It is this individuality that differentiates performance in deploying management skills. We constantly remind our managers and students to enjoy their individuality and to remember that they can use a skill in a way that no one else can.

USES OF THE BOOK

We hope that the book meets the requirements of any learners who want or need to learn more about what they currently do or what they might do in future to develop skills. The book provides a general process that can be used in different situations to facilitate a wide range of skills. We would envisage that learners could use the process on their own or as part of a group, inside work or as part of CPD in studying for a professional qualification. The book is also intended to be used by trainers and tutors to provide a framework for personal and professional development. The learning may come from activities provided by tutors, some described within the book, or through exploring experiences provided by learners. Whatever the source of the experience, the ADAX process can be used to improve performance in skills, to provide a deeper understanding of the skills process and explore insights into individual self-awareness and the learning process itself.

Our approach is by no means the only approach to developing skills. We hope that individuals and tutors who use other processes and approaches may wish to use some of our ideas and material – borrow bits that you find useful.

Figure 22: *Learning requires constant renewal – 'Keep sharpening your saw'*

We have emphasised that the ADAX process is intended for use in developing all skills, and indeed we have used it to assist managers develop personal, interpersonal, task-related and social skills of many types. Different training programmes or courses each have a particular focus for skills development. However, if there are tutors who are unsure about which skills they might try to address with students, we have provided some ideas of groups of work-based skills that might be addressed on either general management or HR programmes. We also provide a framework of personal skills and skills related to learning that can be developed through any management programme. These models can be found in the Appendix at the end of this chapter, along with websites and additional references that the reader might find useful in developing skills or facilitating skills development.

It is also intended that these lists of skills will provide an overview for anyone working alone who wants some ideas about where they might begin. However, if anyone has a clear idea about skills they wish to develop or if they prefer to use organisational frameworks of skills, they might choose to ignore the lists in the Appendix.

Appendix

The following are a selection of frameworks that might be useful for anyone who is unsure about where to begin on skill development.

MANAGEMENT AND HR SKILLS RELEVANT TO PROFESSIONAL PROGRAMMES

We have used these overarching skills to summarise those required throughout the CIPD programme, although the list is not exhaustive.

Personal and interpersonal skills

- time management
- study skills
- self-management – eg motivation
- decision-making
- teamwork skills, including influencing, encouraging others, gate-keeping
- self-presentation
- listening and interpretation of non-verbal information
- negotiation
- advising others
- giving and receiving feedback
- encouraging creativity
- recognising and managing stress

Management/HR skills

- presentation
- developing policy
- implementing policy
- interviewing – eg recruitment and selection, fact-finding
- designing learning interventions
- delivering training
- training evaluation
- appraising others and providing feedback
- coaching others

- interpreting employment law to provide advice
- dealing with grievance and discipline
- preparing for an employment tribunal
- negotiation
- managing change
- HR planning
- using HR/MIS systems
- interpreting data
- developing and monitoring budgets
- project management
- managing others' performance
- consultancy

SKILLS FOR MASTER'S PROGRAMMES

This list is taken from the Benchmarks for Master's Degrees in Business and Management (2007), mainly cognitive and intellectual skills.

- ability to think creatively and manage the creative process, analyse, synthesise and critically appraise
- ability to solve complex problems and make decisions
- ability to conduct research into business and management
- ability to use information and knowledge effectively
- numeracy and quantitative skills
- effective use of CIT
- effective two-way communication
- personal effectiveness
- ability to evoke effective performance in a team
- leadership and performance management
- ability to recognise and address ethical dilemmas and corporate social responsibility issues

During a programme students are expected to demonstrate:

- systematic understanding and knowledge about organisations
- the application of their knowledge to a range of complex situations
- critical awareness of business issues
- the use of appropriate analytical techniques
- creativity in applying knowledge
- the ability to acquire and analyse data
- an ability to conduct research
- that they can communicate effectively.

Graduates in professional practice, in business should:

- deal with complex issues systematically and creatively
- proactively recognise the need for change
- be adaptable, show originality, insight and critical and reflective abilities
- make decisions in complex and unpredictable situations
- evaluate and integrate theory and practice
- be self-directed and able to act autonomously in planning and implementing projects
- take responsibility for continuing to develop skills and knowledge.

The initial framework is more limited to skills associated with study, although it is interesting that the final list of skills expected from Master's graduates in business links very closely with a number of the issues and skills used throughout this book.

NVQ MANAGEMENT SKILLS

A summary of generic management skills identified within National Vocational Qualifications in management is presented below (NVQ Management MSC, 2004).

- setting objectives
- communicating
- planning
- time management
- evaluating
- reviewing
- learning
- obtaining feedback
- self-assessment
- stress management
- reflecting
- prioritising
- questioning
- information management
- presenting information
- influencing and persuading
- risk management
- decision-making
- team-building
- motivating
- monitoring
- providing feedback
- valuing and supporting others

- thinking creatively
- managing conflict
- leading by example
- involving others
- empathising
- acting assertively
- reporting
- negotiating
- consulting
- contingency planning
- problem-solving
- thinking systematically
- delegating

Many of these skills are used differently in different situations and contexts but the list can be a useful beginning.

CIPD GRADUATE-LEVEL COMPETENCIES

We provide students with an audit against these competencies and recommend that they complete the rating themselves and ask a manager or colleague to do an assessment of them, so providing a benchmark against which a development plan can be agreed. The rating can be repeated at a later time (12 or 24 months) to check on progress. The rating form is provided below (adapted from CIPD Graduate competencies).

Core competency	Description	Rating 1 = Never, 5 = Always				
Personal drive and effectiveness The existence of a positive, 'can-do' mentality, anxious to find ways round obstacles and willing to exploit all the available resources in order to accomplish objectives.	**Sets out own professional objectives with a prioritised plan for managing time.** Establishes priorities, tasks and work schedules in advance in order to maximise efficiency and added-value effectiveness and, above all, to ensure the provision of advice, help, guidance and professional services to meet the needs of senior management, line managers and employees generally.	1	2	3	4	5
	Monitors progress and takes remedial action as necessary.	1	2	3	4	5
	Anticipates resource problems and seeks to resolve them proactively.	1	2	3	4	5
	Identifies own motivators and strengths, and uses them to drive personal performance.	1	2	3	4	5

People management and leadership The motivation of others (whether subordinates, colleagues, seniors or project team members) towards the achievement of shared goals, not through the application of formal authority but rather by personal role-modelling, the establishment of professional credibility, and the creation of reciprocal trust.	**Demonstrates a level of knowledge and understanding and ability about managing people and leadership that meets CIPD Professional Standards.** Treats others the way they themselves would wish to be treated.	1	2	3	4	5
	Demonstrates personal commitment to team decisions.	1	2	3	4	5
	Encourages and supports the contributions of others.	1	2	3	4	5
	Helps colleagues when they are under pressure.	1	2	3	4	5
	Adapts personal style to the situation and the needs/expectations of others.	1	2	3	4	5
Business understanding Adoption of a corporate (not merely functional) perspective, including awareness of financial issues and accountabilities, of 'customer' priorities, and of the necessity for cost/benefit calculations when contemplating continuous improvement/ transformational change.	**Understands the business needs and issues of one or more types of organisation.** Understands why 'customer' needs are what they are, given the dual context of internal organisational priorities and external environmental scenarios (both current and predicted).	1	2	3	4	5
	Acknowledges and accepts the significance of relevant business drivers and selected scorecard measures.	1	2	3	4	5
Professional and ethical competence Possession of the professional skills and technical capabilities, specialist subject (particularly legal) knowledge, and the integrity in decision-making and operational activity that are associated with effective achievement in personnel and development.	**Meets a defined range of the CIPD's Professional Standards.** Displays achievement of the CIPD Professional Standards both in general terms and also within defined areas (depending on chosen electives).	1	2	3	4	5
	Conducts self in accordance with the Institute's Code of Professional Conduct.	1	2	3	4	5

Continuing learning Commitment to continuous improvement and change by the application of self-managed learning techniques, supplemented where appropriate by deliberate, planned exposure to external learning sources (mentoring, coaching, etc).	**Adopts a considered approach to continuing learning and personal professional development.**					
	Conscientiously maintains CPD records.	1	2	3	4	5
	Periodically reflects on experience and systematically seeks to improve performance when recurring situations present themselves.	1	2	3	4	5
	Sets self-learning objectives and achieves them through action planning.	1	2	3	4	5
	Accepts constructive feedback positively.	1	2	3	4	5
	Considers implications, and seeks to change behaviour if positive outcomes beckon.	1	2	3	4	5
Adding value through people A desire not merely to concentrate on tasks, but rather to select meaningful outputs which will produce added-value outcomes for the organisation or eliminate/reduce the existence of performance inhibitors, while simultaneously complying with all relevant legal and ethical obligations.	**Identifies opportunities for adding value and makes appropriate recommendations.**					
	Fulfils all promises to 'customers' in terms of timeliness, quality of response and other significant parameters (as perceived by 'customers'), within known areas of technical expertise.	1	2	3	4	5
	Shows commitment to work and targets.	1	2	3	4	5
	Is willing to put in extra effort when necessary in order to ensure that corporate priorities are not jeopardised.	1	2	3	4	5
	If asked, can outline own short-term targets, progress and future actions.	1	2	3	4	5
Analytical and intuitive/creative thinking Application of a systematic approach to situational analysis, development of convincing, business-focused action plans, and (where appropriate) the deployment of intuitive/creative thinking in order to generate innovative solutions and proactively seize opportunities.	**Demonstrates use of a range of thinking abilities, tools and processes – analytical, intuitive, creative.**					
	Provides professional advice in area of expertise.	1	2	3	4	5
	Uses relative inexperience to advantage by questioning established methods, procedures and systems.	1	2	3	4	5
	Introduces new ideas and approaches derived from knowledge of HR in action elsewhere and from previous studies.	1	2	3	4	5
	Thinks through issues clearly; concentrates on facts rather than assumptions.	1	2	3	4	5

'Customer' focus Concern for the perceptions of personnel's 'customers', including (principally) the central directorate of the organisation, a willingness to solicit and act upon 'customer' feedback as one of the foundations for performance improvement.	**Empathises with customers of P&D functions and of employing organisations generally.** Liaises closely and continuously with main 'customers' and develops high level of reciprocal trust/intimacy with them.	1	2	3	4	5
	Takes personal responsibility for resolving 'customer' concerns; asks 'customers' periodically for feedback, and acts on significant lessons gained.	1	2	3	4	5
Strategic capability The capacity to create an achievable vision for the future, to foresee longer-term developments, to envisage options (and their probable consequences), to select sound courses of action, to rise above the day-to-day detail, to challenge the status quo.	**Understands the concept of strategy and the required contributions to it at all levels.** Identifies personal strengths, weaknesses, opportunities and threats against defensible predictions of the future (labour) marketplace.	1	2	3	4	5
	Devises action programmes to capitalise on strengths, reduce weaknesses, seize opportunities and anticipate threats.	1	2	3	4	5
Communication resourcing and interpersonal skills The ability to transmit information to others, especially in written (report) form, both persuasively and cogently, display of listening, comprehension and understanding skills, plus sensitivity to the emotional, attitudinal and political aspects of corporate life.	**Uses 'active listening' with feedback; communicates clearly and positively; generates empathy with others.** Offers support and challenge to the proposals of others, so that in the process these proposals are improved/modified; reinforces the benefits of proposals and recommendations by using relevant facts and figures; anticipates objections and prepares responses.	1	2	3	4	5

REFERENCES AND ADDITIONAL SOURCES OF MANAGEMENT BENCHMARKS OR LISTS

MSC. (October 2004) Management Standards, www.management-standards.org/home [accessed 13 May 2007]

Quinn, R. E., Faerman, S. R., Thompson, M. P. and McGrath, M. R. (4th edition, 2003) *Becoming a Master Manager: A competency framework.*

INDEX